DISASTER

ON THE

SANDUSKY

THE LIFE
OF
COLONEL WILLIAM
CRAWFORD

Robert N. Thompson

AMERICAN HISTORY PRESS
STAUNTON VIRGINIA

Copyright © 2017 Robert N. Thompson

All rights reserved. No part of this book may be transmitted in any form by any means electronic, mechanical or otherwise using devices now existing or yet to be invented without prior written permission from the publisher and copyright holder.

American History Press

Staunton, Virginia
(888) 521-1789
Visit us on the Internet at:
www.Americanhistorypress.com

First Printing May 2017

To schedule an event with the author, or to inquire about bulk discount sales, please contact American History Press.

Library of Congress Cataloging-in-Publication Data

Names: Thompson, Robert N., 1953- author.
Title: Disaster on the Sandusky : the life of Colonel William Crawford / Robert N. Thompson.
Description: Staunton, Virginia : American History Press, 2017. | Includes bibliographical references and index.
Identifiers: LCCN 2017010047 | ISBN 9781939995209 (pbk. : alk. paper)
Subjects: LCSH: Crawford, William, 1732-1782. | Crawford's Indian Campaign, Ohio, 1782. | United States--History--Revolution, 1775-1783--Biography. | Washington, George, 1732-1799--Friends and associates. | Soldiers--United States--Biography.
Classification: LCC E238 .T48 2017 | DDC 973.3/38092 [B] --dc23
LC record available at https://lccn.loc.gov/2017010047

Manufactured in the United States of America on acid-free paper.
This book exceeds all ANSO standards for archival quality.

Praise for *Disaster on the Sandusky*

"Becoming a martyr for the massacre of one hundred Christian Delaware at Gnadenhutten, the torture and death of William Crawford is one of the most repeated stories in American history. *Disaster on the Sandusky* is the first book on the life and times of William Crawford. Robert Thompson has authored a compelling narrative that shines light on Crawford's moral character as well as his flaws as a military leader and how those flaws ultimately led to Crawford's death. An insightful read for students of 18th century frontier history." - **Greg Bray, Executive Director, Pricketts Fort Memorial Foundation, Pricketts Fort State Park, Fairmount, West Virginia**

"Robert Thompson has crafted an engaging and entertaining story of the early history of the American Colonies, the turmoil surrounding early expansion westward, and its subsequent conflicts with the Native tribes already inhabiting the lands.

The book is well-researched and heavily documented, providing more details to the story than most of the early writers. His approach provides a nuanced glance into the life and motivations (good and bad) of two frontier friends—George Washington and William Crawford. One went on to be the "Father of Our Country" while the other has become a largely forgotten character of the early American frontier.

By utilizing multiple original letters, period accounts, and journals the author enables readers to place themselves in the midst of early battles and their associated marches. He also provides a fuller explanation as to why the Delaware executed Crawford and how his death was a form of Native justice rather than just an act of vengeance.

The book is a finely crafted examination of the early American frontier and highly recommended for anyone interested in or studying the original expansion westward and its related conflicts with the Native American tribes." - **Ronald I. Marvin, Jr. , Director/Curator of the Wyandot County Historical Society, Sandusky, Ohio**

For Tom, my brother and lifelong best friend

CONTENTS

Preface		ix
Introduction	A Boyhood Memory	xiv
Chapter 1	Frontier Farmer and Surveyor	1
Chapter 2	The Surveyor Becomes a Soldier	14
Chapter 3	Defeat at the Monongahela	29
Chapter 4	An Officer of the King	47
Chapter 5	Over the Mountains	64
Chapter 6	Lord Dunmore's War	89
Chapter 7	Revolution	109
Chapter 8	War on the Frontier	138
Chapter 9	Expedition to the Sandusky	165
Chapter 10	Battle Island	190
Chapter 11	Trial and Punishment	217
Chapter 12	Legacies	233
Endnotes		251
Bibliography		278
Index		294

PREFACE

The 1782 American expedition to destroy the Native American towns near the Sandusky River in Ohio is one of many small military disasters lost in our historical memory. Moreover, the memory of the man who led that expedition, William Crawford, became just as lost over the course of time. Crawford, a friend and business associate of George Washington, was a noteworthy figure in American colonial frontier culture and politics at the time who became a martyr and folklore hero to white Americans; however, his fame eventually faded. By the early twentieth century, few Americans would recognize his name, let alone know his story.

When I first came upon Crawford in researching an earlier book, the story of his relationship with Washington and the infamous renegade, Simon Girty, intrigued me. My interest was further piqued when I learned more about the Sandusky Expedition, William Crawford's fate, and how both related to the barbaric massacre at Gnadenhutten. Hence, I began to see what else I could learn.

When I began my research, I discovered that the events surrounding the expedition were well documented, but William Crawford was not. To date, no biography on him has ever been published, and what was published about his life is filled with historical inaccuracies and the products of unsubstantiated myths. Therefore, I decided I would not merely tell the story of the disastrous expedition to the Sandusky River, but would also document the life of the man who led it—a man I found to be a fascinating figure, one who was very much a distinct product of the American colonial frontier.

There is a significant amount of historical data about Crawford in the form of dates, places, military ranks and organizations, and numerous business letters between himself and George Washington. This serves to establish Crawford's activities and locations, but it reveals very little about Crawford as a person. There is a glaring lack of information from either Crawford himself or others who knew him regarding his personal opinions, family life, political motivations, or military capabilities. Furthermore, such information as I was able to find seemed to provide more questions than answers. Therefore, I chose to stick to the facts, come to my own conclusions where I could, and not rely on the simplistic popular platitudes that portray him as a martyred pioneer farmer and patriot. Where gaps existed, and there were several, I decided to exercise some historical judgment and lean on whatever logical conclusions I could draw based on available information.

I discovered that there was a fair amount of confusing and conflicting genealogical information regarding William Crawford. This is due in large part to the fact that his name was very common among the colonial frontier population. As a result, some documents and family trees maintain that he had two wives, and others insist he had four legitimate children, not three as indicated in other documents. To eliminate this problem, I decided to use Allen W. Scholl's definitive genealogical study, *The Brothers Crawford*, as my baseline source. Scholl's work is clearly the result of intense research and study in which he reviews the many sources of data and ably refutes the information resulting from legend and folklore.

In cases where there were often great disparities between accounts of the same event and disputed dates, my approach was twofold. First, I granted extra weight to information agreed upon by a majority of sources, and afterward I favored data provided by a primary source. When all else failed, I tried to apply large quantities of common sense.

I must admit that my initial impressions about William Crawford changed as I conducted my research for this book. All of us are complicated beings, driven by different factors at various points in our lives, and William Crawford was no different. As I began to delve into his life, I had already labeled him as one of the many greedy land speculators of the colonial era, a man without any sense of either honor or humanity. Although he was clearly someone long fueled by personal ambition and a measure of greed, in the end, he acted with honor. He took command of the Sandusky Expedition for the best of reasons, although he knew that its chances of success were slim. Therefore, despite his many flaws, I found myself stepping back from my completed manuscript with a measure of respect for William Crawford.

As concerns the Sandusky Expedition of 1782, the works written by a stalwart regional historian, Parker B. Brown, aided me in my research. Brown's work in examining colonial era accounts of the campaign and resolving many discrepancies from previous works simplified my task, and I owe a great debt to his wonderful work on this subject. Also, Brown's efforts helped me examine the many legends that surrounded Crawford's story and weed out those that had no factual basis.

At the same time, I also carefully filtered information written by nineteenth-century historians such as Consul W. Butterfield. Butterfield was a noteworthy regional historian of the colonial frontier. However, his histories of the Sandusky Expedition and the Girty family, as well as the amplifying notes for his books on the Washington-Crawford and Washington-Irvine letters, are heavily influenced by the cultural and racial prejudices of the time. In fairness to Butterfield, he was writing for a target audience of white, late-nineteenth century male readers, and as a result, he told them exactly what they wanted to hear. As a result, Native Americans were always referred to as "savages," the expedition's volunteers were all brave patriots, massacres perpetrated by Americans were either justified or merely some misunderstanding, and the journals of Christian missionaries like David Zeisberger and John Heckewelder were filled with "utter nonsense." However, the facts, when viewed from a twenty-first-century perspective, often tell a far different story.

Regarding the format, I would like to say first that the writers of the eighteenth century and especially, those documenting events via personal journals and diaries, often used abbreviations, capitalization, and spelling that is very different from that which we accept today. In many cases, where I quote directly from one of these documents, I have updated the original spelling and capitalization based on current standards to improve readability and prevent a cluttered narrative that might distract the reader. Also, where the narrative involves Native American figures, I chose to use the names given to them in their native language, as opposed to the ones assigned to them by Europeans. This seems only right because it is more historically accurate to do so. More important, it is right because the European names appear to be based on the notion that these Native Americans were somehow less than human until the white man named them what he willed. This is another example of the extreme cultural, religious, and racial arrogance demonstrated by the British and their American colonists. As a result, I refer to the "Half King" of the Seneca as Tanaghrisson, "Captain Pipe" of the Delaware as Hopocan, and the "Half King" of the Wyandot as Dunquat.

One important lesson I learned during this process is that no author develops a good product in a vacuum, and I want to acknowledge some people and organizations that were a key part of my work. First, I must thank my publisher, David E. Kane, and the entire staff at American History Press, who successfully guided my work through the publishing gauntlet and then provided invaluable advice and insight as it worked its way towards reality. I also owe a debt of gratitude to the Wyandot County Historical Society, who granted the rights for the use of two key images used in this book. I also want to acknowledge their very able curator, Ronald Marvin. Jr., who gave me a wonderful tour of the county museum and its exhibits on William Crawford one warm July afternoon.

In addition, I wish to thank the staff at the State Historical Society of Missouri Research Center at the University of Missouri's Ellis Library for their invaluable assistance in navigating the Lyman Copeland Draper Collection. As any historian researching the colonial frontier era knows, the Draper Collection is a critical resource. Finding the right information among its many documents can be a formidable challenge, but the research center staff made my job an easy one, and for that I am very grateful.

My intent was to write this book as a narrative history, one that tells a great story as much as it recounts historical events. Therefore, making every effort to be as accurate as possible, I also strove to add color and texture to the story's events and characters. This approach meant taking some literary license at times but never at the price of historical precision. As I had never attempted this approach before, I needed someone to guide me in making my manuscript more inviting to those among its readers who were not historians. Luckily, such a person was nearby. My dear friend, Ann Kruse, stepped up to this daunting tasks by applying her

PREFACE

considerable skills as an editor in "humanizing" my narrative, giving it that extra touch that brings life to the characters and authentic drama to the events in William Crawford's life. Without her, the story would not be all I hoped to make it. For that, both my readers and I owe her our deep appreciation and grateful thanks.

Robert N. Thompson
O'Fallon, Missouri

INTRODUCTION

Uriah Springer remembered the ride distinctly. Even as he grew to an age when memories naturally faded, when time covered them in layers of dust, he could still feel the rocking of the old horse beneath him, and his Grandma's strong back against his cheek. As a little boy growing up in southwestern Pennsylvania, Uriah often spent summer days at his Grandma Hannah's farm. The farm was not much: a small log cabin, a springhouse, and a small barn on the southern bank of the Youghiogheny River, just across the water from the borough of Connellsville. His grandfather built the cabin in 1766, as the French and Indian War was finally ending. In those long ago days, Grandpa, Grandma Hannah, and their three children had been the first white settlers along this stretch of the river.

Now, the farm's fields were tended by the few slaves his grandmother could afford to keep, and they produced just enough for themselves, plus a little extra to sell in Connellsville. The farm had woods and meadows to explore, streams to fish, and horses to ride. These were the things a young boy growing up in the Pennsylvania countryside needed for as carefree a summer as one could have in those days when hard work and a difficult, harsh existence was the standard, even for a child.

Then there was the added attraction of Grandma Hannah's stories, tales of the days when marauding and blood-thirsty Indians were nearby, raiding and killing, and when men like George Washington visited Uriah's grandfather, sharing the family's tiny cabin as the men prepared for surveying expeditions down the Ohio River. She told stories of his grandfather's days as a soldier fighting the French and the Indians with Washington, and then serving as a colonel in the Continental Army, as they fought both the British and their Indian allies during the great War of Independence. The life of a soldier, however, meant that Uriah's grandfather was away from his family for months on end, leaving Grandma Hannah to manage the farm as best she could.

In the end, all of Grandfather's years as a soldier would cost the family dearly. The farm would never thrive, and his land speculation schemes with Washington eventually amounted to little. At one point, Uriah's grandmother had faced the prospect of selling her slaves, which would have meant the end of the farm. However, when President Washington heard of her plight, he intervened and provided her with enough money to keep the slaves and save the land. By the day of Uriah's ride, Grandma Hannah had nothing but the farm and her husband's pension from the Revolutionary War.

On that summer day that stood out so clearly in Uriah's memory, Grandma Hannah saddled her favorite horse, a big mare named Jenny, and hoisted her grandson up behind her. Then they rode across the ford on the Youghiogheny. With the river behind them, Jenny trotted past Mr. Rice's farm and followed the road that swung to the left, finally disappearing into the nearby woods. After a while, they came to a clearing, where Uriah's grandmother stopped the horse by an old, moss-covered white oak log. After Grandma helped Uriah slide to the ground, she then eased herself off Jenny's back. Beneath the trees, she invited Uriah to come sit with her on the log, and as they sat there, she became very quiet, and soon began to sob. To young Uriah, it sounded as if her heart was breaking. When he asked her what was wrong, she replied, "Here, I parted with your grandfather."[1]

Years before, on a warm day in May 1782, Grandma Hannah had stood beside the old oak log and had said goodbye to her husband as he prepared to leave for Mingo Bottom on the Ohio River. There, he planned to rendezvous with a group of several hundred American militia volunteers and lead them west, deep into the hostile expanse of the Ohio Country. Their goal was the destruction of the Wyandot, Delaware, and Shawnee towns along the Sandusky River. There, Native American warriors lived who had been raiding American frontier settlements at the bidding of their British allies. The expedition would fail, although

INTRODUCTION

many of the volunteers escaped to safety, but Uriah's grandfather would never return. Instead, he died a cruel death following a trial for crimes he did not commit, and thus became a tragic martyr for white Americans seeking to conquer the new nation's frontier.

His grandfather's name was William Crawford.

Disaster on the Sandusky

Chapter 1

FRONTIER FARMER AND SURVEYOR

The Early Years

Like most children growing up on the colonial frontier, William Crawford spent much of his early life working alongside his parents and siblings—a child in the colonies had little time for play. His life was also far from one of privilege. Unlike the childhoods of the educated men with whom he would collaborate as an adult, for young William there was no wealth, no large estate, and no political connections.

Born on September 2, 1722, in Westmoreland County, Virginia, William came into the world as the fourth in the Crawford family line to carry that name. His father, the third William Crawford, was a twenty-eight-year-old former soldier. His mother, Honora Grimes Crawford, was the twenty-two-year-old daughter of Irish immigrants. Two years after William's arrival, his brother, Valentine, was born, and the brothers would be close for the rest of their lives.[1]

During William's early childhood, the Crawford home often included "redemptioners," European émigrés who had sold themselves into indentured servitude to pay for the cost of their passage to the colonies or, often as not, to secure their release from British debtor prisons. Richard Stephenson, who arrived in North America in 1718 to begin a seven-year term as an indentured servant to the Crawford family, was one of these redemptioners.[2]

In 1725, when William was still a toddler, his father died at the age of thirty-one, a tragedy common in those times when the average male life expectancy was only twenty-seven. The elder Crawford's death came just as Richard Stephenson fulfilled his contract term, and a year later, the former indentured servant married Honora Crawford, becoming the four-year-old William's stepfather. Later that same year, Richard and Honora Stephenson's first child, John, was born, and in 1727, the family moved west to new lands in Frederick County, Virginia, located in the northern, or lower, end of the Shenandoah Valley.[3]

When five-year-old William first arrived at his new home, eight years had passed since the valley's first British expedition in 1719. William now lived in a place that the expedition's members had described as "enchanting"—mountains on either side that seemed to lie one upon the other until they faded into "blue and gold clouds, challenging the eye to define where cloud began and mountain ceased." Since there were no formal land grants at the time William's family arrived in the Shenandoah Valley, Stephenson did like all the other new settlers and simply "squatted" on the land he had selected. Later he would purchase the property after someone eventually obtained a grant from the colonial government. The land he chose bordered on a creek called Bullskin Run. This land emptied into the Shenandoah River about twelve miles south of present-day Harpers Ferry. Years later, in 1750, Stephenson bought additional land and replaced the family's rough log cabin with a sturdy, stone house. The generations of family that followed would add to his initial work, creating a fine Georgian mansion named Beverley; the same mansion stands on the site to this day.[4]

William's childhood was much like that of most frontier children, characterized by a minimum of play and a maximum of work. Frontier parents expected their children to become productive contributors to the family as soon as they were able to do so. Their only treatment as simple children with no responsibilities was during infancy. By the time a frontier child was three years old, they had begun to perform simple chores. The younger children gathered goose feathers, picked berries, and helped process food, while their older siblings plaited straw, weeded the garden, and knitted stockings.[5]

When they were not hard at work in the fields of the family farm, William and Valentine hunted for the plentiful game that lived in the lower valley's forests, and swam and fished in the streams and rivers that

Redbud Run, one of the many creeks in the lower Shenandoah Valley near William Crawford's boyhood home. (*Author photo*)

wound along the valley floor. Although life on the frontier could be challenging, even by the standards of the time, it was still a wonderful place for a boy to grow up. He and his brother could wander the woodlands at will, exploring and creating their own adventures along the way.

The boys enjoyed such freedom because there was almost no threat from Native American raids in the Shenandoah during the early eighteenth century. The Shawnee who had once occupied the valley had abandoned the region ahead of the appearance of the first settlers. Like many tribes along the colonial frontier, European diseases had devastated their nation. Even before the first white trapper had set foot in the valley, dangerous microbes had already established a foothold, carried by Native Americans from the Virginia coastal region who ventured across the Blue Ridge to trade with the Shawnee. These innocent trading expeditions were the first link in a disastrous chain of events. Diseases such as measles and smallpox caused "virgin soil" epidemics, striking down thousands of

Native Americans across both the Shenandoah Valley and the Allegheny Plateau. By the time William and his family arrived, the Shawnee had moved farther west in a desperate attempt to outrun these contagions, leaving the Shenandoah open to British settlement.[6]

The Young Surveyor

When William turned eighteen, his parents decided it was time for him to learn a trade that would provide for his adult future. Although neither Richard nor Honora could read or write, they undertook measures to ensure that their children received an education. The exact means they used to accomplish this are unknown, but the surviving correspondence of both William and his brother Valentine indicate that they had sufficient schooling. Both wrote at a level that was above average for their time, especially among people living in a very rough frontier region. Furthermore, unlike many young men in the area, William had received enough education not only to write well but also to perform complex mathematical calculations with precision.[7]

With their son's abilities in mind, William's parents arranged for him to become an apprentice to a local surveyor named John Vance. In 1740, William moved to the Vance farm to live with the surveyor's family and begin his apprenticeship. As it turned out, William's parents made a very shrewd career choice on his behalf, as surveying was a skill very much in demand on the Virginia frontier. When hunters and trappers originally occupied the region, the land remained unclaimed in any legal sense and appeared an unending expanse of forests and meadows open to any white settler. The colonial government of Virginia revised the land law in 1730, and speculators quickly began to lay claim to the valley, carve up the wilderness, and sell it to eager pioneers. These claims required a survey, as did every individual parcel of land bought or leased by a colonist. This resulted in a steady flow of surveys to the local government and a correspondingly robust stream of business opportunities for the few surveyors in the valley.[8]

For William, life as an apprentice offered more than just tutelage in the science of surveying. John Vance and his wife Elizabeth had five children, among them a lovely daughter named Hannah, who was only a year younger than William. At some time during the first four years of his apprenticeship, William and Hannah began courting and on January 5, 1744 they married. Over the next six years, they would welcome three children into their growing family: Ophelia, who they called "Effie," in 1747; Sarah, whom they always called "Sally," in 1748; and John in 1750.[9]

Hanna Vance Crawford.
(*Wyandot County Historical Society*)

Prior to John's birth, William and Hannah lived with her parents before leasing a portion of her family's land. Then, on August 4, 1750, the Crawfords bought their first property, a 64-acre tract located on a branch of the Shenandoah River called Cattail Run that they purchased from Elijah Teague for the tidy sum of £1 per acre. The land was relatively flat with more than adequate water and so was perfect for farming.[10]

In the decades that followed, the Crawford home was renowned for its hospitality, a reputation that would endure no matter where they lived. Much of the credit for this went to Hannah, who was always ready to help newly arriving settlers. Many others also regarded William as one of Frederick County's most stalwart, honest, and reliable citizens.

He was also a man remembered as being "handsome," with pale skin and deep blue eyes, and at five-feet-ten inches, he was several inches taller than most contemporary men.[11]

Within a few months of buying the Cattail Run property, William quit-rented 128 acres of land bordering his farm from Lord Fairfax. Fairfax, the elder of one of Virginia's "first families," was a wealthy, powerful landowner who managed thousands of acres in the valley from his estate, Belvoir, near the site of present-day Springfield, Virginia.[12]

About the time William rented the additional acreage from Lord Fairfax, he heard that a new surveyor had arrived in the valley to look at lands granted to the wealthy English nobleman. Rumor said that the newcomer had a close, almost familial relationship with the Fairfax family. William decided to seek out this man to offer his assistance. After all, it was likely the new arrival could use an experienced, local surveyor who knew the area and its inhabitants. At the same time, William might establish a business relationship with someone who clearly possessed close ties with one of the colony's most powerful and prestigious families.

William was probably surprised to find that the man assigned the considerable task was so young—eighteen years old—and presented such an imposing figure. At six feet, three inches tall he towered over most men, and had broad shoulders and long, muscular arms. Although it was obvious that he came from a wealthy family, there was not a single sign of softness in his appearance; he radiated a steely, resolute toughness. Even at eighteen, he seemed to be someone that was not to be trifled with. Along with his height and imposing physical traits, his piercing blue-gray eyes struck William. When he introduced himself, William could not help but notice that the he stared directly at him, almost to the point of looking right through him. Nonetheless, he was also courteous and friendly, though somewhat reserved and even a bit socially awkward. When they shook hands and agreed to work together on some upcoming surveys, neither of them realized it was the beginning of a relationship that would last the rest of their lives and one that would forever alter William's fortunes.[13]

The young man was George Washington.

Young Washington

George Washington first arrived in the Shenandoah Valley in 1749 and met William a year later. Washington's father, Augustine, had died when he was only eleven years old, but even before the elder Washington's death the relationship between father and son had been tenuous at best. In fact, in the thousands of pages of journals and personal correspondence Washington would write during his lifetime, he never mentioned his father once. His mother, Mary Ball Washington, was an arrogant, selfish, domineering woman who seemed determined to keep George forever under her thumb.

As a result, Washington looked elsewhere for adult role models, particularly among the older men of his acquaintance: Lawrence Washington, George's older half-brother; Lawrence's father-in-law, Colonel Thomas Fairfax; and the colonel's son, George William Fairfax were some who profoundly influenced him. To the youthful Washington, these men were everything he aspired to be—intelligent, cultivated, and urbane; but also brave, dynamic, and ambitious. With these men as role models and ardent supporters, Washington began seeking a path that would provide him the prominence he desired, while, most importantly, allowing him to escape his mother.[14]

In 1746, Colonel Fairfax offered George an opportunity to serve as a midshipman in the Royal Navy; after three years of service, he would have been eligible to take the examination for a royal commission as a lieutenant in His Majesty's Navy. In spite of this, his mother refused the offer on George's behalf, more determined than ever to keep her son at home.[15]

With a navy career out of his reach, Washington turned his attentions to surveying. Blessed with a natural gift for mathematics, especially geometry, the profession was a logical choice for young George. Armed with his father's old surveying tools, Washington began to run lines at his home farm, as well as at neighboring plantations. At age fourteen he received formal instruction from three prominent local surveyors—George Byrne, James Genn, and George Hume. Hume seemed to have had a particularly strong influence on his skills, and under the old Scotsman's instruction, he mastered the neatness in writing and precision in drawing which would reflect in all of Washington's later surveys.[16]

This training led to what might have been the first great adventure of Washington's life. In 1748, Lord Fairfax, Colonel Fairfax's cousin and owner of thousands of acres in the Virginia frontier, returned to America after a long stay in England. Upon his arrival, His Lordship began the process of surveying and selling part of his holdings. The land Fairfax wanted to sell was along the south branch of the Potomac, just across the Blue Ridge. He assigned George William Fairfax to lead a surveying team, and George invited Washington, who was only sixteen, to serve as a member of the team. The expedition not only honed Washington's surveying skills; it also instilled a love of the frontier that he would never lose.

The early experience in the Valley also provided Washington with an opportunity to impress Lord Fairfax, who quickly took to this vigorous and ambitious young man. As a result, Fairfax became Washington's first benefactor, and it would have been hard to find one more influential in Virginia politics and society. The teenager so impressed His Lordship that the following summer he authorized Washington to cross the mountains into the Shenandoah on his own. Armed with a new commission as a surveyor from Culpeper County, Washington finally had the means to escape his mother and the mundane life of a planter.

George began his surveying work in the valley, charging about £1 more per thousand acres than the going rate set by the Virginia Assembly. Despite his higher rates, he did so much business that he opened an office in Winchester. From 1749 through 1751, he surveyed over two hundred lands and at least four of these, in 1750, involved William Crawford. The first of these was a survey of land on August 20 for William's stepfather, Richard Stephenson. Washington hired Crawford as a chainman, and given William's experience as a surveyor and the fact that this was his stepfather's land, it was a logical move.[17]

The experience of having William on his survey team must have been a positive one because Washington used him in that capacity again the next day while surveying land for his older half-brother Lawrence. Afterward, William worked as a chainman on at least two more of Washington's

*Washington's November 10, 1750 survey for John Vance,
William Crawford's father-in-law, with William Crawford
serving as lead chainman. (Library of Congress)*

surveys, both conducted in the fall of 1750. During this time, the two men developed a friendly, professional relationship, and Washington became a regular guest for meals in the Crawford home. During this time, however, circumstance and broader events would conspire to draw them into different and far more dangerous work—the work of a soldier.[18]

Land Speculation and the Politics of Empires

Land speculation on the frontier would have a substantial impact on Crawford's and Washington's lives for almost twenty-five years, and the seeds were sown before the two men even met. In 1748, Lawrence Washington joined several other partners in petitioning George II for the rights to 500,000 acres of land on the Allegheny Plateau. As was required at the time, they also requested permission to trade with the Native Americans. Later that year, the King consented to the petition, agreeing to an immediate grant of 200,000 acres along the Ohio River, and promising 300,000 additional acres in seven years; however, there were strings attached to the grant. To preserve its rights, the new company had to build and maintain a fort and bring in one hundred settlers within those first seven years. With the grant in place, Lawrence became one of four managing partners of the new Ohio Company, and young George Washington saw first-hand how lucrative land speculation could be. At the same time, this speculation led to an unintended and unanticipated chain of events that would stretch far beyond the banks of the Ohio.[19]

As the Ohio Company moved into the wilderness beyond the Alleghenies, they hired a team led by frontiersman Christopher Gist to carve out an eighty-mile-long road into the dense forest. Soon, the company was negotiating with the local Native American tribes and seeking additional investment from men eager to profit from these new lands. Much of this added investment came from Virginia Lieutenant Governor Robert Dinwiddie, and between 1750 and 1753, the business of land speculation became inexorably merged with Virginia's colonial policies.

Robert Dinwiddie, the Crown's Lieutenant Governor of Virginia. (*New York Public Library*)

FRONTIER FARMER AND SURVEYOR

When Gist and his men cut their road across the mountains, the French government took notice and was not pleased by what it discovered. The French also claimed the lands on the Allegheny Plateau, and they saw the Ohio Company's activities as a direct challenge to their sovereignty over that portion of New France. In 1752, Louis XV dispatched a new governor to North America, Ange de Menneville, Marquis de Duquesne, with orders to halt Virginia's expansion into the Ohio Country. Duquesne's first move was to send Pierre Paul de La Malgue, Sieur de Marin, from Montreal to the southern shores of Lake Erie with a force of nearly two thousand men, instructing him to begin building a chain of forts intended to solidify French claims to the region. The governor also ordered Marin to expel every English trader and settler forcibly from the territory, planting iron tablets every few miles proclaiming French ownership.

By May 1753, the French had made fast work in accomplishing Duquesne's orders. First, they completed a fort at Presque Isle, near present-day Erie, Pennsylvania, and began building a new road south to Fort Le Boeuf, located outside today's Waterford, Pennsylvania. By July, the French had made significant progress in establishing this new network of outposts, and they waited to see how the British might react.

They did not have long to wait. The intense French activity set off alarms that spread rapidly from the frontier to the colonial government in Williamsburg. British traders west of the mountains sent urgent messages to Lieutenant Governor Dinwiddie as soon as French troops and agents moved below Lake Erie. This area was considered part of Virginia because the original Virginia Company grant of 1609 stated that Virginia was bounded two hundred miles north and south of Old Point Comfort (in present-day Hampton, Virginia) and west and northwest by the Pacific Ocean. The traders informed Dinwiddie that not only were the French quickly building forts, they were also undoing years of fragile negotiations with the Native Americans above the Ohio, turning them against the British in the process.[20]

For his part, Dinwiddie could see his personal investments, as well as the Ohio Company, quickly going to ruin. He immediately implemented a counterstrategy designed to portray the French moves as threatening the very safety of the British Empire in North America. He informed all the other colonial governors about the French actions in an attempt to unify the colonies against this new threat, but also ensured to make authorities in London aware of the rapidly evolving situation. On May 21, 1753, Dinwiddie wrote to James Hamilton, the governor of Pennsylvania, telling him of the "great fears and apprehensions of the French designs to settle the Ohio." He went on to tell his fellow governor,

> I have some time ago heard of their robberies and murders, and if they are allowed a peaceable settlement on the Ohio I think the consequences will be attended with the ruin of our trade with the Indians, and also in time will be destruction to all our settlements on the continent…And we further think it would be absolutely necessary, for all the colonies to join together, in raising a proper force to prevent the French settling on the lands of the Ohio.[21]

Next, Dinwiddie wrote to the Board of Trade in London telling them, "I hope you will think it necessary to prevent the French taking possession of the lands on the Ohio, so contiguous to our settlements, or indeed in my private opinion they ought to be prevented making any settlements to the westward of our present possessions." The letter was read before the board on August 9, and the board directed the Earl of Holderness, the King's secretary of state, to respond to Dinwiddie in the strongest terms. The earl's message to Lieutenant Governor Dinwiddie read,

> . . . if you shall find, that any number of persons, whether Indians, or Europeans, shall presume to erect any fort or forts within the limits of our Province of Virginia . . . . You are to require of them peaceably to depart, and not to persist in such unlawful proceedings, & if, notwithstanding your admonitions, they do still endeavor to carry on any such unlawful and unjustifiable designs, we do hereby strictly charge, & command you, to drive them off by force of arms.[22]

As all this was going on William continued to work his farm, supplementing his income with surveying jobs. He and Hannah had a good life, absent from any severe difficulties other than the daily challenges that came with life on the colonial frontier. Nevertheless, events in Versailles, the Ohio Country, Williamsburg, and London caused storm clouds to build on the horizon, clouds that would soon envelop William, changing his life forever.

Chapter 2

THE SURVEYOR BECOMES A SOLDIER

Washington, the Ambitious Military Officer

While William's life followed its normal routine in the fall of 1753, matters were very different for his friend George Washington. After learning of London's instructions to Governor Dinwiddie, Washington left Mount Vernon for the colonial capital in Williamsburg. Upon his arrival there, he offered his services to the governor and proposed that he carry Dinwiddie's message to the French. Why Dinwiddie selected an untried twenty-two-year-old surveyor for this crucial mission is a mystery. Clearly, something about Washington impressed the governor, and on October 27, 1753, he issued Washington his official orders to serve as His Majesty's envoy.

Those orders directed Washington first to Logstown, a small outpost on the Ohio River about fifteen miles northeast of what is now Pittsburgh. Once there, he was to seek out the sachems of the Six Nations, among them Tanaghrisson of the Seneca, known to the British as "Half King." Tanaghrisson was a viceroy of the Iroquois Confederation appointed to oversee its people in the Ohio Country and Allegheny Plateau, including the Seneca, Delaware, and Mingo nations. Washington was to tell Tanaghrisson and the other sachems about his mission, and to ask their assistance in delivering Dinwiddie's message to the French. The text of that message accused the French of "…injuries done to the subjects of Great Britain, in open violation to the Laws of Nations, & the treaties now subsisting between the two Crowns." Dinwiddie's note also demanded that the French justify their encroachment on British territory and told them that, if they did not do so, he would demand their "peaceable departure." The governor crafted his message in very diplomatic terms, but he made certain the French understood that Dinwiddie would use force to remove them.[1]

On October 31, Washington departed from Williamsburg, carrying Dinwiddie's message. By November 14, he had arrived in Wills Creek (present-day Cumberland), Maryland. There he hired his brother's Ohio Company scout Christopher Gist as his guide, as well as four of Gist's men, to help him make the journey to Logstown. Twenty-five days later Washington and his men arrived at the Ohio River outpost, where he soon made contact with Tanaghrisson. Washington told the Seneca viceroy about his mission and requested his assistance in traveling to see the French. Tanaghrisson readily agreed and sent word for warriors to join him in Logstown that night to accompany himself and Washington on their journey. On the morning of November 30, Washington, Gist, Gist's men, Tanaghrisson, and the Seneca warriors departed for the nearest French outpost, Fort Venango.

After a five-day trek in cold rain they arrived at the fort. Washington informed garrison commander Captain Philippe Thomas Joncaire that he had an urgent message from Governor Dinwiddie to convey to the French colonial authorities. Joncaire told Washington they would have to continue on to Fort LeBeouf, some fifty miles away, and deliver Dinwiddie's message to General Louis Le Gardeur de St Pierre de Repentigny. That evening, Joncaire hosted a dinner for Washington, and the young Virginian shared wine and conversation with the officers assigned to the stronghold. During dinner Washington cleverly gathered intelligence information by engaging his hosts in what they thought were innocent conversations. These friendly chats revealed that recent orders from Montreal directed the French officers to cleanse the Allegheny Plateau of all Englishmen, a task the officers were determined to carry out. The next morning, Joncaire attached four French soldiers to Washington's group, presumably to keep an eye on them, and they set off, arriving at Fort LaBeouf four days later.[2]

Washington delivered the message from Dinwiddie to Repentigny. After a series of meetings with his officers, the French general suggested that Washington travel on to Montreal so the young Virginian could personally deliver Dinwiddie's note to the governor of New France. Washington told him that such a journey would exceed his orders, so Repentigny offered to forward the message to French authorities at the provincial capital. Washington agreed to this proposal, and the next morning, his party departed from the French fort. Within a few days, Tanaghrisson said goodbye, as he and his warriors returned to their village, leaving Washington, Gist, and his men to make their way back to Virginia.[3]

Washington arrived in Williamsburg in mid-January 1754, and he went straight to Governor Dinwiddie. After Washington had shared the details of his expedition and his meetings with Repentigny, Dinwiddie told him to transcribe the story of his journey for publication. Within a few weeks, the governor made certain that the details of Washington's mission to the French were printed in numerous American newspapers and were distributed in London as well. Meanwhile, despite the fact that the French had not yet sent an official response, Dinwiddie decided to take unilateral action.

Perhaps Washington's report describing French commitment to remove by force all British inhabitants from the Allegheny Plateau moved the governor to act, or perhaps it was just a product of the governor's combative nature. Whatever his reasons, Dinwiddie chose to take the offensive and follow a path almost certain to provoke a confrontation with the French.

Before Washington could leave Williamsburg to return to Mount Vernon, Dinwiddie commissioned him as a major in Virginia's service. The governor ordered Washington to go to Frederick County and enlist "50 men of the militia, who will be delivered to you by the commander of the said county pursuant to my orders." In addition to the men from Frederick County, the governor tasked Washington to gather fifty more men from the militia of neighboring Augusta County. Once this small force was trained and equipped, Dinwiddie told Washington that he was to march "to the Fork of Ohio, with the men under your command & there you are to finish & complete in the best manner, & as soon as you possibly can the fort which I expect is there already begun by the Ohio Company."[4]

THE SURVEYOR BECOMES A SOLDIER

A young George Washington in his Virginia Regiment uniform. (*New York Public Library*)

As it happened, Dinwiddie's ideas about enlisting men for this expedition proved far too ambitious. Washington's recruiting campaign did not go well, as few men wanted to march into a hostile wilderness where they might confront French soldiers and their Native American allies. By early February in 1754 neither Frederick nor Augusta Counties had recruited their fifty men, and Washington returned to Williamsburg in defeat. Dinwiddie decided to up the ante by issuing a proclamation on February 19 that offered land grants east of the Ohio River to all volunteers. Even so, as March arrived Washington still had made little progress. Because he could not find the men he needed in the Shenandoah Valley counties, he decided to see if he might be more successful in Alexandria.

While Washington labored to find recruits, Dinwiddie announced that the men Washington was trying to enlist would be formed under the banner of the "Virginia Regiment." The governor also revealed that he was appointing Joshua Fry as commander of this new regiment with the rank of colonel. Fry was an Oxford-educated college professor who possessed some militia experience but no actual military training. Washington considered Fry old and slow, but worst of all Washington had assumed that he, and not Fry, would be given command of the regiment. He had even gone so far as to lobby for the assignment with members of the House of Burgesses. Although very disappointed, Washington took some solace from the news that the governor promoted him to lieutenant colonel and made him second-in-command of the Virginia Regiment.[5]

Within days of Fry's appointment, Dinwiddie learned that the French were pushing south with several hundred men toward the strategic juncture of the Allegheny, Monongahela, and Ohio Rivers, where they planned to construct a new fort, Fort Duquesne (site of today's Pittsburgh). On March 15 he wrote Washington, ordering him to move forward immediately without Colonel Fry, who would have to catch up with the regiment later. Washington quickly completed preparations to leave Alexandria and head west for the Shenandoah with the recruits he had managed to gather, an ill-equipped group of 134 men, whom he referred to as being "loose, idle persons that are quite destitute of house, and home."[6]

As he prepared to march, Washington learned that Adam Stephen, a physician and recent arrival from Scotland, had assembled a small militia company of twenty-five riflemen in Winchester. He wrote Stephen, directing him to prepare to join Washington's regiment, and told Dinwiddie on March 20 that, "I have given Captain Stephen orders to be in readiness to join us at Winchester with his company as they were already in that neighborhood—raised there."[7]

Unknown to Washington, his former surveying partner, William Crawford, was a member of Stephen's militia company. Once Governor Dinwiddie issued his February 19 proclamation, both William and his brother, Valentine, enlisted in the king's service. One has to wonder what led William to take this action, as he had no military experience of any kind. Moreover, his surveying business was doing well, the farm was thriving, and he was a family man in his early thirties. Why he would join what was clearly a dangerous expedition led by an inexperienced militia lieutenant colonel lay either in his confidence in Washington's abilities, or more likely in Dinwiddie's promise of a piece of 200,000 acres of land east of the Ohio River to every man who joined.[8]

Once Washington arrived in Winchester in early April 1754, William and the rest of Stephen's company joined the regiment. After gathering supplies, the contingent began their journey to the northwest. A few days into the march, Washington received a dispatch informing him that on April 17 nearly 1,000 French troops with 18 pieces of artillery had seized Washington's objective—the Ohio Company's fort. Now he would have to abandon any hope of taking it. Given how badly the French outnumbered Washington's little regiment, it might have been prudent to cancel the expedition immediately. Instead Washington held a council of war with his officers on April 20 to discuss the situation and determine their course of action.

The courier who brought word of the fort's capture also carried a message from Tanaghrisson. In this dispatch, the Seneca viceroy stated his contempt for the French and his determination to fight alongside Britain. "We are now ready to fall upon them," he wrote, "waiting only for your succor. Have good courage, and come as soon as possible; you will find us as ready to encounter with them as you are yourselves." Unknown to Washington, the source of Tanaghrisson's enthusiasm for a fight was a recent meeting the Seneca held with a French emissary.[9]

The French had dispatched an officer to meet with Tanaghrisson to try to persuade him to abandon any alliance with the British and their forces from Virginia. Tanaghrisson took the French message as an implicit threat and told the officer that the French had no business intruding on the Iroquois Confederation's hunting grounds. Tanaghrisson then placed his hand on the officer's chest and pushed him away, forcefully telling the Frenchman he would not "allow his Brothers the English to be routed from the Land, which the Half King by the Directions of the Six Nations had allowed them to build and fortify." The French emissary responded with outrage at Tanaghrisson's words and actions. Tanaghrisson ordered the French to depart immediately, threatening to unleash his warriors if they did not do so. The sachem was not one to take a threat lightly, and he was now determined to resist the French alongside Virginia and Great Britain.[10]

With this news from Tanaghrisson, Washington saw a new opportunity. He proposed to his officers that they move forward, saying, "it would be proper to advance as far as Red-Stone-Creek, on Monongahela, about thirty-seven miles on this side of the fort [Duquesne], and there to raise a fortification, clearing a road broad enough to pass with all our artillery and our baggage, and there to wait for fresh orders." His officers agreed, and William and the other soldiers continued their march the next morning.[11]

After several weeks of cutting down trees and hacking through underbrush, the regiment carved out an eighty-mile road, the first to cross the mountains into the Allegheny Plateau. This also placed the Virginians deep into the territory disputed with France, and Washington was concerned they might run into French scouting patrols at any moment.

On May 11 a friendly trader told Washington that a small French detachment under the command of Ensign Michel Pépin had arrived at Christopher Gist's small settlement, some fifty miles away. Reportedly, Pépin was the vanguard for a fifty-man French force moving down from Fort Duquesne to meet the Virginians. Washington immediately issued orders to Adam Stephen to take his company, William included, and head for Gist's settlement. Washington told Stephen to determine Pépin's whereabouts and "in case they were in the neighborhood, to cease pursuing and to take care of themselves."[12]

As William and his fellow militiamen moved out the next morning, he likely experienced feelings of both apprehension and excitement. He may also have felt a great sense of relief, as this assignment would mean leaving the heavy labor of road building behind him for a while. However, the weather soon dashed any exuberance he might have felt. A torrent of heavy rain began to fall, flooding every stream and river in the company's path, thus slowing their progress to a crawl. The company had set out with only a four-day supply of rations, and after three days slogging through the relentless rain, the men's rations were almost spent. At this point, Stephen paused the march and sent some of the men out to kill game, while the remainder built crude rafts.

After three more days of marching and crossing raging streams with their makeshift rafts, William and his comrades arrived on the Monongahela near its confluence with Redstone Creek. Here they met several traders who told them that, due to the bad weather, Pépin's party and the larger force under Ensign Jumonville had returned up the Ohio to Fort Duquesne. Although this information indicated a reduced threat to the Virginians, Stephen still wanted to return to Washington with more substantial intelligence on the enemy. Therefore, he hired a local man to venture to Fort Duquesne, collect what information he could regarding the French forces, and return with it, all for a small payment of £5. As Stephen's hired spy departed for the fort, the company set up camp and waited for his return.

Five days later, the spy arrived safely from his trip to the French stronghold. As Stephen debriefed him, the company commander found the information very detailed and complete in every possible way. In fact, to Stephen's great chagrin, he realized that the information was too good for the money spent and suspected that the man had taken a similar payment from the French for the exact location of Stephen and his men. As a result, the Scotsman decided it was time to leave and return to the main body of the regiment as quickly as possible.[13]

As William and the rest of Stephen's company made their way back, the regiment continued building a road towards Redstone Creek, a task that local traders told Washington would be nearly impossible. Although "impossible" might have been too strong a term, it was very close to the truth. Two weeks of backbreaking labor only gained the regiment about half the distance to their objective. On May 24 they reached a large open spot in the forest called Great Meadows, about twenty-five miles from the Ohio River.[14]

Lighting the Fuse

Six days before arriving at Great Meadows, Washington learned that a company of one hundred Virginians accompanied by fifty militiamen from New York was nearby and would soon reinforce his regiment. This news gave Washington more confidence about the safety of his command. However, once the regiment made camp at Great Meadows, Washington received a message from Tanaghrisson informing him that the French were on the march again, and were now actively searching for the Virginians. Tanaghrisson also knew the French troops' primary mission was not to search for Washington. Their real objective was to intercept the Seneca leader, who was en route to Winchester with a small group of warriors and family members to meet with Governor Dinwiddie. Once the French found Tanaghrisson, their orders were to turn him back. Failing that, they were to kill his entire party. On May 27, three days after Washington received Tanaghrisson's message, Christopher Gist arrived at Great Meadows to report that Pépin and fifty French soldiers were at Gist's settlement. Combined with the message from Tanaghrisson, Gist's story convinced Washington that he should try to defend his current position at Great Meadows.[15]

Around 8:00 p.m. that evening, Washington received another message from Tanaghrisson. In it, he told Washington that warriors had discovered the tracks of two men near the Seneca's current encampment, only a few hours' march from Great Meadows. After following the tracks they had come upon a French camp nearby. After receiving this message, Washington immediately sprang into action by placing a heavy guard on the camp at Great Meadows. Next, he assembled a small force of forty men (including William and the rest of Stephen's company) to accompany him as he set out to discuss the situation with his Seneca ally.[16]

Marching through the forest in heavy rain and deep darkness, William and his comrades stumbled over rough terrain and one another, with some losing their way on the narrow trail. Despite these obstacles, Washington and his men arrived at Tanaghrisson's camp in the early hours of May 28. The two leaders conferred, and Washington assured the sachem that reinforcements were on the way. In his assurances Washington stretched the truth, telling Tanaghrisson there would soon be enough men to defeat any French force sent from Fort Duquesne. Washington proposed that they join forces and immediately attack the nearby French encampment, and Tanaghrisson readily agreed.

Given that there was no state of war between Great Britain and France, Washington had made a remarkable suggestion to Tanaghrisson. Yet, given Washington's ambitions and youth, perhaps this was not very surprising. Once Dinwiddie made him an officer in the colonial militia,

THE SURVEYOR BECOMES A SOLDIER

Washington began to yearn for a royal commission, believing that a career in His Majesty's army might be his destiny. Making an assault on the French might help achieve that goal. While Governor Dinwiddie had planted the explosives for war between the two empires through his demands to the French; young Lieutenant Colonel Washington was now about to light the fuse.

As two Seneca scouts ran ahead through the forest to reconnoiter, Washington, with his forty militiamen, and Tanaghrisson, with fifteen warriors, set off for the French camp. The scouts quickly returned, saying that the French force of about thirty soldiers was encamped nearby in a slight depression beneath a rocky outcropping, and they apparently had not posted any sentries. Hearing this news, Washington decided to divide his force into three groups. The first, under his personal command, would move around to the right of the French camp, and Stephen's men would march to the left. The Seneca, meanwhile, were to position themselves at the rear of the camp to cut off any escape route. With the orders given, all three groups moved out, took their assigned posts, and made themselves ready.

Once in his position on the left flank of the French camp, William Crawford crouched behind the cover of some nearby rocks. His rifle was loaded, the flint in place, and he was ready to fire. For a while, the only sounds he heard were the birds in nearby trees, the clatter of pans in the enemy camp below, and the unintelligible chatter among the French soldiers while cooking their breakfast. Suddenly, just as the sun crept above the horizon, an explosion of musket fire interrupted the peaceful tranquility of the morning.

What happened next remains a historical controversy to this day, as various British and French accounts differ markedly. All versions agree that the shooting erupted suddenly, leaving ten Frenchmen dead, including their commander, Ensign Jumonville. Twenty-two others were captured, among them Jumonville's second-in-command, Ensign Pépin. There is also agreement that French fire killed one of Washington's men and wounded two others. Moreover, after the French surrendered, the Native Americans scalped their dead, later sending the scalps to other tribes as grizzly trophies designed to enlist their participation in a new war with France. This is where the agreement ends.

Washington maintained that, as his soldiers took their positions, Jumonville's men discovered the Virginians and the French troops began shouting the alarm. At that point, Washington ordered his troops to open fire. The French returned fire, much of which they directed at Washington's right column, and the fight "only lasted a quarter of an hour, before the enemy was routed." In his account Adam Stephen wrote, "A smart action ensued: their [the French] arms and ammunition were dry being sheltered by the bark huts they slept in, we could not depend on ours, and therefore, keeping up [withholding] our fire, advanced as near as we could with fixed bayonets, and received their fire." According to Stephen, William and the rest of the Virginians on the left rushed into the French camp shortly after the firing began to find Jumonville already dead.[17]

For their part, the French asserted that Jumonville was on a diplomatic mission to deliver a message to Governor Dinwiddie. This meant that the ensign was actually an envoy, just as Washington had been the year before. They stated that after the first two volleys from the Virginians, Jumonville's interpreter shouted over the din of the rifle fire in an effort to get the Virginians to cease fire so that Jumonville could explain the reasons for his mission. At that point, the French claimed that the Virginians did stop shooting, which allowed Jumonville to read his message aloud through the interpreter. But before Jumonville could finish one of Washington's men shot him through the head. This act, the French argued, was the assassination of a diplomatic messenger, and one ordered by George Washington. Washington later declared the story of a diplomatic mission was nonsense. Moreover, he stated that Jumonville's men were spies and suggested that the French prisoners he sent back to Winchester be hanged.[18]

A third account of the skirmish provides its own interesting picture of what happened that May morning. This account was provided by a Native American veteran of the battle to Colonel James Innes during a British conference with Seneca, Delaware, and Shawnee delegates at Wills Creek in October and November 1754. The Native American, only referred to by Innes as the "Chief Warrior," told the British officer that Jumonville's men had detected the Virginians and that "Col Washington begun himself and fired." The French returned some sporadic shots before taking "to their Heels and running." The retreating French soldiers ran directly into Tanaghrisson and his warriors, and "Eight of them met with their Destiny by the Indian Tomahawks, upon which the other remaining Survivors turned short and ran the other Way." Seeing that they were surrounded, the French, now led by Pépin, surrendered to one of Tanaghrisson's war chiefs, Monacatootha, who took the prisoners to Washington. When Tanaghrisson arrived on the scene, the Seneca leader told Pépin, "I will let you see that the Six Nations can kill as well as the French, which you said we know nothing of, and as you came after me to take my Life and my Children's." Tanaghrisson then raised his tomahawk to kill the French officer, but Washington stepped between Pépin and Tanaghrisson and convinced the Seneca viceroy not to kill the Frenchman.[19]

Whatever the truth, Crawford had seen his first combat and the events in which he participated would ignite a global war between the world's two greatest empires.

A re-creation of Washington's Fort Necessity at Fort Necessity National Battlefield in Fayette County, Pennsylvania.
(*Author photo*)

After the fight with Jumonville's men, Washington decided to build a small stockade at Great Meadow, naming it Fort Necessity. The reinforcements Washington had promised to Tanaghrisson did arrive, but, in the end, it was not enough. On July 3, 1754, a French force of more than 700 men arrived and made quick work of Washington and his command of just over 300 soldiers. After a few hours of fighting, the French proposed that Washington surrender. Seeing his position was truly hopeless, Washington was forced to accept humiliating terms. Worst of all, an error made by his translator during a review of the official surrender document led Washington to sign an admission that he had knowingly assassinated Jumonville while the Frenchman was on a diplomatic mission.

A Brief Respite

The survivors of the defeat at Fort Necessity retreated to Winchester. There they reunited with other members of the Virginia Regiment, including William, who was not present during the battle. In all likelihood he was detached from the command at the time of the French attack, either on scouting duties or guarding the French prisoners who were on their way to Winchester.

Washington was now in full command of the regiment, since Colonel Fry had died at Fort Cumberland on May 31 following a fall from his horse. Washington moved on to Alexandria, and he worked to find new recruits and supplies. In early August, Dinwiddie proposed that he move his men to Wills Creek in preparation for a new fall and winter expedition, one designed to dislodge the French from Fort Duquesne. The idea shocked Washington, and he made it clear that his regiment was in no condition for such a campaign.

There were several reasons for Washington's reluctance. First, his commissariat had no money to buy supplies, and even if he did have the funds the area around Winchester could not provide the food and other provisions his men needed. There was also the issue of his men's ability to survive the cold, wet weather they would encounter on such an expedition. Washington wrote to William Fairfax expressing his concerns for his men's survival under such conditions:

> Neither can men, unused to that life, live there, without some other defense from the weather than tents: this I know of my own

knowledge, as I was out last winter from the 1st of November till sometime in January; and notwithstanding I had a good tent, was as properly prepared, and as well guarded, in every respect, as I could be against the weather, yet the cold was so intense that it was scarcely supportable. I believe out of the 5 or 6 men that went with me, 3 of them, though they were as well clad as they could be, were rendered useless by the frost, and were obliged to be left upon the road.[20]

Perhaps Washington's greatest concern, however, was morale. While William and the others in Adam Stephen's company were happy to be home in Frederick County where they could again see their families, the remainder of the regiment was in a state of near mutiny. In his letter to Fairfax, Washington mentioned the "sufferings our soldiers underwent in the last attempt…to take possession of the fork of the Allegany and Monongalia" before adding that,

You also saw the disorders those sufferings produced among them at Winchester after they returned. They are yet fresh in their memories, and have an irritable effect…they got some intimation that they were again ordered out, and it immediately occasioned a general clamor, and 6 men to desert last night; this we expect will be the consequence every night, except prevented by close confinement.[21]

With men steadily deserting in response to the rumored campaign, William and the rest of Stephen's company were the only reliable men left in the regiment. Washington ordered them to scout the surrounding hills and forests for signs of Native American activity. Although the lower Shenandoah had long been safe from Native American raids, Dinwiddie's policies and Washington's recent actions against the French had changed the situation. The French had encouraged their Native American allies to move down from the Alleghenies and attack British settlements that had never before experienced raids. Even though the men in William's company did their best to prevent these attacks, they had little success.

Raiding parties continued to attack isolated farms throughout the Shenandoah Valley, killing adult males who defended their settlements and carrying away dozens of women and children into captivity.[22]

By the fall of 1754, London had issued new policies, so Dinwiddie scrapped his plans for another campaign. The leadership in Whitehall appointed Horatio Sharpe, the Governor of Maryland, as a lieutenant colonel and placed all colonial forces raised for service against the French and Indians under his direct command. In response to this news, Dinwiddie decided to divide the Virginia Regiment into independent companies, with no Virginia officer to be higher in rank than captain. Because this was a huge demotion, Washington angrily resigned his commission, and by mid-November, he was home at Mount Vernon. In the meantime, Adam Stephen acted as the senior officer from Virginia, and the sad remnants of the Virginia Regiment languished in Winchester for the winter, poorly supplied, awaiting orders.[23]

As it turned out, they did not have long to wait.

Chapter 3

DEFEAT AT THE MONONGAHELA

The Stage for War is Set

By the middle of the eighteenth century, France and Great Britain had been battling for the eastern half of North America for more than 150 years. During this era, the fighting was almost incessant as the two countries fought four wars, three of which involved North America: King William's War (League of Augsburg War, 1689-1697), Queen Anne's War (War of the Spanish Succession, 1702-1713), and King George's War (War of the Austrian Succession, 1745-1748). Each of these wars would end via treaty, and each of those treaties would sow the seeds for the next conflict.

One reason for the long lasting and bitterly contested French and British quarrel is that each country's approach to colonization was unique. Although both nations' interests were mercantile, France took a subtler approach to establishing relationships with the Native Americans. While the French did occasionally engage in battle with nations such as the Iroquois, Natchez, and Fox, they never sought to truly conquer them. Instead, they preferred to pay the Native Americans very high duties for exploiting the wilderness they occupied.

New France consisted of a string of isolated, primitive trading posts scattered across a broad backwoods. The only large settlements were clustered between Quebec and Montreal, and New Orleans and Mobile. For the most part, the Native Americans tolerated the French. Though they resented their presence, their hostility was not strong enough to push them into war. The French never suggested that Native Americans were French subjects, and they made sure that goods dispensed to them were always considered "rent," or distributed in direct payment for furs. The French clearly understood that their survival relied upon maintaining good relations with the Native Americans.[1]

The French also integrated themselves into tribal life. It was common for a Frenchman to speak one or more Native American languages, and to be thoroughly familiar with Native American customs. Intermarriage was common and was more readily accepted in New France's colonial society than that of Britain. More importantly, the French understood the various tribes' ambitions and politics. This helped them negotiate with the Native Americans and maintain stable diplomatic and military relations.

The British perspective on the Native populations of the New World was entirely different. British colonization began shortly after the 1604 Treaty of London between Great Britain and Spain. In that treaty, James I recognized and accepted existing Spanish properties in the Western Hemisphere, but retained the right to take whatever remained "unoccupied." The fact that thousands of Native Americans already "occupied" much of North America did not matter in the least. The British approach to colonization would be one of physical occupation and legal ownership based upon the tenets of European culture and custom.

With the establishment of the Jamestown settlement in 1607, the British embarked on a program of brutal and violent conquest. They unleashed an endless flood of settlers armed with "muskets, diseases, and ploughs" upon the lands between the Atlantic Ocean and the Appalachian Mountains. The British made little, if any, attempt to accommodate the various Native American nations that already lived and hunted there, and as a result, they quickly earned their hatred.[2]

The pinnacle of British arrogance lay in their belief that they could seize and colonize land based on their monarch's divine right and "superior" religion. Employing religious dogma from the time of the Crusades, the British believed that a Christian king possessed the right of eminent domain over any lands held by a non-Christian heathen people. As Anglican minister Richard Eburne explained, the passage in Genesis 1:28, which reads "…and God said unto them, be fruitful and multiply and replenish the earth, and subdue it" provided additional justification for the British to seize Native American lands. According to Eburne, this commandment from God to Adam and Eve awarded Christianity a grand charter with the "privilege to spread themselves from place to place, and to have, hold, occupy, and enjoy any region or country whatsoever which they should find either not occupied." Native Americans would argue that their lands were indeed "occupied," but the British had an answer for that as well. If one does not use English and European agricultural techniques, he is not "replenishing" the land and therefore has no rights to it.[3]

It was not surprising to anyone that a majority of the woodland nations sided with France in the coming war. Native American leaders who stood with the British, such as Tanaghrisson, were a small minority. A greater number of the Native American tribes recognized the difference between the French and British approaches to colonization and reacted accordingly. While British settlers seized every bit of land in their path and threatened the Native Americans' very way of life, the French asked for nothing but access to good trade. Therefore, most of the woodland nations believed their best strategy was to side with France and make war on Great Britain and her colonists.

Braddock Arrives

As the winter of 1754 approached, intense diplomatic activity was underway in London and Paris. British and French diplomats frantically exchanged notes and viewed maps of the Allegheny Plateau, each of which depicted each sides' version of the boundaries between New France and Britain's American colonies. While the French were conciliatory, the British were not, and no compromise seemed within reach. By the spring of 1755, despite the fact that there was no formal state of war, the two sides broke diplomatic relations.

The reason for the steady decline in diplomatic progress and its eventual failure was a decision made by King George II's government in December 1754. At that time, Whitehall resolved to send two full regiments of British Regulars to America under the command of General William Braddock. Hearing this, one French minister said, "War alone can end our differences.... If they are determined at London to kindle a war, all we can say to forestall that evil will not prevent it." On December 22 Braddock sailed from Cork, Ireland for Hampton Roads in Virginia. Twenty-four days later his two regiments followed, a total of one thousand troops from Sir Peter Halkett's 44th Regiment and Colonel Thomas Dunbar's 48th Regiment.[4]

Braddock was an odd choice for this pivotal command. Although he had been in the army for forty-three years, the sixty-year-old general had never held an independent command at any level. Nevertheless, he would now oversee all British forces in North America. The reasons for his assignment lay in Whitehall's debate over the strategy for the coming campaign in America and the political machinations among its ministers.[5]

When His Majesty's government first heard that the French had erected Fort Duquesne, the King's privy councilors met to determine Great Britain's response. They soon found themselves divided on what approach to take to what they interpreted as an affront to British sovereignty. King George II opposed dispatching a British army to North America to fight the French. Great Britain had just negotiated the treaty ending the last war with France, and the King did not want to start another. The man in charge of colonial policy, the Earl of Halifax, countered that they needed to employ a joint Anglo-American army, and he proposed a grand campaign to seize Fort Niagara, a French stronghold in western New York. This, Halifax argued, would make their position at Fort Duquesne untenable and force the French to evacuate it, eliminating the need for the British to mount a direct attack over the Allegheny Mountains, a formidable obstacle.

In the end, the king's son, Prince William Augustus, the Duke of Cumberland and head of the British army, overruled Halifax. Prince William despised the French, and many in Great Britain considered him a brutal, cruel man. His repression of the Scots after the rebellion of 1745 had earned him the sobriquet of "The Butcher of Culloden." Not content with the slaughter of the Scottish army on Culloden Moor, Prince William had ravaged the Scottish Highlands with a search and destroy campaign that wiped out the clan system and saw the imprisonment and execution of hundreds of Scots. Prince William, true to form, convinced his father

General Edward Braddock, commander of His Majesty's forces in North America. (*New York Public Library*)

that they needed to send a British army to the colonies. He also proposed a direct assault on Fort Duquesne, and he directed that Braddock, the Prince's own man, lead that force.[6]

Braddock's selection to lead the British forces was therefore based on his political connection to Prince William and his own steadfast commitment to discipline. The latter was important because Braddock would need a colonial militia to supplement British Regulars. Both Whitehall and the Prince hoped Braddock could bring the unruly militiamen to heel, and make them perform like British soldiers. Whitehall gave Braddock the mandate to conduct an ambitious campaign that would lead to the seizure of Fort Duquesne, in addition to all the other existing French forts along the frontier.

Braddock's many shortcomings began to show soon after he arrived in America in early February 1755. Success in the coming campaign depended on Braddock working closely with the colonial governments. His army needed money from the colonies for supplies, and American officials had important advice to provide on warfare with the Indians. Yet, rather than cooperating and listening, Braddock fought continuously with the colonial authorities over matters involving both money and strategy. In doing so, he made his contempt for them and all Americans very clear. Pennsylvania's chief justice, William Allen, wrote that Braddock was "an improper man, of a mean capacity, obstinate and self-sufficient, above taking advice." Meanwhile, Washington, who returned to duty in May 1755 as one of Braddock's aides-de-camp, said that the general "represents us in a light we little deserve; for instead of blaming the individuals as he ought, he charges all his disappointments to a public supineness, and looks upon the country…as void of both honor and honesty."[7]

Braddock's most serious flaw was his stubbornness. His overall tactical approach included overconfidence in his Regular troops and a determination to employ standard European tactics. Despite advice from Americans who had fought the Native Americans for decades, Braddock dismissed any proposal for using the techniques proven effective by both frontiersmen and American colonial troops. This meant that rather than fighting from the cover of concealed positions, Braddock wanted his men to engage the enemy by standing upright in the open while firing disciplined volleys from a line formation.

Perhaps worst of all, the general refused to employ any large numbers of Native American warriors as either scouts or fighters. All attempts by American officials to add Native warriors to the ranks of Braddock's army failed as a result of the general's sense of racial and cultural superiority. In many cases, Braddock immediately sent home warriors who arrived in camp to volunteer their services. Other Native Americans often stormed out of camp on their own after the general informed them that their lands belonged to His Majesty and that, following a British victory, he would not allow them to remain on them. As a result, Braddock's army marched west from Fort Cumberland on June 10, 1755 with only seven Mingo warriors, led by their chief, Scarouady, accompanying it.[8]

Into the Woods

In the weeks before the army departed, colonial militiamen from Maryland, New York, Pennsylvania, and Virginia had joined the British

Regulars at Fort Cumberland. William Crawford was among them, still serving under Adam Stephen. Stephen's company, now numbering about sixty men, formed a "Ranger" unit, one specializing in Indian-style warfare. Nonetheless, because Braddock still refused to consider such tactics, he ordered the militia trained in standard European methods. Not surprisingly, his efforts were not very successful, and he complained bitterly about the militiamen, especially those from Virginia. Braddock reported that "the whole of the forces are now assembled, making two thousand effectives, the greatest part Virginians, very indifferent men, this country affording no better." Braddock also ordered the mixing of colonial units with British Regulars, placing the colonials under the overall command of British officers.[9]

From the moment the integration of Regulars and militia began it damaged morale, although not in the way one might guess. Instead of reducing the spirits of American colonials, it adversely affected the British Regulars. As soon as they merged with the two British regiments, the Americans began to entertain their new British comrades with tales of what lay ahead. These stories began with descriptions of the dense forest between Fort Cumberland and Fort Duquesne, particularly the woods on the far side of the Alleghenies. The Americans told the British soldiers that the forest was so thick that you could walk for miles without seeing sunshine, even at noon on a clear summer day. They said these woodlands would be unlike anything the British soldiers had ever seen, which, of course, was true. Henry Bouquet, a Swiss-born British officer, commented that a European "must have lived some time in the vast forest of America; otherwise he will hardly be able to conceive a continuity of woods without end." The Americans told the Regulars that what lurked in the darkness of that forest was far worse.[10]

The American militiamen described their Indian opponents as well-armed, highly skilled "savages," who would ambush the army repeatedly during the day and capture or kill every careless sentry at night. Those killed outright, the colonials said, would be the lucky ones. Any British soldier wounded or captured could look forward to being scalped, painfully mutilated while alive, or taken back to an Indian village. Once there they would be slowly tortured and then burned at the stake. This combination of an unfamiliar, dark, and forbidding landscape filled with savages waiting to take one's scalp was more than unnerving for many British Regulars; it was terrifying.

By June 18, the column had barely made any progress into the forest, only advancing about two miles a day and marching a mere thirty miles from Fort Cumberland. Braddock ordered William's unit of Rangers and a small contingent from South Carolina to guard the huge supply train at the rear of the column. That train consisted of massive ammunition wagons, a large herd of cattle, and wagons filled with food for the men and fodder for the horses.

Re-creation of the type of ammunition wagon used by Braddock's army. (*Author photo*)

As the army moved on the impenetrable gloom, hot temperatures, and lack of breeze took their toll. As the troops rested from another hard day of marching, news arrived that an additional 500 French troops were moving to reinforce Fort Duquesne. Speed was now essential, so that night Braddock held a council of war to discuss the situation. At that meeting, Washington made the argument that Braddock needed to abandon his supply train and hurry forward with a smaller force of handpicked men supplied by only packhorses and a few small wagons. For once, Braddock heeded the advice of a colonial. He immediately organized a force of thirteen hundred men to move ahead, while the rest of the army established a base camp under Colonel Dunbar.[11]

As Braddock's men moved closer to their objective, Native American warriors scouting on behalf of the French began to pick off stragglers. They horribly mutilated those they killed, exactly as the American soldiers had warned. Nerves among Braddock's Regulars began to fray, and British troops screamed in alarm and fired at nonexistent threats in the night. Braddock ordered that all troops sleep with their arms, and then doubled up the number of sentries.

At the rear, William saw his share of fighting. The experience Stephen's company had gained in dealing with Native American raids in the Shenandoah gave them the advantage in an ongoing series of skirmishes against their attackers. The Rangers trailed about fifty miles behind the main column, escorting a small group of wagons as well as a herd of one hundred cattle. From the moment they left Colonel Dunbar's camp Stephen deployed the men carefully by ordering them to cover the company's flanks and to scout ahead for signs of Native American activity. As Stephen later recalled, "vigilance" was "the only thing can secure one against such an enemy."[12]

As it turned out, this vigilance was necessary as warriors ranged down from Fort Duquesne and harassed the Rangers day and night. William and his comrades always got the best of them by breaking up every attempted

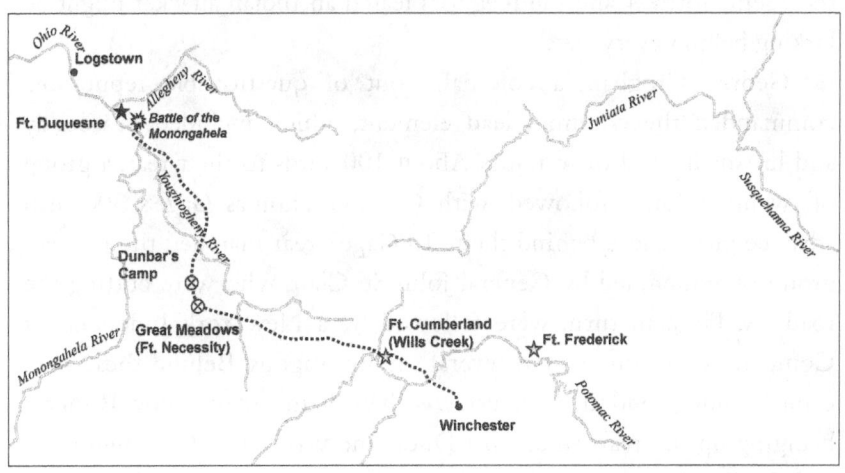

Map of the route taken by Braddock's army. (*Drawn by the Author*)

ambush, and having "the first fire on them" at every attack. By July 5, the Rangers had caught up with Braddock's column without the loss of a single man, wagon, or steer.[13]

On July 8, the army arrived on the banks of the Monongahela River, only eight miles southeast of Fort Duquesne. This meant they would reach their objective late the following day. Braddock now had to decide on the best way to make their final approach to the fort. The most direct path led through an area called "The Narrows," but the terrain there was rough. Scouts told Braddock that The Narrows also offered the enemy numerous opportunities for an ambush. The scouts recommended crossing the Monongahela, marching up the west bank of the river to a point known as Frazier's Cabin, and then crossing the river again, just a few miles southeast of Fort Duquesne. Braddock agreed, and then issued his orders for the following day.[14]

In the morning, the British army made its way across the river, as planned, but not without difficulty. The slopes leading down to the Monongahela were steeper than the scouts had reported, making the movement of artillery very challenging. To make matters worse, it was a sunny, hot day, without even a slight breeze to cool the air, as the army struggled across the river for the second time. As they reentered the woods on the other side of the river tensions increased. The army was very near the enemy fortress, and the Regulars feared an Indian attacker might be lurking behind every tree.

George Croghan, a colonial scout of questionable reputation, commanded the column's lead element, which included Scarouady and his small band of warriors. About 100 yards to their rear, a group of twenty soldiers followed, with Colonel Thomas Gage's 300-man advance guard close behind them. To Gage's rear marched the pioneer group of axmen, led by General John St. Clair, who were cutting the roadway. They, in turn, were followed by a New York Independent Company, two cannon, and several supply wagons. Behind these men came Braddock and the main body, with William and his fellow Rangers bringing up the rear. Since Fort Duquesne was only a few miles away and the French were nowhere to be seen, Braddock decided to march a few more hours and then encamp for the night. They would make the final approach to the French fort the next day after a night of rest.[15]

Meanwhile, the French command at Fort Duquesne was in turmoil. Despite the fact that their Native American allies had been making raids on Braddock's army for over a week, the fort's commander, Colonel Contrecoeur, did not hear about the British army's advance until July 6. Disappointed that his Indian forces did not do more damage, Contrecoeur complained that the British were "so constantly on guard, always marching in battle formation, that all the efforts that our detachments put forth against them are useless." While the French commander initially thought the enemy force was small, estimates from Native American scouts placed Braddock's strength at three to four thousand men and artillery. Contrecoeur's total strength was only about 250 French and Canadian troops and an unknown number of Native American warriors. These warriors soon made it clear they were not sure they wanted to oppose such a formidable British force. Moreover, the fort was not ready to defend. The French had built 10-foot deep earthen ramparts topped by a twelve-foot high wooden stockade wall, but this could only fend off infantry. Braddock's artillery was another matter. There was no possibility the fort would survive a sustained cannon barrage.[16]

Contrecoeur and his officers debated whether to burn and abandon the fort or make some kind of stand against Braddock's overwhelming strength. The debate became moot on July 7 with the arrival of Captain Daniel Hyacinthe Mary Lienard de Beaujeu. The governor of New France ordered de Beaujeu, an experienced frontier officer, to take command of Fort Duquesne. Not surprisingly, Contrecoeur refused to relinquish command to a junior officer. In an attempt to sooth his superior's ruffled feathers, de Beaujeu offered to act as second in command, but his offer was premised on Contrecoeur authorizing de Beaujeu to assemble a force to attack Braddock's column as it tried to cross the Monongahela. Contrecoeur accepted the proposal.[17]

With the news on July 8 that Braddock was only a few miles away, de Beaujeu gathered the warriors in the fort for a grand council meeting. At first, the Native Americans remained reluctant. "No, Father," they told him, "you want to die and to sacrifice yourself; the English are more than four thousand, and we, we are only eight hundred, and you want to go and attack them. You see clearly that you have no sense. We ask until tomorrow to make up our minds." The warriors and their chiefs deliberated. When de Beaujeu asked them about their decision, they told him once more that they would not go. De Beaujeu replied passionately, saying, "I am determined to confront the enemy. What would you let your father go alone? I am certain to defeat them!" He then sang war songs with the warriors, eventually convincing all but one tribe, the Potawatomi from the Detroit region, to make the attack. Around 9:00 a.m. on July 9 de Beaujeu and a force of 72 French troops, 146 Canadians, and 637 warriors marched from Fort Duquesne to ambush the British.[18]

De Beaujeu may not have had a clear idea of Braddock's numbers as he left Fort Duquesne, but both French and Indian scouts had provided him with an accurate assessment of the approach path the British would use. This was crucial to his plan for the battle. He knew he had to head for the fords on the Monongahela rather than The Narrows, and he was keenly aware of the close order formation Braddock's army was using as they marched. His plan was to envelop British as they crossed the river, employ the cover of the dense forest, and cut them down with a relentless attack on both flanks. This tactical approach pleased the Indians who were supremely confident of its chances for success. As one Delaware said, they would "shoot um down all one pigeon."[19]

Who Would Have Thought It?

De Beaujeu intended to attack the British as they were midstream crossing the river, but he was too late. As he approached the Monongahela, Braddock's army had already made both river crossings and was pressing forward toward Fort Duquesne. Just after 1:00 p.m. on July 9 Croghan and the Indian scouts discovered the French force moving down the trail through the forest. They dashed back to warn Gage's advanced guard, but de Beaujeu was hot on their heels. As soon as Croghan found Gage, de Beaujeu appeared in the trail behind him dressed in Indian garb. Suddenly, and to both armies' complete surprise, the French and the British had collided head-on in the forest above the Monongahela.

As De Beaujeu waived his hat and shouted an order for his men to disperse along the British flanks, Gage's Regulars quickly formed to fire a series of volleys in return. In minutes, both sides were fully engaged in a vicious firefight, with Captain de Beaujeu falling dead as one of the battle's first casualties.

It was at this moment that the close contact between American militiamen and the British soldiers had its inevitable impact. Within minutes of the first shots and with the Americans' horror stories fresh in their minds, the British troops abandoned all sense of military discipline, and their defense quickly disintegrated into complete panic. As the Indians, Canadians, and French troops swept down the British flanks, they kept up a hot, steady fire. What terrified the Regulars most, however, was a virtually invisible enemy. As soon as the French and Indians would fire they would quickly shift their position. As a result the British countered with volleys aimed at nothing but the lingering smoke from the enemy's rifles. As one British soldier recalled, "...the French and Indians crept about in small parties so that the fire was quite round us, and in all the

In this painting by Edwin Willard Deming, Braddock's British Regulars attempt to fight back against the French and Indians in the forest near the Monongahela.
(*Wisconsin Historical Society, WHS-1900*)

time I never saw one, nor could I on enquiry find anyone who saw ten together." Braddock's men fell one after another. In the advance guard alone, the French and Indians killed or wounded fifteen out of eighteen officers along with at least 150 of their 300 men.[20]

The British soldiers quickly realized that massed volleys, bayonet charges, and artillery were of little use. The officers lost control of their troops, and they retreated toward the rear and collided with St. Clair's pioneers. The soldiers began to clump together in ranks ten-men deep, wildly firing at an unseen enemy. They then withdrew in total disorder towards the river and the safety of the main body of the British army. Washington later reported their conduct writing, "In short the dastardly behavior of the Regular troops exposed all those who were inclined to do their duty, to almost certain death; and at length, in despite of every effort to the contrary, broke & run as sheep before hounds, leaving the artillery, ammunition, provision."[21]

At the rear of the column, William and the other Rangers could clearly hear the opening salvos of musket fire echoing through the dense forest. The volume and intensity steadily increased, and there could be no doubt a major battle was underway. Within minutes, officers were dashing about on horseback, shouting commands with desperate urgency. Despite lacking orders to do so, Adam Stephen quickly deployed his small command to defend the rear of the army. William and the other Rangers moved into the woods in a crescent formation on either side of the trail, positioning themselves behind trees and rocks. It did not take long before they witnessed what was happening at the head of the column, as the first panicked British troops dashed by in their flight to safety. William could see the looks of intense fear and panic on their faces. Still the Rangers waited in the forest, rifles at the ready, watching for the first signs of the enemy's approach.[22]

Within minutes of the first shots, General Braddock rode forward and tried to organize resistance, but to no avail. The French and Native American attack took on the shape of a widening half-moon that threatened to envelop Braddock's entire army. The Regulars had become an undisciplined mob, and the only soldiers who were

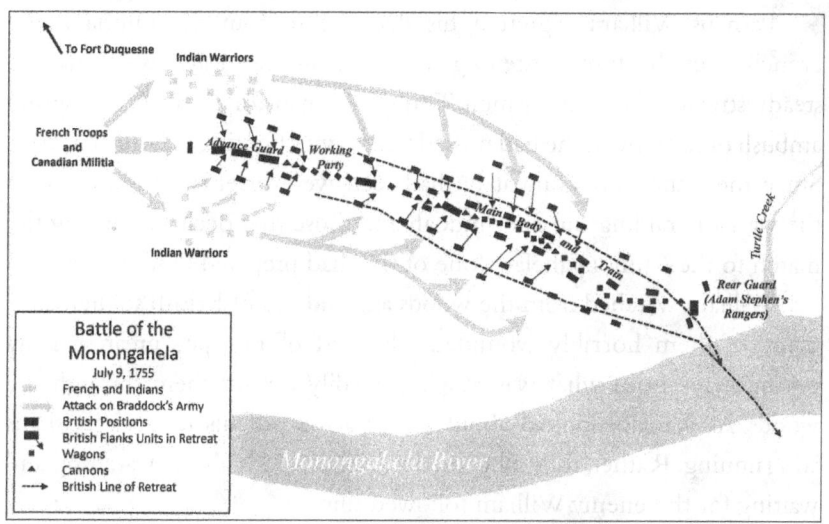

Map of the battle between Braddock's army and a combined force of French troops, Canadian militia, and their Native American allies. (*Drawn by the Author*)

putting up a fight were the colonial militia, the very men Braddock had characterized as being unruly and untrustworthy.

Every American militiaman did what their long experience had taught them to do—use the same tactics as the Native Americans by taking cover in the trees and then returning fire. Despite the wisdom of this course of action, British officers, including Braddock, rode among the Americans swatting them with the backs of their swords, calling them cowards, and ordering them back into formation. As the militia formed their effective defense, many of them died as victims of the wild, undisciplined firing from the British Regulars. Washington later wrote in a letter to Governor Dinwiddie that "it is conjectured (I believe with much truth) that two thirds...received their shot from our own cowardly Regulars who gathered themselves into a body contrary to orders 10 or 12 deep, would then level, fire, & shoot down the men before them."[23]

As the French and warriors blasted away at them from the surrounding forest, Braddock's Regulars retreated, steadily melting away toward the river. Eventually, as retreating British soldiers began crossing the Monongahela, the French attack reached what had been the rear of the army. William and the rest of Stephen's Rangers continued to wait.

Perhaps William regretted his decision to join the militia as he crouched in the forest, listening to the firing ahead and watching the steady stream of retreating men. Though he had fought in Washington's ambush of Jumonville, he had missed the heavier fighting at Fort Necessity. Since then, the only combat he had seen were brief skirmishes against the warriors raiding the Shenandoah and those that occurred during the march to the Monongahela. None of that had prepared him for this.

William watched from the woods as hundreds of British soldiers fled, many of them horribly wounded. The best of Europe's greatest army ran in terror from what was moving steadily toward them through the woods. As William looked about him, not one of his fellow Virginians was running. Rather, they all peered into the woods ahead, watching and waiting for the enemy. William followed suit.

As the minutes passed, the sounds of the battle came closer, and the Rangers made ready to open fire. The French and Indians had abandoned their usual stealthy movement and instead were crashing headlong through the woods trying to reach the river to cut off the rest of Braddock's army. The Rangers held their fire until they had clear targets, as the first of the enemy appeared, one Ranger fired, and the rest soon followed. Unlike the pointless volleys of the Regulars, William and his fellow colonials carefully aimed at each target before firing, then quickly reloaded, found another target, and fired again. The resulting brisk covering fire quickly caused the French attack to lose its momentum. The French and Native Americans had already inflicted a great deal of damage on Braddock's command, but now, with an organized and well-deployed resistance in front of them, their eagerness for the fight waned.

As the Rangers fought, William may have seen his old surveying partner, Washington, pass by, heading toward the river crossing. Washington was not fleeing in panic like the others. Instead, he was carrying General Braddock in his arms. The general, who had five horses shot out from under him during the melee in the forest, had been mortally wounded when a musket ball pierced his arm and ribs before lodging in a lung. Washington and two soldiers assisted the general and laid him in a tumbrel cart found near the river crossing. Before crossing the river, they paused near the Rangers, who were the only remaining line of defense. At that

Re-creation of a Tumbrel Cart similar to that in which Washington placed a mortally wounded Braddock. (*Author photo*)

moment, one militiaman heard the general state his change of regard for the Virginians. Braddock, he recalled, cried out, "My dear blues (the color of the Virginian's uniforms) give 'em to the fire, you fight like men and will die like soldiers." Minutes later, Washington led the cart across the river to safety, surrounded by British Regulars who splashed into the Monongahela, desperately seeking refuge on the far side.[24]

Finally the firing began to subside, and William's Rangers made their own crossing, hurrying to catch up with the shattered remains of Braddock's army. Their action had likely saved the survivors of the army. One British officer later reported that "The Rear Guard (tho' only a [Captain's] Command) did more execution than the whole, among the Enemy, as the officer had time to recollect himself. Consequently made a disposition and extended his Guard in advantageous posts behind trees by which he both repulsed and killed a great number."[25]

As he lay in the cart bleeding, Braddock ordered his army to make a stand. But no one was listening, and the rout continued unabated. The forest floor north of the river was littered with casualties who soon would be killed, mutilated, and scalped. In total, sixty-three out of eighty-six officers, both British and colonial, had been killed or wounded. Out of 1,373 soldiers, there were 456 enlisted men dead and another 421 wounded, a staggering casualty rate of over sixty-four percent. Among the colonials, losses were particularly severe. Washington, who was one of the few Virginia officers to remain unscathed, wrote Dinwiddie that, by his count, only about thirty Virginians had survived the ghastly battle.[26]

As night began to fall, the unorganized remnants of Braddock's army finally paused to rest and count their losses. Dazed and in severe pain, Braddock ordered the army to retreat down the road they had built during the last month, sending Washington ahead to bring reinforcements. Four days later, as the army passed near the remains of Fort Necessity, Braddock died. In his final moments, the general looked into Washington's eyes and whispered his last words: "Who would have thought it? We shall better know how to deal with them another time."[27] Washington, who had now returned to the column, buried the general in the middle of the roadway, hoping the grave would go unnoticed by the Indians.

Monument at Braddock's grave, Fort Necessity National Battlefield in Fayette County, Pennsylvania. (*Author photo*)

Chapter 4

AN OFFICER OF THE KING

Retreat and Stalemate

With Braddock's death, Colonel Thomas Dunbar now assumed command of the British army. Dunbar, who had remained behind the main column during the battle with the French, wanted no further disasters, so he directed the army to destroy most of their supplies and return to Fort Cumberland. The soldiers set fire to wagons, smashed dozens of gunpowder barrels, and dumped over 1,000 artillery shells into streams. Dunbar also ordered that many of the wounded be left behind. One unhappy British officer wrote later that he considered Dunbar's decision to retreat to the fort a heinous act, because it left "the road...full of dead and people dying who with fatigue or wounds could move on no further; but lay down to die—this melancholy [account] convinces, what use our staying, would been of, to save the life of many a poor fellow."[1]

It took nine days for the British forces to reach Fort Cumberland and Stephen's Rangers, William Crawford among them, provided an effective rear-guard the entire way, preventing or turning back several Native American ambush attempts. On July 22, the army reached the fort, although at this point they were an army in name only. Morale had been completely shattered, especially among the Regulars. Although the remaining fifteen hundred men still greatly outnumbered the French at Fort Duquesne, Dunbar and the other British officers had no stomach for a return expedition. This was probably a wise move, but Dunbar's next major decision was an act of pure cowardice.

On August 2, Dunbar issued orders for all British Regulars to march to Philadelphia. There he intended to await further instructions from

Whitehall. In an act Governor Dinwiddie termed "monstrous," Dunbar left Fort Cumberland in the hands of only 160 colonial troops, abandoning hundreds of nearby frontier settlers to their fate. Benjamin Franklin wrote that Dunbar "was requested to afford some protection to the inhabitants; but he continued his hasty march through all the country, not thinking himself safe till he arrived in Philadelphia, where the inhabitants could protect him."[2]

The French now saw an opportunity to push the British completely out of the frontier. Captain Dumas, who replaced Contrecoeur at Fort Duquesne, sent war belts to every Native American village in the Allegheny Plateau, urging them to join him in driving the British away. War belts were made of wampum, a type of shell bead. These belts contained symbolic messages, and the Native American nations used them to communicate messages of peace, friendship, or, in this case, the need to make war on a common enemy. Encouraged by the news of Braddock's dramatic defeat and Dunbar's withdrawal, the tribes responded by flocking to Fort Duquesne. Dumas supplied the eager warriors with weapons and sent them out to raid British colonial settlements. Within a few months, French officials were boasting that French and Indian forces had "disposed of more than 700 people in the provinces of Pennsylvania, Virginia, and Carolina, including those killed and those taken prisoners."[3]

It was now clear to every colonial government that relying on the British army for protection was foolhardy. To meet the threat to his frontier settlements, Governor Dinwiddie re-formed the Virginia Regiment, authorizing funding of £40,000 to supply and equip one thousand men and two hundred Rangers. On August 14, 1755, Dinwiddie placed Washington in command. Washington's first act was to order William and the rest of Stephen's Rangers back to Winchester, where Washington set up his new headquarters. This did little to stop the Native Americans, who ransacked the Shenandoah Valley during the late summer and early fall of 1755. Adam Stephen wrote, "They go about and commit their outrages at all hours…and nothing is to be seen…but desolation and murder heightened with…unheard of instances of cruelty. Smoke of the burning plantations darken the day, and hide the neighboring mountains from our sight."[4]

By late November, the raiding died down, and William could spend some much needed time at home. He had been gone for almost eighteen months serving in the militia and undoubtedly missed his family. His children had grown while he was gone. Effie had just turned seven, Sally was six, and young John was five. Hannah had done her best to keep the farm going, but the intense Native American raiding activity meant that she and the children had spent a great deal of time at her parent's nearby farm, and the Crawford farm had suffered as a result.

The life of a settler's wife was difficult, even by the standards of eighteenth-century American colonial society. Normally, Hannah's daily tasks included caring for the children, maintaining the fire in the fireplace, making and mending clothing, and cooking and preserving food for storage. Cooking and making certain that there was sufficient food stored to last through the coming winter typically consumed most of her time. On the frontier, however, just watching the children was a constant trial. The Crawford home, like most in the area, was a busy, cluttered place that was not particularly safe for children. There was an open fire with kettles of hot water and pans with hot boiling food, all at floor level. Outside the cabin, there were privy holes, unfenced ponds, and open wells that posed great danger.[5]

In addition, Hannah, during William's absence, also had to tend to the crops, harvest them, and make repairs to their home. Because of increased raiding by Native American warriors, she had to accomplish all this with a rifle handy and the children close at hand. Although it is likely that her father and father-in-law lent whatever support they could in maintaining the farm, the pressure and the constant fear of a Native American attack must have been overwhelming.

The fear and intense anxiety created by the mere possibility of a Native American attack cannot be overstated. At times, it must have felt like there was a constant stream of rumors and reports regarding yet another Indian "outrage" on either lives or property. It might be a neighbor reporting a stolen cow or pilfered food supplies, but more often than not, settlers learned that a nearby farm had been burned to the ground, its occupants murdered, scalped or taken captive. Consequently, even sending the children to the woods to gather berries, go out after dusk to get water from the well, or go to the barn in the morning to milk a cow was cause for anxiety, trepidation, and genuine foreboding. One frontier settler's wife remembered:

> The fears of the night were horrible beyond description, and even the light of day was far from dispelling painful anxiety. While looking from the windows of my log-house and seeing my neighbors tread cautiously by each hedge and hillock, lest some secreted savage might start forth to take their scalp, my fears would baffle description…Imagination now saw and heard a thousand Indians; and I never went round my own house, without first looking with trembling caution by each corner, to see if a tomahawk was not raised for my destruction.[6]

While William was back with his family Washington was in Winchester, reorganizing the Virginia Regiment. One action he took was to appoint Christopher Gist as a Captain in command of a company of Rangers. He ordered Gist to begin recruiting "woodsmen" to his command. In filling out Gist's new company, Washington appointed William as an Ensign (equivalent to a Second Lieutenant) effective December 27, 1755, with orders to report to Washington's headquarters in Winchester on February 14.[7]

William was pleased that his friend awarded him an officer's commission. He was a good choice for the position, for he knew the lower Shenandoah very well and had gained considerable experience while a Ranger under the tutelage of Adam Stephen. Moreover, at thirty-three years of age, his maturity might prove invaluable in commanding the sort of tough frontiersmen Gist was recruiting as scouts. On January 6, 1756, William traveled to Winchester to attend a session of the Frederick County Court, where he took the oath for his commission along with seventeen other new regimental officers.[8]

On April 7, Washington ordered Gist's company to move north to store supplies at Maidstone-on-the-Potomac, a house owned by Evan Watkins, a man who operated a ferry across the Potomac to the Maryland side (today's Williamsport, Maryland). Washington wanted to establish a supply depot and garrison at Maidstone to support forays over the mountains by Gist and his men. His secondary purpose was to provide protection from renewed Native American raids occurring upriver.[9]

As soon as William arrived at Maidstone with Gist's company, Washington sent him new orders. On April 25, Washington directed him to select twenty men from the company and then march south. His new detachment was to actively patrol the area in the vicinity of Jost Hite's house on Opequon Creek, about six miles south of Winchester. Washington also ordered Crawford to range down towards Bullskin Creek, and "to act rather as a reconnoitering party, than as an offensive one." Washington made it clear that he was to use his knowledge of the area to avoid battle with the Indian raiding parties. William was almost certainly glad to be returning close to home, especially since these raiding parties were a threat to his own family.[10]

The frontier war did not go well for Virginia between the spring and fall of 1756. During that time Washington's regiment skirmished with the Indians on twenty different occasions, and suffered over one hundred casualties. In a letter to John Robinson, the colony's treasurer, Washington noted that "upward of fifty miles of a rich and once thickly settled country…now quite deserted…from Maryland to the Carolina line; great numbers below that, removed through fear…and the whole settlement deliberating whether to go or stay."[11]

Amid so much disaster, there was also considerable turmoil as Washington and Dinwiddie clashed repeatedly over strategy. Washington proposed the construction of a chain of forts to protect the region. The governor flatly rejected this, saying the plan was too expensive. As an alternative the governor suggested that Washington relocate his headquarters from Winchester to Fort Cumberland, a garrison Washington thought was useless and should be abandoned. At the same time, Washington's regiment had constant desertions, small mutinies, and numerous courts martial.

In July 1756, Washington, at the behest of Dinwiddie, ordered Captain Gist to relocate his company to Fort Cumberland, and in the autumn the governor ordered a reluctant Washington to also move there. As a result, both William and his commanding officer were now far from where they would have preferred to be—William far from Hannah and his children, and Washington far from Winchester; where he thought his regiment would be most effective.

When spring of 1757 arrived the Native American raids along the frontier renewed, but little went right for the Virginians. In May 1757, Governor Dinwiddie issued orders to reduce the number of captains serving in the regiment. As a result, Washington was forced to demote Christopher Gist to the rank of lieutenant and dissolve his company. He ordered William and the rest of Gist's men to merge with Captain Robert Stewart's company stationed at Maidstone, but before Crawford and his men could march to their new posting, Washington moved Stewart's company to Fort Loudon in Pennsylvania. It seems Stewart's men had been at Maidstone so long that their training had suffered. Moreover, Washington did not want Gist's men back at Maidstone, since many of them were from Maryland and their friends across the Potomac kept encouraging them to desert.[12]

While Stewart's company was at Fort Loudon, William began serving as Washington's provost marshal, a position which put him in charge of prisoners and of hunting down deserters. On July 20, 1757, Washington ordered him to go in pursuit of Private William Smith, a deserter from the regiment, saying "If he should resist, and stand upon his defense, contrary to the laws of the country; you are in that case, to fire upon him as an enemy." The pursuit did not take long, and by July 25 Smith had been captured. He was soon sitting in the docket at a court martial convened for him and seven other deserters, all of whom were officially listed as being in William's custody. The court found all eight prisoners guilty and sentenced them to be hanged or shot by firing squad. Washington pardoned five of these men, but Smith and another man were hanged on July 28. Apparently pleased with William's performance, Washington promoted him to lieutenant on July 27 and transferred him to Robert Spotswood's infantry company in Augusta County in the Shenandoah Valley.[13]

Crawford spent the remainder of 1757 scouting the Virginia frontier in an attempt to stop raids, though he could hardly prevent them. The frontier was too expansive and the enemy too skilled for a small, scattered regiment to prevent their attacks.

The year 1758 saw a shift in the English strategy toward the larger war with France. In what had become a worldwide conflict, Great Britain began to turn the tide under the leadership of their new prime minister, William Pitt, who decided to shake up the British command structure in America.

A New British Commander

In the spring of 1758, Pitt's government appointed General John Forbes as the British commander for His Majesty's forces in Pennsylvania. The commanders who served before him had been unable to accomplish much, and their relationships with the colonial governments were rocky at best. As a result, none had held the post for very long. Although Forbes, like Braddock, had never held an independent command, he was ordered to undertake a new campaign to seize Fort Duquesne. Unlike the generals before him, Forbes was not arrogant; he was a tough, hardworking officer. This gave him a decided advantage in dealing with colonial officials. The general also had an honest, forthright manner. This gave pause to some colonial officers, including Washington, who had become used to playing politics and effusively complimenting their British superiors in order to gain favor. This sycophantic approach did not work with John Forbes.

Although Forbes's personality was better suited to working with colonial officials than his predecessors, he still found the process to be slow and frustrating. Although Forbes stumbled at times, he was very successful in getting both funds and men from the provincial authorities. He eventually received £100,000 from Pennsylvania alone and gathered two thousand men from Pennsylvania and another twenty-seven hundred from Virginia to add to his existing force of two thousand British Regulars.[14]

At the same time, Forbes shared two characteristics with previous British commanders: a personal loathing of the Indians and a low opinion of colonial military officers. He refused to allow Native American warriors in his ranks, despite considerable advice to do so. He soon recognized, however, how important it might be to create rifts in the alliance between the Native Americans and the French at Fort Duquesne. He used the services of a missionary named Christopher Post to break up the French-Indian alliance by dispatching Post to the major Native American towns west of the Alleghenies. He brought wampum belts to convey a message assuring the tribes that Britain had no post-war designs on their lands. At first, no tribe abandoned the French, but as Post continued meeting with Native American leaders, he started to create doubt in their minds about the prudence of their alliance with France.[15]

For his senior colonial military officers, Forbes felt mostly disgust. At first, Forbes said, "I flattered myself that some very good service might be drawn from the Virginia, & Pennsylvania forces." As time passed, he found himself frustrated by the behavior, character, and military capability of the officers leading those forces. In a letter to Prime Minister Pitt, Forbes referred to the colonial officers as,

> ...an extremely bad collection of broken innkeepers, horse-jockeys, and Indian traders and that the men under them, are a direct copy of their officers...as they are a gathering from the scum of the worst of people...who have wrought themselves up, into a panic at the very name of Indians who at the same time are more infamous cowards, than any other race of mankind.[16]

George Washington was among those Forbes detested, although from the moment Forbes arrived in Pennsylvania, Washington had taken great pains to curry favor with his new commander. In April 1758, he wrote General John Stanwix asking him to bring his name forward to General Forbes, saying,

> ...mention me in favorable terms to General Forbes (if you are acquainted with that gentleman) not as a person who would depend upon him for further recommendation to military preferment, for I have long conquered all such expectancies (and serve this campaign merely for the purpose of affording my best

endeavors to bring matters to a conclusion) but as a person who would gladly be distinguished in some measure from the *common run* [italics in original] of provincial officers; as I understand there will be a motley herd of us.[17]

Given his previous campaigns for a royal commission, the comment regarding Washington's shunning of any "military preferment" came across as disingenuous to both Stanwix and Forbes. Moreover, Washington's next actions garnered Forbes' intense ire and betrayed some of his own post-war ambitions, ambitions that would become a major force in William Crawford's life.

Choosing a Road

Virginia provided so many troops to General Forbes that Governor Dinwiddie decided to create two full regiments. The old Virginia Regiment now became the First Virginia, with Washington in command and Crawford serving as an infantry officer. Forbes placed the new regiment, the Second Virginia, under the authority of Colonel Henry Bouquet, a Swiss-born officer and veteran of the Dutch and Sardinian armies. As summer arrived, William and the First Virginia sat idle around Winchester as Colonel Bouquet took the Second Virginia west from Lancaster, Pennsylvania toward Fort Duquesne.

By June 24 Bouquet had arrived in Raystown, Pennsylvania and constructed a new garrison, Fort Bedford. In early August, General Forbes arrived at the fort and contemplated a critical decision about the best route to use in approaching Fort Duquesne. He could take the most direct path by continuing west over the mountains. This strategy would mean that his troops would have to hack a new road through the wilderness, as Braddock had once done. The other option was to use the path built by Braddock's men, consequently named the Braddock Road. This option meant Forbes would only have to cut his way thirty-five miles to the south towards Fort Cumberland, and then pick up the Braddock Road. He knew the choice might prove critical in the campaign, so he sought

Washington's advice. This was clearly an opportunity for Washington to shine by demonstrating solid military judgement and singular dedication to a greater cause, but he squandered his chance.

In a protracted series of letters sent to Colonel Bouquet, Washington advised Forbes to follow the Braddock Road, but Washington's supporting analysis was both flawed and dishonest. He told Bouquet that the Braddock Road was only nineteen miles longer than the road proposed west from Fort Bedford. Bouquet and Forbes only had to read a map to see this was not the case. In addition, Washington's contention that construction of a new road would delay an attack on Fort Duquesne for a year did not hold up under objective scrutiny. To make matters worse, as Forbes indicated a clear preference for the direct route from Fort Bedford, Washington continued to write letters that made specious arguments to support his own position. Having lost patience with the Virginian, Forbes angrily ordered him to desist in advocating the use of the Braddock Road and to move his regiment to Fort Bedford immediately.[18]

Re-creation of Fort Ligonier in Ligonier, Pennsylvania.
(*Author photo*)

This entire process seems out of character for Washington, but he had very personal reasons for pushing the Braddock Road plan. At the time, the road was the only path across the mountains to the far side of the Alleghenies, and it lay in an area controlled by Virginia. The new route west from Fort Bedford would create a road within Pennsylvania's control. For much of the next twenty years, Virginia and Pennsylvania would dispute which colony had legal claim to the land both around Fort Duquesne and into the Ohio Country. The citizens of the colony that managed access into the region would have the best opportunity to grab up new lands after the war. Beyond his fading hope for a royal commission, Washington's greatest ambition was to acquire as much land as possible west of the Alleghenies. Once this land was in his possession, great wealth from land speculation would surely follow. Therefore, if Virginia controlled the only road over the mountains, it would be of great personal benefit to George Washington.

Having failed to sell his Braddock Road plan, a chastened Washington moved the First Virginia to Fort Bedford, where they idled as Forbes' pioneers built the new road. Forbes' decision for the direct road to Fort Duquesne could not have pleased the Pennsylvanians more. One colonel with Forbes' army wrote to a member of the Pennsylvania provincial government, "The Virginians are much chagrined at the opening of the road through this government, and Colonel Washington has been a good deal sanguine and obstinate upon the occasion."[19]

The Final March on Fort Duquesne

With October's arrival, the leaves began to turn and the nights grew cooler. The advanced elements of the army under Colonel Bouquet had arrived at Fort Ligonier, only fifty miles from Fort Duquesne. Bouquet's men lingered there into November as Forbes and his officers debated the next move.

Meanwhile, things at Fort Duquesne were not going well. The French commander, Francois-Marie Le Marchand de Lignery, had only one thousand men and his Indian scouts reported that Forbes' army included five thousand soldiers. The fort itself would not stand up to any sustained bombardment, and de Lignery's Native American forces were deserting at a steady rate. The commander was becoming a desperate man. By October, he thought that one French victory might stall Forbes until spring, allowing him time to reinforce his garrison.

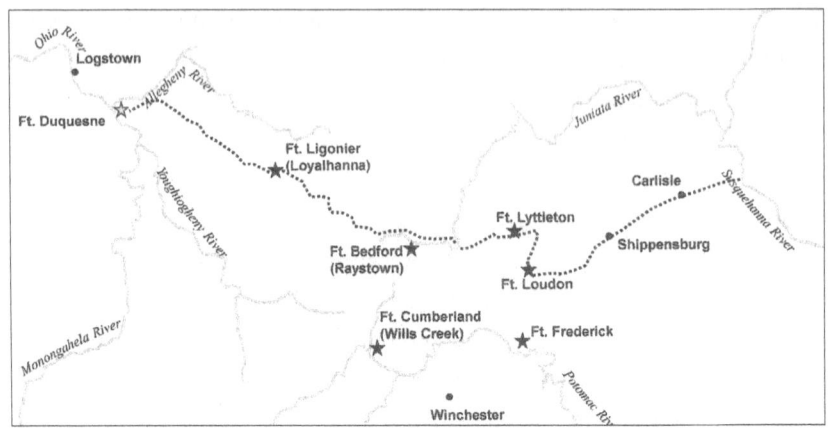

Route of march for the Forbes' Expedition. (*Drawn by the Author*)

De Lignery decided to send a French force of Louisiana and Illinois militiamen towards Fort Ligonier in hopes of instigating a fight. On October 12 the French soldiers ran into elements of the Second Virginia Regiment and an intense skirmish followed. Neither side could gain a tactical advantage, and the French eventually withdrew to Fort Duquesne, having lost nine men to sixty-one Virginians killed, wounded, or missing. Although the numbers favored de Lignery's men, the Native American warriors were so disgusted by the French militia's retreat that nearly all of them decided to abandon the French.[20]

The First Virginia moved forward to Fort Ligonier along with General Forbes. The general was plagued by two critical problems preventing a final push to Fort Duquesne. First, he did not have any reliable information about the strength of the French garrison. One estimate suggested there were four thousand French troops waiting for him there. Forbes believed that the French more likely had about twelve hundred troops, but without solid information, he decided to delay action while his scouts tried to gather accurate intelligence. His second problem was the weather. On October 8 a hard rain began to fall and continued to do so for the next three weeks. Although the French were doing little damage to him, "General Mud" was defeating Forbes and his army. On October 16 Forbes wrote to General Abercrombie, commander-in-chief of British forces in North America, saying "I am ruined and undone by rain, so pray God send us a few fair days—At present cannot move one yard." He ordered Bouquet to reconnoiter all possible routes to Fort Duquesne, including the Braddock Road, which required a crossing of the Monongahela River. When Bouquet rode out with a small group of scouts to check the Braddock Road, they discovered that the rains had swelled the waterway so much that they would not be able to cross it.[21]

Luckily, as October came to a close, so did the rains. Forbes ordered the rest of his army from Fort Bedford to Fort Ligonier, and they arrived on November 2. His entire force was now within striking distance of Fort Duquesne, and Forbes wanted to rapidly advance before the roads became blocked by the snow. This was critical for two reasons: the men were without winter clothing and the enlistments for most of the colonial troops would expire on December 1. That meant much of Forbes' army would soon pack up and head home.[22]

On November 11, Forbes held a council of war with his staff and regimental commanders to determine a course of action. The discussion was lively as the officers weighed the advantages and disadvantages of every possible option. In the end, the clear consensus was that the army should wait until spring before advancing further, especially since they still did not know the strength of the French garrison at Fort Duquesne. Luck is sometimes the best friend a general can have, and luck was about pay a visit to John Forbes.

At dusk the next evening thirty Canadians and over one hundred warriors under the command of Lieutenant de Corbiere attacked British troops guarding the army's horses near Fort Ligonier. As soon as the sound of battle reached the fort, Forbes dispatched Washington and five hundred men from the First Virginia to march directly toward the gunfire. In the meantime, Colonel Hugh Mercer directed another group from the regiment in a maneuver to the rear of de Corbieres' men. All the First Virginia had done since leaving Winchester was march and drill—William was about to see his first action of this campaign.

Moving swiftly through the growing darkness, the Virginians marched at the quickstep towards the rifle fire echoing from the paddock near the fort. Within minutes, William and his men could see the flashes from the rifle barrels of both their own guards and the French raiding party. They moved up adjacent to the guards, fell into line, and engaged the enemy with volleys of rifle fire. The rapid response from the British surprised Lieutenant de Corbieres, and he could see that he was clearly outmanned and outgunned. He ordered a quick retreat, but before all of his men could escape the Virginians had captured three prisoners: two warriors and a third man named Johnson, a British subject who had joined the French army.[23]

As de Corbieres withdrew into the woods, a dense fog began to form and the forest became impenetrable. Washington ordered his men to follow the retreating enemy force. In single file, the militiamen moved off as fast as the darkness and fog would allow. Meanwhile, Mercer's men had circled around de Corbieres' original position, as ordered, but the enemy had escaped. This now put two friendly groups of soldiers heading directly toward one another. When Mercer saw the shadowy figures of Washington's men looming before him in the fog, he mistook them for French forces and ordered his troops to open fire.

The bright flashes of musket fire they saw exploding in front of their position shocked William and the others in Washington's command. Thinking the French had decided to make a stand, Crawford deployed his men into line. As they raised their rifles to commence firing, another blast of muskets erupted at them from the gloom ahead. As their fellow soldiers fell around him, William and the other officers shouted the order to return fire. As the battle gained in intensity Washington's voice was suddenly heard thundering above the roar of the guns, ordering his own men as well as those on the opposite line to cease fire. Yet the firing did not stop. Out of the fog, William saw Washington ride between the two sides, once again commanding everyone to cease fire. Now, at great risk, Washington rode up to Mercer's line and, slapped his men's muzzles upright with his sword. Tragically, the brief firefight between friendly forces had led to the deaths of two officers and thirty-five soldiers. In William's initial action of the campaign, the Virginians had killed more of their own men than the enemy's.[24]

Following the friendly fire incident, the interrogation of the three enemy prisoners brought Forbes the information he had long sought. Johnson, a British national, was informed that he could be shot for treason, and this threat brought forth a wealth of detailed information from the man. He told his interrogators about Fort Duquesne's weak defensive state, and most important, he told them that de Lignery now had less than one thousand men in the garrison. Upon hearing that news Forbes decided that he had to move immediately.

The general ordered formation of a strike force of twenty-five hundred men organized into three elements: William's First Virginia under Washington's command and two others led by Bouquet and Lieutenant Colonel Archibald Montgomery. The three units marched out from Fort Ligonier on the morning of November 15. Bouquet and Montgomery's commands advanced, while the Virginians cut the road ahead. This time, the road was built only wide enough for a few pieces of artillery and a small wagon train to pass through, so the work went quickly. By the first night, William and his fellow soldiers had advanced six miles, and by November 18 they had cut the road to within thirty miles of Fort Duquesne.

The next morning Bouquet's men arrived, with Montgomery's not far behind. Washington ordered Crawford's regiment forward, advancing toward the headwaters of Turtle Creek. By the morning of November 21 the weather had become favorable and all three elements joined only twenty miles from Fort Duquesne. General Forbes now moved forward from Fort Ligonier to join the strike force. He ordered Bouquet to take the lead, and by evening the army arrived at its final assault position only twelve miles from Fort Duquesne. The commissariat issued rations to William and the other soldiers who were making preparations for the attack on the French. Forbes sent scouting parties forward, and the general anxiously awaited their return with updated intelligence on the fort's defenses.

The scouts returned on November 24, and reported having heard explosions and seen dense smoke rising from the direction of Fort Duquesne. Forbes dispatched a light horse unit to determine what was happening, and immediately moved the entire army forward in an attack formation. As they closed in on Fort Duquesne Washington ordered the First Virginia into line, and they advanced quickly towards the smoke in the distance. Marching briskly through the woods, William and the

Virginians were anxious to finally see what had been their objective for over three years—the French "Gibraltar" on the Ohio. However, when they cleared the trees and the fort came into view, all they could see were the charred remains of its buildings, with lonely chimneys standing above the smoldering rubble. De Lignery, upon learning that a large British force was closing in, had chosen to destroy the fort and withdraw. The bastion the British had sought to capture since 1753, the same one which had cost so many lives, was, in the end, taken without firing a single shot.[25]

On November 27, Forbes wrote Prime Minister Pitt reporting the fort's capture and adding, "I have used the freedom of giving your name to Fort Duquesne." With that, Forbes immediately began construction of a new and far more substantial garrison, Fort Pitt. This complex would become the major British stronghold on the frontier for years to come.[26]

Forbes assigned a garrison of two hundred men to the new fort, and ordered the rest of his army to head east into winter quarters. The First Virginia would return to Fort Cumberland, and Washington would travel to Williamsburg to lobby for funds. Before he left, he promoted William to the rank of captain. Washington had come to appreciate his skills as a soldier and leader, skills he would call upon again in the future.[27]

As Crawford prepared to move his company to Fort Cumberland, he discovered that he did not have sufficient transport to relocate their supplies and equipment. Luckily, he found a local teamster in the vicinity and decided to press him and his wagon into involuntary service. The teamster, a large, muscular fellow, was enraged and at first refused to cooperate. But after realizing that William had many troops behind him, the teamster felt he had little choice in the matter.

He told William that he objected to being forced into service and thought he ought to have a fair chance to decide the matter. "I will fight you," he said, "or any man in your company; if I am whipped, I will go with you, without no grumbling, but if I conquer, you must let me off." Crawford considered the teamster's proposal, and not wanting to appear cowardly in front of his men, he agreed to the fight.

Both men began to strip off their coats and shirts in preparation for combat. As William removed his uniform, the men of the company closed in around him and one young soldier named Daniel approached him. "Captain," he whispered, "you must let me fight that fellow. He will whip you, and it will never do to have the company whipped." William thanked him but said he was certain he was capable of beating the man. The young soldier politely insisted he reconsider and the rest of the men added their agreement. William looked around him at the faces of his men and reluctantly agreed to young Daniel's suggestion.

Daniel, who was tall, lean, and muscular, approached the teamster with his fists raised and the fight began. Within minutes, the young soldier had beaten the teamster badly. The teamster congratulated Daniel on his skill and agreed to take William and his men's supplies to Fort Cumberland. William shook Daniel's hand and thanked him for saving the honor of the company. Luckily, the young soldier survived the war and went on to serve as a general during the American Revolution. His full name was Daniel Morgan, and in 1781 he would lead the American army to a crucial victory at Cowpens in South Carolina.[28]

A few weeks later, as the newly promoted Captain Crawford and the other Virginians rested at Fort Cumberland, Washington arrived in Williamsburg and surprised many by resigning his commission. With Fort Duquesne vanquished at last and the prospect of a royal commission now gone, he decided to return to Mount Vernon and marry his fiancée, the widow Martha Custis. Meanwhile, his friend, William Crawford, remained in the regiment and would do so for another year.

Chapter 5

OVER THE MOUNTAINS

Peaceful Pursuits

In early 1760, as British success on the battlefield continued, the war with France entered its final phase. Amid a decline in Native American raiding activity William resigned from the First Virginia Regiment, returned home, and resumed his life with Hannah and their children. William's younger brother, Valentine, also left military service and took a civilian job as a teamster for George Washington, transporting produce from Washington's lands in the Shenandoah to Mount Vernon and markets in Alexandria.

In May 1760, Washington visited his Frederick County plantation in the lower Shenandoah near Bullskin Run. While there, he met with Crawford to tour a place called the "bloomery." Washington referred to it as "the place that has been so often talked of for erecting an Iron Work upon." An iron bloomery smelted iron ore into impure wrought iron bars which could then be used by local artisans and blacksmiths. This bloomery had been established in the lower Shenandoah in 1742 by a group that included William's stepfather, Richard Stephenson. William proposed turning it into a full-fledged ironwork and sought Washington's participation. At first Washington seemed impressed by the site's potential, but he chose not to join William's venture. In the end, the ironwork never became a reality, and by 1765 William instead had decided to leave his farm in the Shenandoah and seek a new home beyond the mountains, even though it would violate British colonial policies.[1]

After the signing of the Treaty of Paris in 1763, the war with France officially ended. The treaty stripped France of its Canadian possessions and confirmed British ownership of all the lands west of the Alleghenies. Given Britain's previous dealings with the Indians, France's Native American allies were understandably concerned about the future of their lands, but the war with France led to critical changes in British colonial settlement policy. These changes placated the Native nations, but troubled settlers, land speculators, and colonial governments.

Although His Majesty's government may have been fighting for power and trade during the war, most American colonists fought for reasons entirely their own. Those like William, who already lived on the frontier, supported the British war effort to protect their families and settlements. Others, like George Washington, backed the war in order to expand colonial boundaries and ensure their right to continue land speculation. Although the end of the war furthered the goals of colonists like Crawford and Washington, the British government had to turn its attention to financial concerns. By 1762, Britain had accrued an overwhelming debt of £133 million with annual interest charges amounting to over £4.3 million from the war with France. The British could not afford more conflict and wanted peace with the Native American nations of the Allegheny Plateau, even if this meant making concessions that were unpalatable to the American colonists.

Previously, in 1758, the British government had begun imposing policies to close the frontier to future settlement and make peace with the Native populations. In October, while William was busy advancing on Fort Duquesne with Washington and Forbes, the Council of Easton had been held near Philadelphia. The attendees included over 500 Native Americans from thirteen different nations, as well as colonial officials from Pennsylvania, including the British Indian Superintendent, Sir William Johnson. In the treaty negotiated by the Council, Pennsylvania returned all lands west of the Alleghenies to the Iroquois Confederation, prohibited white settlement there, and allowed the Shawnee, Delaware, and Mingo to once again live on their lands.

The British did not stop there. Over the next five years, His Majesty's government increased and fortified the anti-settlement policy. In 1761, Colonel Bouquet, who was now commander at Fort Pitt, issued a proclamation reminding everyone of the ban on settlement and expanding it to include all of western Maryland and Virginia. He also announced that British and colonial authorities would arrest anyone caught violating the ban and bring them to Fort Pitt for trial by court martial.

Two years later, the British decided to take sterner measures. On October 7, 1763, King George III's government issued the Proclamation of 1763, a formalization of the policy banning settlement west of the Allegheny Mountains. It ordered any British subject currently living there to leave the frontier and return east of the mountains. It also restricted and regulated any contact by whites with Native Americans. For example, traders wanting to do business with the Native Americans had to be licensed by the appropriate colonial governor. In addition, all colonists were prohibited from buying land directly from the Native Americans. This policy slowed the flow of new settlers to a trickle, but there were still those willing to defy it for the prospect of new lands and the opportunity they offered. William Crawford was among them.

Spring Garden

William apparently liked the lands he had seen in western Pennsylvania when he served with Braddock and later with Forbes. As he entered his forties, perhaps William experienced some sense of wanderlust, or maybe the war left him with a desire to start anew. Whatever the reason might have been, in the fall of 1765 William and his half-brother, Hugh Stephenson, set out on horseback up the Braddock Road and over the Alleghenies looking for a good piece of land.

William selected a small meadow nestled in a bend of the Youghiogheny River at a spot on the Braddock Road then called Stewart's Crossing, across from what is now Connellsville, Pennsylvania. He and Hugh surveyed the tract at just over 376 acres, much of it heavily forested. In a flat open space near the river, they built a one-room cabin that would be the Crawfords' new home. It measured about eleven feet by sixteen feet and had two small openings in the logs that served as windows, one beside the door overlooking the river, and the other facing the hills.

The size of William's new cabin was not unusual, as log homes in this region were typically small and had few amenities. Often the floors were packed dirt, and many homes lacked even one piece of iron hardware in their walls or roofs because, as one settler recalled, "Such things were not to be had." William and Hugh did better than most by laying in a split log floor, dressed with an ax to be as smooth and level as possible. With a roof made of rough planks, the cabin was humble but solid. When the two men finished the cabin, Crawford named his new farm "Spring Garden."[2]

Re-creation of the Crawford's cabin at Spring Garden, located in Connellsville, Pennsylvania. (*Author photo*)

William next began the difficult process of clearing the land. The dense forest surrounding Spring Garden had to be cleared because it placed much of the land in a dark shade for a substantial portion of the growing season. To accomplish this, William borrowed the Native Americans' "slash and burn" method. First, he and Hugh used axes to clear an area of small trees. Then they girdled the larger trees and stripped off as many of their branches as possible. After drying the branches for burning, they stacked them at the bases of the girdled trees and set them afire. This killed the trees, allowing William and

Hugh to cut them down easily. One observer of this process said,

> The general mode of clearing the land in this country, where timber is of no value, and labor is of great, is by cutting a circle round the tree, through the bark, quite to the wood, before the sap rises, which kills it; and they cultivate the ground below immediately, leaving the trees to rot, which happens within a very few years, and they never bear leaves more.[3]

When this procedure was completed, the two men cleared the "deadenings" away, and the fields were almost ready for the next year's planting. After wintering in the new cabin, they returned over the mountains to the Shenandoah.

Once back in the valley, William and his family prepared for the challenging move to the new homestead. Packhorses would be needed for the journey because many places on the Braddock Road had grown too narrow for wagons. William and Hannah loaded the horses carefully since they could only take the necessities to start their new life at Spring Garden. They left all of their furniture behind but packed as much bedding, clothing, cooking utensils, and farming tools as possible. In addition to the family and the horses, the family dogs and several cows would also make the journey. In the spring of 1766, William and his family left the Shenandoah Valley for the final time.

Their little caravan moved slowly over the rough terrain, making only a few miles each day. Spring rains and melting snows had swollen the creeks, forcing the Crawfords to take special care with their crossings to ensure that they not lose a single packhorse or cow. Finally, after more than a month on the Braddock Road, they reached Spring Garden.[4]

During the next two years William steadily cleared more and more land and built both a small barn and a stone springhouse. He purchased two black slaves, Daniel and Dick, to help him work the farm, and the three men planted crops between the dead stumps of the trees that had been killed the year before. In the Shenandoah Valley, there had been enough open farmland to plant crops in rows and use horse-drawn plows, but at Spring Garden that was impractical. Instead, William used the

Native American method of planting on small mounds of soil, a technique that reduced frost damage by trapping the cold air near the ground in the small valleys created between the mounds of earth. Once the crops were established, they produced just enough food for the Crawfords' subsistence.[5]

The same year that the Crawfords arrived on the Youghiogheny, their friends from Virginia, the Lawrence Harrison family, settled nearby on New Haven Hill and the Harrison's son, William, married the Crawfords' daughter, Sarah. In addition, Hannah's brother, John Vance, also arrived, settling a few miles away in what would become Tyrone Township. Since it was so close to the Braddock Road, the Crawford home became a welcome respite for travelers and became known for its "remarkable" hospitality. One man recalled that almost everyone coming across the mountains rested a few days at Spring Garden. Anyone needing a meal, drink, and a place to sleep was welcomed with open arms. In this regard, Hannah received the most credit. She was "so dearly appreciated by pioneers in search of homes in the wilderness, and so, of all the women on the frontiers of Western Pennsylvania, none were more highly respected and lovingly remembered."[6]

But, as time passed, William spent less time farming and more time surveying, almost all of which was for his old friend, George Washington.

Surveyor and Land Agent

In the years after he resigned from the First Virginia Regiment, Washington's ambitions for land speculation had not diminished. Initially, he tried to resurrect his brother's land firm, the Ohio Company, but the company lost its royal land grants when the war with France made it impossible to place one hundred settlers on the land by the deadline of December 1755. Washington sent his former aide, Captain George Mercer, to London to request an extension now that the war was over, but he was rebuffed. To make matters worse, in 1767 the British Secretary of State revoked all previous western land grants and announced that everything west of the Alleghenies now belonged to the King.

Washington remained undeterred. He believed that the potential for wealth from the western lands was enormous, telling one acquaintance that he expected to make a five hundred percent profit from wilderness lands within twenty years. The main challenges were surveying the lands and then gaining legal title to them. Both problems, especially obtaining legal title, were further complicated after the Proclamation of 1763. Due to the decree, no colonial government would grant title to illegally surveyed lands west of the mountains, especially since George III now owned all of them. Washington decided to move forward regardless of the laws. He planned to secretly survey good tracts of land and later establish a claim for the title once the British government gave in to the increasing pressure from land speculators and settlers.[7]

In 1767, a rumor began to circulate among colonial political circles that Pennsylvania might soon allow surveying of lands west of the Alleghenies. Regardless of whether this was true, Washington thought this was the perfect time to begin secretly charting land. Late in the summer of 1767, he mentioned his plans to Valentine Crawford during one of Valentine's trips to Mount Vernon with produce from the valley. After Valentine had returned across the Alleghenies, he told William about Washington's scheme. William asked his younger brother to inform Washington that there was available land near Spring Garden. On September 13 Valentine arrived at Mount Vernon with William's message. Washington wrote a hurried letter to William explaining his interest and then followed it four days later with one written more "deliberately, and with greater precision."[8]

In his letter dated September 17, Washington proposed a partnership between himself and William. He asked that, for now, William simply identify suitable lands with rich soil and level topography near William's home on the Youghiogheny. Surveying of these lands would follow in the spring of 1768, all at Washington's expense. Next, Washington proposed that the two men meet the following April, at which time they could develop a strategy for identifying and surveying more lands, including the possibility of finding tracts along the Ohio River. The April meeting would also give them an opportunity to discuss what percentage William would receive once these lands were titled and sold to new settlers.[9]

What would they do about the fact that surveying lands was illegal? In his September letter Washington pointed out to William that starting a process to have clear title was also in William's interest, as Spring Garden was subject to the 1763 decree. So far, no one at Fort Pitt had confronted the Crawfords about their farm, but that could change at any time. Washington went on to say that he believed he was merely securing these lands "in the King's part," since the prohibition against owning the land would eventually change. "I can never look upon that proclamation in any other light," he wrote, "...than as a temporary expedient to quiet the minds of the Indians."[10]

Washington also insisted their activities be kept a closely held secret. He had been a member of the House of Burgesses since 1758, and if his opinions and schemes were made public, he would be officially censured. This would damage his reputation and political standing, both of which were of utmost importance to him. Washington also urged William to remain silent because if knowledge of their plans got out "it might give the alarm to others," thus allowing them to grab up land before he and William could stake their own claims. Their plan was to have William seek out potential acreage under the "guise of hunting game."[11]

William's reply was enthusiastic. On September 29 he wrote Washington agreeing to every aspect of the proposal and detailing suitable lands he had already identified. William wrote that even before receiving Washington's first two letters, he had decided upon the cover story of being a hunter. He added that he believed acting as a trader with the Indians might even be a more effective ruse. The Indians, he wrote, treated those they traded with very well. William asked Washington to consider funding a trading license available from the colonial authorities at Fort Pitt. Moreover, William thought some Indians might be willing to allow survey and sale of their lands, although such activities were also illegal under the Proclamation.

William wrote that one of the tracts he had already identified was along Chartier's Creek, about twenty-five miles below Fort Pitt. He described it as rich bottom land, well-timbered, with access to a ready water supply; it encompassed between two to three thousand acres. Because surveyors from Fort Pitt had recently been seen lurking about, he proposed building a small cabin there and clearing a little land before someone else could claim it.

As to the land further into the Allegheny Plateau and the Ohio Valley, what Washington had referred to as the "King's part," Crawford confirmed that he would "heartily embrace [his] offer upon the terms [he] proposed." He added that he would attend to those lands as soon as he secured the ones closer to home, such as Chartier's Creek. At that point he could "examine all the creeks from the head of Monongahela down to [Fort Pitt], and in the forks of the river Ohio and New River," trying to inspect as much as possible before Christmas. William assured Washington that he would lose no time in this task and that Washington could depend on him. Finally, he promised to keep the entire endeavor a "profound secret" and proposed that he travel to Mount Vernon to provide a "satisfactory account of what transacted" as soon as the weather would allow him to head south in the spring.[12]

On March 25, 1768, after the snow had melted and the Braddock Road was passable, William began the trip to Mount Vernon, one he would repeat many times over the next few years. On April 1 he arrived at Mount Vernon, where he and Washington spent the next six days going over the details of their plan for land acquisition. It was the first time the two men had seen one another in almost eight years, and their first opportunity to discuss their scheme in person. One has to wonder at William's reaction upon seeing his partner's landed estate. For a man who lived in a one-room frontier cabin, Mount Vernon must have seemed luxurious beyond William's wildest dreams. As their meetings concluded, Washington paid William £20 for surveying expenses. William returned to Mount Vernon for four days in July to give Washington an update on his progress.

In late 1768, circumstances took a dramatic turn for the better as far as land speculation was concerned. The British Indian Superintendent, Sir William Johnson, successfully negotiated the Treaty of Fort Stanwix with the Iroquois and the Treaty of Hard Labor with the Cherokee. These treaties moved the 1763 proclamation line west from the Alleghenies to the Ohio River, opening up most of the eastern Ohio Valley to settlement.

Throughout the next year William diligently identified and surveyed land for Washington. In a letter dated January 1769 William told him that he had engaged a surveyor for two tracts of 332 and 333 acres, respectively, and that he would soon make claims on additional acreage near the Pennsylvania line. In early March, William paid another visit to Washington at Mount Vernon, conferring with him for four days. Following this visit, Washington asked John Armstrong, a former Pennsylvania colonel from the Forbes expedition, to help William contact officials at the Pennsylvania land office who would give title to the lands which William was surveying. In October, William found and surveyed another seven hundred acres for Washington in Pennsylvania. However, he had not been able to claim any land further west in the Ohio Valley, a situation Washington moved to resolve.[13]

The Soldiers' Land Grant

In February 1754, when Governor Dinwiddie had called for militia volunteers, he had promised to divide 200,000 acres among the men who signed up. This contingent included men like Washington, William, and all the other original members of the Virginia Regiment. At this point no one who had fought against the French had received a single acre. With a new governor now in place, the Baron de Botetourt, Washington decided it was time to petition the administration on behalf of his former soldiers.

On December 8, 1769, he wrote de Botetourt, referring to Dinwiddie's proclamation as a "mutual contract between the government and adventurers; the latter of whom, always conceiving that the lands were as firmly engaged to them as their pay." He reminded the governor that the men who answered the call to arms in 1754 had "toiled, and bled for the country," and that many were now poor people with large families. Washington's message was very effective. It was also hypocritical, since Washington intended to profit mightily from this. A week later, Washington delivered, and the government accepted, a petition from his men asking that all soldiers receive a share of a grant of 200,000 acres along the Monongahela River, New River, Great Kanawha River, or Sandy Creek. In agreeing to the petition, de Botetourt asked that, if possible, Washington locate a single tract of 200,000 acres for the soldiers, but agreed that up to twenty separate blocks would be acceptable. The governor allotted fifteen thousand acres per officer and four hundred acres for each enlisted man, and directed that the surveyor for the grant be someone appointed by William and Mary College.[14]

The next day, December 16, Washington placed a notice in two different Williamsburg newspapers, Purdie and Dixon's *Virginia Gazette* on December 21 and Rind's *Virginia Gazette* on December 28:

Mount Vernon, Fairfax County, Dec. 16. [1769]

His Excellency the Governor, by and with the advice and consent of his Majesty's Council, having been pleased to grant 200,000 acres of land on the Great Kanawha, &c. to the officers and soldiers who embarked in the service of this colony, agreeable to a proclamation issued the 19th of February, 1754 (by the Hon. Robert Dinwiddie, Esq; then Lieutenant Governor). And having moreover been pleased to require, that I should receive the several and respective claims of every person who engaged in the service aforesaid, before the battle of the Meadows, in 1754, I do hereby give this public notice thereof, requesting that every officer and soldier, or their representatives, will exhibit their respective claims to a share of these lands, properly attested to me, before the 10th day of October next ensuing, in order that the whole may be laid before his Lordship and Council, and finally adjusted. And to the intent that no unnecessary application may be made, it is hereby signified, that no person who entered into the service of this colony after the said battle of the Meadows (which concluded the campaign of 1754) is entitled to any part of these 200,000 acres of land, as they were given to the first adventurers, under the proclamation aforesaid.

George Washington[15]

Washington then used his influence in Williamsburg to ensure William and Mary College appointed William Crawford as the surveyor.

On December 20 Josiah Johnson, the master of the grammar school at William and Mary, replied to Washington's request saying that Washington could "depend upon my concurrence." The next day, James Horrocks, President of William and Mary, added his assent, writing, "I am of opinion it would be advisable for Mr. Crawford to be here as soon as possible, I mean with his own convenience, as I see no impediment to retard or prevent his success."[16]

With the arrival of spring, William was again in residence at Mount Vernon, arriving during the afternoon of March 1. Three days later, he set out for Williamsburg to meet with officials at William and Mary, and returned to Mount Vernon on March 22. With William's appointment as surveyor now secure, Washington gave him £8, 15s to buy surveying instruments in Philadelphia, and an additional £57 to survey and obtain rights to tracts of land along the Monongahela and Youghiogheny Rivers. With their business concluded, William headed back to Spring Garden by way of Philadelphia.[17]

Upon his return, William learned that Pennsylvania's governor had appointed him a Justice of the Peace for Cumberland County, the first of several such commissions. A year later, when the colonial government carved Bedford County from the borders of Cumberland County, Governor Thomas Penn appointed him Justice of the Peace for the new county. Later, in 1773, when Westmoreland County would be created from Bedford's boundaries, the governor again would commission William, this time as one of the Justices of the Court of General Quarter Sessions of the Peace, and of the County Court of Common Pleas. Since William's name was first on the list of justices, he became the President Judge of Westmoreland County and the first person to hold that office. All of this confirmed that the former Virginian was now viewed as a loyal citizen of Pennsylvania and one respected by the colony's leadership. As later events would prove, William's loyalties lay elsewhere, and perhaps they lay where he saw the greatest personal advantage.[18]

In early August 1770, the process of rewarding the soldiers their grants from the governor finally began to move forward. On August 2 Washington journeyed to Fredericksburg to meet with the original veterans of the Virginia Regiment and their representatives regarding their land grants.

The group discussed Washington's plans and agreed to a scheme whereby the officers would divide the costs of the surveys proportionately according to their original ranks. They authorized Washington to begin collecting the required funds immediately and approved William as their surveyor. They also resolved that Washington, William, and Dr. James Craik, the former regimental surgeon, should travel west to the Ohio Valley to locate the best areas for future surveys.[19]

A Journey Down the Ohio

On October 5 Washington left Mount Vernon on horseback to join Crawford and begin their expedition down the Ohio River. Traveling with him to Spring Garden were Dr. Craik and two servants. They arrived at the Crawford cabin eight days later, where they received an enthusiastic greeting from William, Hannah, and their son, John. After a day of rest, Washington spent October 15 viewing the land William had surveyed and acquired for him along the Youghiogheny. Washington's Bottom, as it later came to be known, was twelve miles downriver from Spring Garden. After seeing it, Washington described it in his diary "as fine a land as ever I saw." William's selection clearly impressed him; he noted that the acreage contained a "rich meadow" and was well watered.[20]

The next afternoon three other expedition members arrived at Spring Garden: Robert Bell, a veteran of the Virginia Regiment; William Harrison, Crawford's son-in-law; and Daniel Reardon, a young man William had hired to help him with his surveys. Following their arrival, William said goodbye to Hannah and John, and the six-man party left for Fort Pitt, stopping overnight at John Stephenson's home.[21]

The group arrived at Fort Pitt on October 17 and found it much changed from their previous visit in 1758. What had been a smoldering ruin in the wilderness when Washington last saw it was now a bustling frontier outpost that included a well-constructed, formidable fort and a busy trade center. They took lodging at Widow Myer's Tavern (located approximately at Sycamore and Sixth Street in present-day Pittsburgh), a popular meeting place for frontier militia, traders, and trappers. Shortly after settling in their rooms, they received a dinner invitation from George Croghan. Croghan, the former scout who led Braddock into the French and Native American attack in 1755, was now a colonel in the militia, and he asked Washington, William, and Dr. Craik to dine with him at the officer's mess the following evening.[22]

During their meal at the fort on October 18, Croghan invited them to dine with him again the next night, but this time he proposed that they meet at Croghan's home about four miles up the Allegheny River from Fort Pitt. The next day, as William gathered supplies for the journey, Washington received a note from Croghan telling him that Kanaghragait, known to the British as "White Mingo," would also be at Croghan's home that evening. Apparently, the Native American leader had a message from both his people and the chiefs of the Six Nations to deliver to Washington.

Upon their arrival, Kanaghragait presented Washington with a string of wampum and began speaking. He told Washington that he remembered him from Washington's 1753 mission to the French and bid him welcome to the Ohio Country. Kanaghragait continued, saying that it was their desire that the "people of Virginia would consider them as friends & brothers linked together in one chain." Kanaghragait added that he hoped Washington would tell Virginia's governor that, despite "some unhappy differences" between them in the past, it was their desire to live in peace and harmony with the whites. He concluded his remarks by noting that because Virginians did not trade with them as much as Pennsylvanians, there was some fear among his people. They worried the Virginians "did not look upon them with so friendly an eye as they could wish."[23]

Washington reassured Kanaghragait, saying that all "injuries & affronts" between them had been forgotten and that "nothing was more wished and desired by the people of Virginia than to live in the strictest friendship with them." Washington added that Virginians did not conduct as much trade as the Pennsylvanians, which was why they had not spent much time among the Native tribes. He said that he would be sure to acquaint the governor with their desires. Although Washington was likely being honest in his remarks, the very purpose of his trip—identifying lands for white ownership along the Ohio and

Great Kanawha Rivers—would soon create a great collision of cultures between the American colonists and Native Americans.[24]

The basis for this coming clash was the basic concept of land ownership. Within the Native American villages of the Ohio Country, each community controlled its own territory using two parallel systems of land use. First, as a collective group, the inhabitants of each village owned a large area of "hunting territory," available to anyone from the village. At the same time, members of each extended family, led by the family matriarch, farmed their individual parcels of land. These fields remained in the possession of the family as long as they continued to cultivate them. Once a family abandoned a field, the ownership reverted to the entire community, and the village council would assign it to another family matriarch. Essentially, the Native Americans viewed "ownership" as being a temporary condition that existed only as long as a family made use of the land for their benefit.[25]

This system was far removed from the traditional English concept of possession, and the idea that one could sell perpetual ownership of the land was even farther from the Native Americans' beliefs. Native Americans enjoyed a spiritual relationship with not only the land but also with all the creatures that shared it with them. They believed that all entities, both animate and inanimate, had souls and were equals in the universe. In the words of Makataimeshekiakiak, a chief of the Sauk nation called "Black Hawk" by whites, "Land cannot be sold. The Great Spirit gave it to his children to live upon, and cultivate, as far as is necessary for their subsistence; and so long as they occupy and cultivate it, they have a right to the soil—but if they voluntarily leave it, then any other [Indian] people have the right to settle upon it."[26]

The British and their colonists never understood that when the Indians gave land as a gift or token of friendship, they were not surrendering it forever. Instead, they believed they were granting their British friends the temporary right to make use of the land, just as their village councils had done for members of their own tribes. To the Native Americans, the British had very limited rights to the ground granted to them. If a settler stopped farming the land he received from the tribe or if he failed to abide by the terms of their agreement, the land reverted back to the village, just as it would for any tribe member. Therefore, what many settlers saw as a sale of real property was often merely a limited, rent-free loan of the land by the Indians. If Kanaghragait and his people realized that William and Washington's expedition would result in a flood of settlers and the cruel destruction of their way of life, it is doubtful they would have been so accommodating and friendly.[27]

Both William Crawford and George Washington were ambitious men. While a healthy amount of ambition is no sin, in this case their desire for wealth via land speculation posed dire consequences. It meant that they would be willing to force the Native Americans off their land at gunpoint, destroy their culture and way of life, and even kill them by the score without mercy. Their ambition, along with that of many other Americans, would soon become nothing more than naked greed, and eventually it evolved into a bloody and cruel avarice. By the late eighteenth century, the population of the Native American peoples had diminished from an estimated high during the Pre-Columbian era of 18.1 million to only about 600,000. This loss of life was due to primarily to European diseases that arrived beginning in the seventeenth century, but the warfare produced by the clash of cultures between whites and natives also took a huge toll.[28]

After their dinner on October 19 Croghan accompanied William and Washington to Fort Pitt. As they traveled, the former scout told them that he had hired two men to escort them down the Ohio. The first was an Oneida called Pheasant, and the second was Joseph Nicholson, a well-known trader and interpreter. These two men would join William, Washington, Craik, Bell, Harrison, and Reardon, completing a 10-man expedition party.[29]

On the morning of October 20, the group embarked down the Ohio in two large canoes. The first two days of travel were uneventful, and on October 22, they arrived at Mingo Town (present-day Mingo Junction, Ohio), seventy-three miles from Fort Pitt and home to about sixty Mingo families. Here, one of the tribesmen told William that Indians had killed two traders at Grape Vine Town, some thirty-eight miles further downriver. When William relayed this information to Washington, they discussed whether they should proceed or not, but ultimately they chose to continue the journey. Eventually the expedition members would discover that instead of "two" murdered traders, only one man had died by drowning in the river, and no Native American had taken any part in his demise.[30]

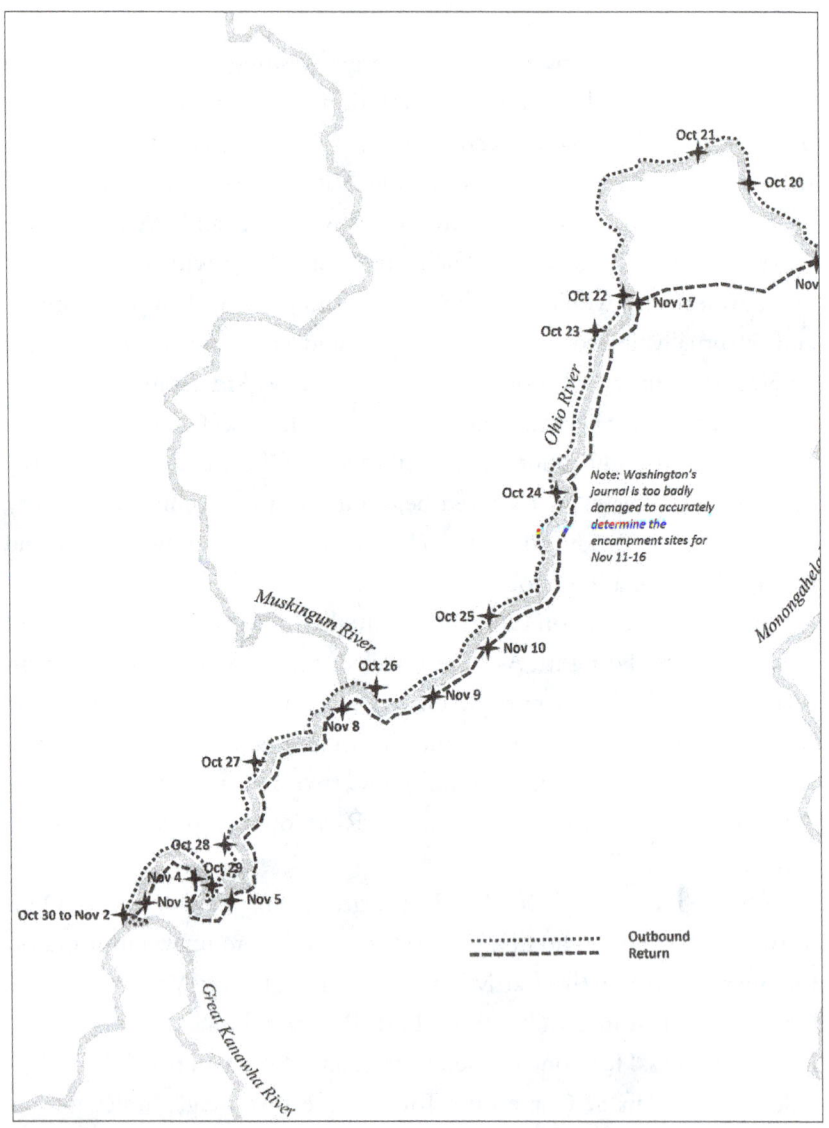

Map of Crawford and Washington's journey down the Ohio River to the Great Kanawha.
(Drawn by the Author)

The weather during the journey was characteristic for the Ohio Valley in late October and early November. There were clear, crisp, glorious days on the river, as the expedition paddled the canoes past wooded hills turning bright with fall colors. There were also days of cold rain, and on October 22 it even began to snow. In his journal of the trip, Washington recorded the day as "Very raw & cold. Cloudy, & sometimes snowing & sometimes raining."[31]

As they continued down the Ohio, William and Washington took notes on the land they saw along the river, recording those locations that might be suitable for a survey. On the return trip, they would decide on which areas they wished to claim.

A few days after leaving Mingo Town, the expedition traveled down what is known as the "long reach" section of the river, one with few curves that stretched from present-day Paden City to Raven Rock, West Virginia. They next passed the mouths of the Muskingum and Hocking Rivers before arriving at a point about 230 miles downriver from Fort Pitt on October 28. As they steered their canoes to the shore, they found the camp of a Seneca hunting party led by Guyasuta, a chief whom Washington had met during his mission to the French in 1753.[32]

Guyasuta, who was now fifty-six years old, was a war chief who did not achieve his office by heredity. Rather, he earned that title through deeds of bravery and leadership as a young man, and his reputation as a warrior and inspiring orator was well known throughout the Ohio Country. He had successfully led Seneca warriors along with Native fighters from other tribes against the British during the French and Indian War, achieving a great victory against the combined Anglo-American forces of General James Grant in September 1758. In that battle, Guyasuta ambushed Grant and inflicted 342 casualties before the British Regulars and American militia fled.[33]

Guyasuta greeted Washington with enthusiasm and great kindness, insisting the explorers spend the night in the Seneca camp. The next morning, Guyasuta joined William and Washington at their fireside and spoke to them. Like Kanaghragait, the Seneca chief told them about his people's desire for peace, friendship, and trade with the whites. Guyasuta also told them that, in addition to these things, the Seneca wanted to continue their lives as they had done for generations on the lands given to all by the Great Spirit.

Later that morning, the explorers bade goodbye to Guyasuta and his party and continued their journey downriver. Sadly, just as with Kanaghragait, the colonials did not take heed of the desires of the Seneca leader. Either that or they simply did not care.[34]

Finally, on October 31, they reached the mouth of the Great Kanawha River, 266 miles from Fort Pitt (near present-day Point Pleasant, West Virginia). Over the next two days, they ventured up the Great Kanawha, but only traveled about fifteen miles before turning back and beginning the return trip up the Ohio. As they retraced their journey, William and Washington began to mark the land they wanted to claim. At the mouth of the Great Kanawha, they marked two maple trees and a hopwood on the east side of the river as a corner of the soldiers' land, intending to take in a single survey all the bottom land from there to the rapids in the Great Bend. Next, they marked ash and hopwood trees on the west side of the river mouth to identify the beginning of a survey of all the bottomland on that side, a total of some eighty square miles.[35]

On November 5, as the party approached the Great Bend and its rapids, William and Washington disembarked on the south side of the river. They hiked across the neck of land that made up the inside of a sharp curve in the Ohio. They found the ground there to be quite desirable, with Washington writing that it was "as high, dry, & level as one could wish." He added, "The growth in most places is beech intermixed with walnut & ash, but more especially with poplar (of which there are numbers very large). The land towards the upper end is black oak, & very good. Upon the whole a valuable tract might be had here, & I judge the quantity to be about 4,000 acres." In fact, it was 4,395 acres, and William marked it for a future survey.[36]

On November 17 they reached Mingo Town and waited for the horses that would carry them on the final leg of the journey. Three days later the horses arrived, and they set out for Fort Pitt, arriving at the garrison on November 21. They rested there for two days, before leaving for Spring Garden, which they reached on November 24. Washington left for Mount Vernon the next day, and William's adventure into the Ohio Country came to an end.[37]

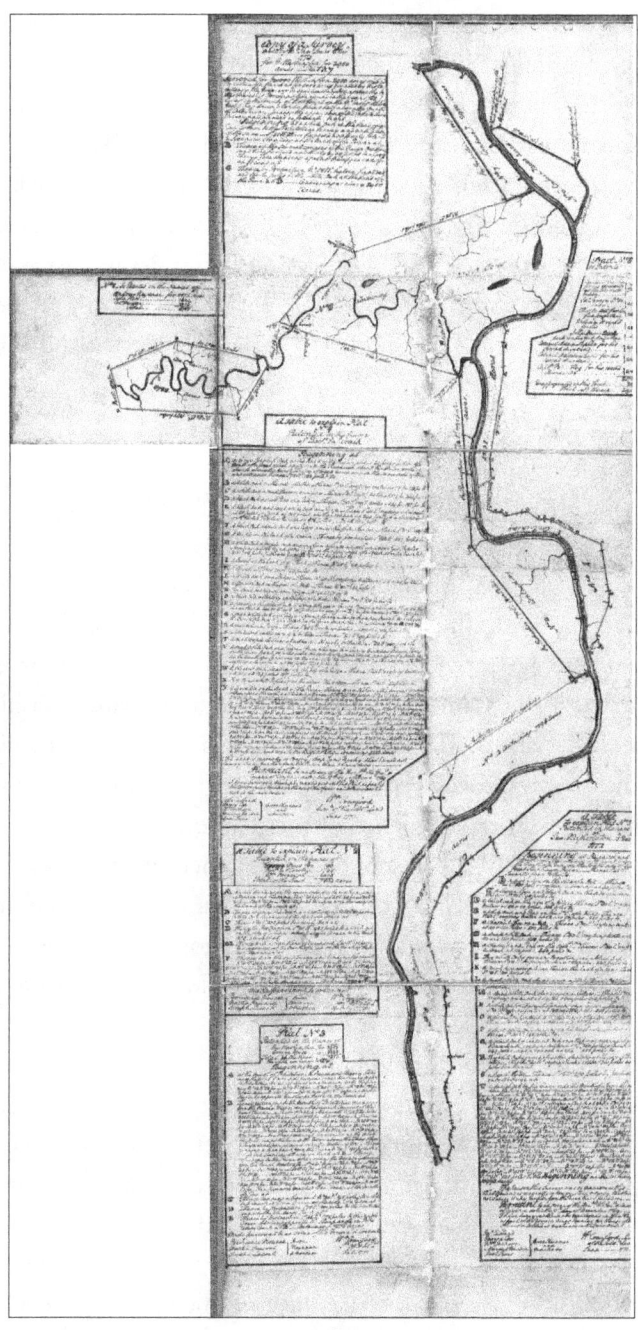

Crawford's survey of Washington's lands along the Great Kanawha.
(*Library of Congress*)

At some point during his visit to the Crawford home, Washington discussed the possibility of buying the Great Meadows land where he had defended Fort Necessity, and had later buried General Braddock during the disastrous retreat from the Monongahela. Although Washington did not record his feelings when he passed this spot on the Braddock Road, it clearly must have meant something significant to him. On December 6 William wrote Washington that, "Agreeable to your desire, I have bought the Great Meadows' from Mr. Harrison, for thirty pistoles, to be paid to Mr. Jacob Hite," and he included a proposed draft of the lines for Washington's approval.[38]

Washington Moves to Buy His Soldiers' Land

In early March 1771, Washington traveled to Winchester to convene another meeting with the former officers and men of the Virginia Regiment. There he provided a formal report on the success of the expedition down the Ohio. After hearing about the lands Washington and William had marked, the members voted unanimously that Crawford continue the survey process on both sides of the Great Kanawha, and later do the same on the branches of the Monongahela and the Tygart Valley. On April 20 William responded to instructions from Washington on the surveys, saying that he would start soon and hoped to be finished by August, adding that he would "run out lines going down the river and coming back; as then the stream will be low, and I can measure up the beach." William also added a comment that indicated Washington had concerns about the soldiers' land surveys, saying, "You may depend on my being as cautious as you could wish in every particular concerning the soldier lands." Although Washington's original letter did not survive, it is very likely that this "cautious" approach involved Washington's attempts to buy up the rights to his former soldiers' land shares, and to do so as cheaply as possible.[39]

In January 1770, months before the first meeting of the regiment in August and the expedition down the Ohio, Washington had written his brother, Charles, in Winchester. In this letter, Washington asked that

Charles determine if any former soldiers would sell their land rights at bargain basement prices. He wrote, "I should be glad if you would (in a joking way, rather than in earnest at first) see what value they seem to set upon their lands, and if you can buy any of the rights of those who continued in the service till after the Cherokee Expedition, at the rate of about five, six, or seven pounds a thousand acres I shall be obliged to you, & will pay the money upon demand." He added that he thought a few of the men might need "a little ready money" and "would gladly sell."[40]

Later on, Washington wrote to many of the individual soldiers whom Charles had identified. Washington told them that much of the land was "very hilly and broken." This was false. He added that there were rumors about a new charter government for the Ohio Valley, and their shares might come to nothing because of it. This was also fictitious. For these reasons, he wrote, selling to their old commander at any price might be their best course of action.[41]

The dishonesty of this act apparently did not trouble Washington. He wrote a friend that he saw no reason why he should not have all the best lands for himself, saying, "I might add without much arrogance, that if it had not been for my unremitted attention to every favorable circumstance, not a single acre of land would ever have been obtained." Again, as in the Braddock Road episode with General Forbes, it was not Washington's finest hour. It is likely that William was aware of the scheme, so this does not speak too highly of his integrity either.[42]

Over the next three months, from May through July 1771, William traveled down the Ohio and conducted Washington's surveys. He plotted a 10,990-acre tract running for more than seventeen miles on the south bank of the Great Kanawha from two miles above its mouth at the Ohio. The three surveys that followed included tracts of 4,395; 2,448; and 2,314 acres on the east bank of the Ohio between the Little Kanawha and Great Kanawha Rivers. In early August, Crawford wrote Washington that he had completed the work and would make a draft of the surveys before his next visit to Mount Vernon.[43]

The facet of William Crawford's integrity demonstrated in his work as Washington's land agent also found expression in his personal life. In

Crawford's 1771 survey of lands along the north bank of the Ohio.
(*Library of Congress*)

January 1773 a young Presbyterian minister, the Reverend David McClure, was making the journey to his assignment as a missionary with the Delaware living along the Muskingum River. As he traveled, he kept a diary in which he recorded some highly negative views on the people inhabiting the frontier. On February 5, 1773, for instance, he wrote, "Drinking, debauchery & all kinds of vice reign, in this frontier of depravity." A few weeks earlier, he had stayed with the Crawfords at Spring Garden, recording that "The Captain was very hospitable." Then, McClure added a sentence in Latin that read, "Sacred things are not observed much in his home. He has a virtuous wife, but, alas, that man at this time lives in fornication, and he keeps a scandalous woman, so people say, not far from his home." This diary entry might be dismissed as the writings of an over-zealous minister, but two years later another person would report a similar story and reveal the identity of this woman.[44]

That person was Nicholas Creswell, an Englishman visiting the Pennsylvania frontier on business. During July and August 1775, he stayed at the Crawford home on several occasions and seems to have been treated very hospitably. On August 9, however, he made a very odd and disturbing entry in his journal: "Mr. Berwick and I set out this morning to Major Crawford's, but met him at his mistress's. This woman is common to him, his brother, half-brother, and his own son, and is his wife's sister's daughter at the same time. A set of vile brutes."[45]

This information indicates that William had an illicit relationship with Ann Connell, the daughter of Hannah's sister, Elizabeth Vance Matthews. Ann was born about 1741 and her husband, James Connell, had died just before the Crawfords moved to Spring Garden. This event had prompted her to follow her Aunt Hannah over the Alleghenies. She arrived on the Youghiogheny shortly after the Crawfords, and William built her a cabin just north of his family's home at Spring Garden. As best can be determined, this ignoble behavior by not only William but also his brother, Valentine; half-brother, John Stephenson; and even his son, John, resulted in four illegitimate children. None of these men ever acknowledged Ann's children as theirs, even when they wrote their wills. Of course, if the behavior and relationships Creswell described were accurate, each child's relative paternity may have been impossible

87

to know. How Ann ended up in this situation and the dynamics of her circumstances are unknown. Regardless of what drove her into this sort of relationship, it does not speak highly of William's moral character.[46]

Chapter 6

LORD DUNMORE'S WAR

Land and the Colonial Boundary Dispute

Over the next two years, William strengthened Washington's claims by building cabins on several tracts of land, while fighting off squatters who had begun arriving in droves to grab up any unoccupied ground. During that same period, a new governor arrived in Williamsburg, John Murray, Fourth Earl of Dunmore. Lord Dunmore was a politically ambitious and aggressive man who would be the last royal governor of Virginia. As soon as he arrived in September 1771, Washington began ingratiating himself to him. He then presented his first petition to him on the subject of the soldiers' lands in 1772. In the years that followed, William Crawford would be pulled into the orbit of Washington's relationship with Lord Dunmore and the rapidly evolving political turmoil between Virginia and Pennsylvania.

In April 1773, Washington wrote Lord Dunmore about the governor's upcoming July visit to Fort Pitt. The governor had invited Washington to accompany him, but personal business would prevent Washington from doing so. Nevertheless, Washington still wanted his views on the western lands laid before Dunmore, so he proposed that during his trip the governor stop at Spring Garden to confer with William. Lord Dunmore agreed, and in early July he made a visit to the Crawfords' cabin. William presented Washington's arguments on the validity of his claims and surveys, and after Dunmore had departed William wrote Washington, "Lord Dunmore had promised me...he would patent these lands for me if I would send him the draft of the land I surveyed on the mouth of the Little Kanawha." Whether he knew it or not, William had just drawn himself into a long

John Murray, Fourth Earl of Dunmore, the last Royal Governor of Virginia.
(*New York Public Library*)

standing dispute between Virginia and Pennsylvania, one that Lord Dunmore was aggressively intensifying.[1]

The events generating the boundary dispute between the two colonies had been churning for over eighty years. The region around Fort Pitt was included in the original Virginia Company grant of 1609. Then, in 1681, the Crown defined the Pennsylvania grant as being bounded to the west by a line five degrees west of the Delaware River and paralleling it. This meant that Pennsylvania extended south to the thirty-ninth parallel and included the region surrounding Fort Pitt, an area falling within the boundaries of the Virginia Company grant.

For twenty years before Lord Dunmore's appointment as governor, Virginians acted on the belief that their colony owned the lands near Fort Pitt and many of them, including William Crawford, had flocked to the area in the years following the end of the French and Indian War. At the same time, Pennsylvania had surveyed and awarded lands to Pennsylvania settlers. Then, in 1771, Pennsylvania appointed magistrates and began plans to erect a courthouse and jail at the settlement outside Fort Pitt, since renamed Pittsburgh. However, the many Virginian residents of the area insisted on only recognizing the authority of Virginia's colonial government.[2]

For his part, William adroitly played both sides. After all, he was one of the Pennsylvania magistrates appointed by Governor Penn, but at the same time he was the surveyor and land agent for a well-known Virginian, George Washington. Moreover, William was now meeting privately with Virginia's governor to defend the sanctity of the claims and surveys he had executed for Washington. As tensions between the two colonies escalated, William would continue to keep a cautious foot in each of the warring camps.

In 1771, George Croghan, the scout, trader, and garrison commander at Fort Pitt, joined with Michael Cresap, a Maryland trader, to create an association whose goal was to resist any attempts by Pennsylvania officials to apply the laws of that colony to the disputed area. The following year, Croghan drove Pennsylvania tax collectors off his property, threatening them with death. Given Croghan's mischief, Governor Penn requested that General Thomas Gage, who had been serving as commander of British forces in America since 1763, immediately replace the militia garrison under Croghan's command at Fort Pitt with British Regulars. Gage had no desire to be pulled into the dispute and refused Penn's request. This did not deter Penn, and in early 1773 Pennsylvania created Westmoreland County near Fort Pitt and appointed new magistrates, of whom William was the ranking member.[3]

During Dunmore's July 1773 visit to Fort Pitt he met Dr. John Connolly, a local physician who had served with the British Army in Martinique and on the colonial frontier. Connolly found His Lordship to be "a gentleman of benevolence & universal charity, & not unacquainted with either man or the world." Dunmore was equally impressed by Connolly, to whom he granted "2,000 acres of land at the falls of the Ohio." Connolly soon became Dunmore's "agent provocateur" and lead agitator in western Pennsylvania. Over the course of the coming months, Connolly raised a rowdy, thuggish group of militia to defend Lord Dunmore and Virginia's interests, using them to harass Pennsylvanian officials and even arrest their magistrates.[4]

As this political turmoil swirled around him, William still somehow managed to appear loyal to each side. In early January 1774, William entertained Connolly at Spring Garden to discuss the status of his surveys for Washington. Afterward, he relayed the contents of their meeting to Washington, adding that Connolly told him that Lord Dunmore would lay down these lands as counties eventually and that His Lordship had promised William a position as surveyor for one of them.[5]

Yet, four months later, in April, William wrote a letter to Governor Penn, detailing the "very extraordinary occurrences" surrounding Connolly's activities in and around Fort Pitt. He described Connolly's militia as being "composed of men without character and without fortune." William also discussed the harassment of magistrates, such as himself, saying "…it will become both fruitless and dangerous for them to proceed in the execution of their offices." However, he betrayed that his real purpose in writing was to convince Penn to negotiate a temporary boundary line with Lord Dunmore quickly. In speaking for the other magistrates, William said, "They presume not to point out the measures proper for settling the present disturbances, but beg leave to recommend the fixing of a temporary line with the utmost expedition, as one step, which, in all probability, will contribute very much toward producing that effect."[6]

Then, as it appeared that the dispute might boil over into open warfare between the two colonies, events along the Ohio River shifted the political dynamics from land disputes to war with the Shawnee and Mingo nations.

A New War Begins

The surge in settlement west of the Alleghenies following the Treaty of Fort Stanwix led to steadily increasing hostility in the Native American villages of the Allegheny Plateau and the Ohio Country, especially among the Shawnee. As early as 1773, colonials traveling along the frontier were seeing evidence of the tribe's growing anger first hand. In February of that year, David Jones, a Welsh Baptist missionary, faced two open threats in the course of a single evening. First, a warrior threatened him with a large knife because he would not share his tobacco. It was only the intervention of the warrior's mother that prevented Jones from being killed. Later that night, a warrior known as Old Will entered the lodge where Jones was sleeping, and a comrade warned Jones to hide beneath some blankets in the loft. Old Will asked where Jones had gone, making threats and shouting, "Oh! If I could get one stroke, one stroke!"[7]

Within a year of Jones' encounters, the number of violent acts committed by both whites and Native Americans began to increase rapidly. On October 9, 1773, a party of Shawnee, Delaware, and Cherokee warriors raided into southwestern Virginia. There they tortured and killed two whites, one of whom was Daniel Boone's son, James. A few weeks later, Shawnee warriors captured seven men who were camping along the Ohio. They made threats against their captives, but cooler heads prevailed and the warriors soon released the men. As the settlers were headed home, another group of more than twenty-five Shawnee recaptured them, took their possessions, and sent them on their way with a warning to all Virginians—stay off the Ohio or be killed. In April 1774, the situation escalated toward general warfare when a small Cherokee raiding party attacked three traders, leaving one trader dead and another wounded.[8]

For their part, the settlers were not without blame, since they had made several brutal attacks against the native inhabitants of the region. On April 27, 1774, a party of Virginians led by Michael Cresap killed two Native American employees of a local trader. Cresap and his friends next murdered and scalped two other Native Americans and then attacked a Shawnee encampment located along Captina Creek (near present-day Wheeling, West Virginia). On April 30, a separate band of Virginia hunters and some "ruffians" led by Daniel Greathouse, a Virginia settler, lured a Mingo hunting party into their camp and then ambushed them, killing nine.

Greathouse's attack was especially bloodthirsty and had far-reaching implications. Among the Mingo casualties were the mother, brother, and sister of the Mingo war chief, Tahgahute, who called himself John Logan. Tahgahute, who had always been a loyal friend of the settlers and a voice for peace among the tribes, now swore he would avenge these deaths. After sending the surviving members of his camp to the Shawnee village of Kispoko Town, Tahgahute led a band of eight warriors on raids against the frontier settlements of Virginia in a classic mourning war. Once he had killed nine colonials, Tahgahute ended his campaign and went home.[9]

War was a distinct part of Native American society, with its own set of common practices and fundamental beliefs. In general, wars between the woodland nations were relatively short-lived, and far less brutal than those between European nations. Although a few conflicts were fought for territorial gain and trade advantage, most were an extension of a blood feud for an alleged wrongdoing that resulted in the death of a tribal member, a type referred to as a "mourning war." Native Americans did not see the battlefield as a unique cultural zone in which killing was sanctioned to the exclusion of other acts of killing which white men might define as murder. Therefore, the Europeans believed murder to be a crime requiring blood revenge, but Native Americans maintained that any killing by enemies demanded such revenge whether in or out of battle. Therefore, what Greathouse and his companions had done demanded revenge by Tahgahute on Greathouse's "tribe."[10]

The damage done by these attacks on both sides could not be undone. While many key Shawnee leaders were doing their best to restrain their war chiefs and preserve some semblance of peace, voices in the settler community called out for vengeance. In response, Lord Dunmore began assembling a militia army to move against the Shawnee in what eventually became known as Lord Dunmore's War.

On May 8, 1774, Crawford wrote Washington, detailing events on the frontier. He told him about Cresap's and Greathouse's attacks, noting that the latter had "killed and scalped ten." William also noted the alarm among the local populace writing, "Our inhabitants are much alarmed, many hundreds having gone over the mountain, and the whole country evacuated as far as the Monongahela; and many on this side of the river are gone over the mountain. In short, a war is every moment expected."[11]

The threat of a new war with the Native Americans was of great concern to William, his family, and his neighbors. In response, he and others living near Spring Garden erected two blockhouses, one on

William's land and another on Valentine's nearby farm. This was an all too regular practice on the Allegheny Plateau. Across the region, people came together to build blockhouses and small forts where local families might take refuge during periods of Native American raids. The surge in raids beginning in 1774 led to an increase in the building of these refuge forts. Within a few years, there were forty-five of them in the upper Monongahela Valley alone. Although some of these were merely two-story log fortifications, others included sleeping quarters and corner blockhouses, all of which were surrounded by twelve-foot-high stockade walls whose foundations were sunk deep into the earth.[12]

Any advance warning of a potential attack was crucial, so the militia employed what they called "Indian spies." These men were essentially scouts who constantly patrolled the woodlands watching for any signs of raiding party activity in the vicinity. Should they discover footprints or other evidence, such as the remains of a recent campsite, the scouts tried to determine the tribe, the size of the party, and if there was hostile intent. They then sent word to the nearest militia commander and "would fly from Fort to Fort and give the alarm."[13]

One settler later wrote of those nights when, as a child, his family received the alarm from scouts, what they called an "express," and hurriedly gathered what they could before fleeing to the safety of the refuge fort:

> I well remember that, when a little boy, the family were sometimes waked up in the dead of night by an express with a report that the Indians were at hand. The express came softly to the door, or back window, and by a gentle tapping waked the family. This was easily done, as an habitual fear made us ever watchful and sensible to the slightest alarm. The whole family were instantly in motion. My father seized his gun and other implements of war. My stepmother waked up and dressed the children as well as she could, and being myself the oldest of the children I had to take my share of the burdens to be carried to the fort. There was no possibility of getting a horse in the night to aid us in removing to the fort. Besides the little children, we caught up

what articles of clothing and provision we could get hold of in the dark, for we durst not light a candle or even stir the fire. All this was done with the utmost dispatch and the silence of death. The greatest care was taken not to awaken the youngest child. To the rest it was enough to say Indian and not a whimper was heard afterwards. Thus it often happened that the whole number of families belonging to a fort who were in the evening at their homes were all in their little fortress before the dawn of the next morning.[14]

Sometimes the settlers only stayed at the fort for a few days, but at the height of the raiding in the mid-1770s, they often remained for months at a time. Given the small size of many of the blockhouses and forts and the number of settlers seeking refuge, these visits could become quite unpleasant. Noise, crowding, disease and the typical human filth that accompanies such conditions made for a difficult, even miserable stay.

At the close of his letter, Crawford added news that revealed his true sentiments in the Virginia-Pennsylvania dispute. "I am now setting out for Fort Pitt at the head of one hundred men," he wrote, "Many others are to meet me there and at Wheeling, where we shall wait the motions of the Indians, and shall act accordingly." William was now openly serving Lord Dunmore and pledging his allegiance to Virginia. The following January, Governor Penn removed him from his magistrate position for serving the interests of Lord Dunmore and Virginia.[15]

In July, as he gathered his army in the Shenandoah Valley, Dunmore directed two hundred men under Major Angus McDonald, a Virginia frontiersman, sheriff, and landowner, to march to the mouth of Wheeling Creek on the Ohio and erect a fort. McDonald's men soon arrived there and began construction of Fort Fincastle. The governor then ordered William and his company, which had grown to 200 men, to relieve MacDonald's command and complete the fort's construction. MacDonald moved forward into the Ohio Country but was unsuccessful in initiating any major battle with the Shawnee or Mingo. He fell back to Fort Fincastle, but Lord Dunmore then recalled all his forces, including William's company, to the Shenandoah Valley[16]

This painting by Cecy Rose, "Shawnee Sentinel," depicts a resolute Shawnee warrior similar to those who resisted Lord Dunmore's forces.
(Courtesy of the artist)

Lord Dunmore reorganized his army, assigning the five hundred men of the Frederick Regiment to William and promoting him to colonel. He then formed another contingent, the Berkeley Regiment, led by William's old commander, Adam Stephen. The governor then sent Stephen's regiment west to Fort Fincastle while Dunmore accompanied William and the Frederick Regiment to Fort Pitt which the governor renamed "Fort Dunmore." Arriving there in early September, they were joined by a battalion of two hundrd men under Dr. Connolly, whom Dunmore had elevated to the rank of lieutenant colonel. William and his regiment only stayed at the fort until September 20, when the governor ordered William to take his men to the mouth of the Hocking River on the Ohio where he had surveyed land for Washington. Once there, William wrote Washington that he was "to erect a post on your bottom, where the whole of the troops are to rendezvous. From there they are to proceed to the Shawanese [sic] towns, if the Indians do not comply with his Lordship's terms; which are, to give six hostages for their good behavior."[17]

William's regiment moved down the Ohio by canoe and arrived at Washington's land on the Hocking River without incident. There they erected a stockade and named it Fort Gower, in honor of the Earl of Gower, a friend of Lord Dunmore in the British House of Lords. Within a few days, the Berkeley Regiment under Adam Stephen joined Crawford and the Frederick Regiment at Fort Gower, bringing their combined strength to about thirteen hundred men, all under Lord Dunmore's personal command. Meanwhile, the governor had formed two additional regiments under General Andrew Lewis, a Virginia surveyor and frontiersman, and marched them to the mouth of the Great Kanawha River. There they established Camp Point Pleasant (site of today's Point Pleasant, West Virginia).

The Shawnee, the Mingo, and their allies had observed the movement of both Lord Dunmore's and Lewis' forces. They correctly

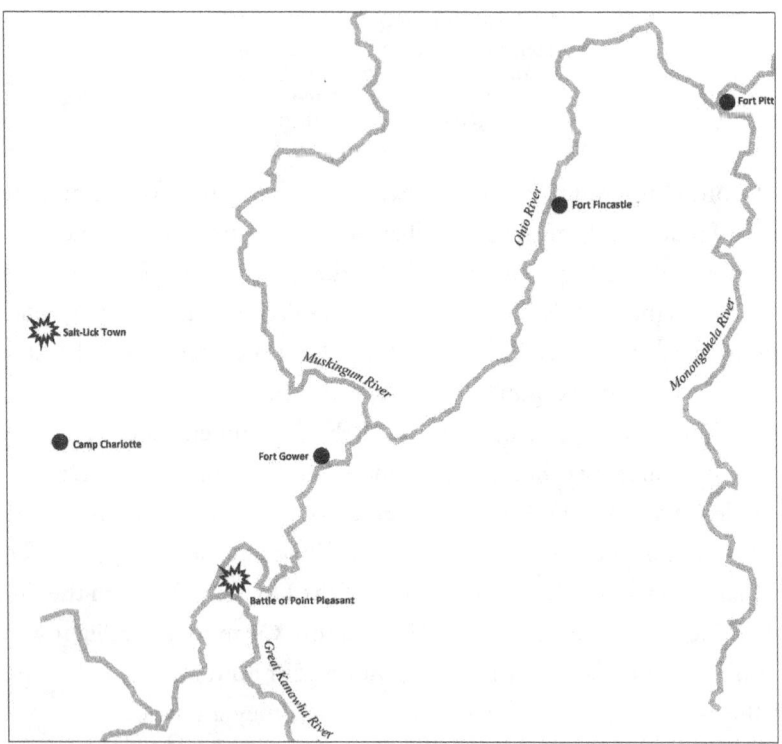

Map of the key places in Lord Dunmore's War of 1774.
(Drawn by the Author)

assumed that the Virginians planned to unite the two wings of their army and move against the Native American towns in the Ohio Country. The leader of the alliance, the Shawnee chief Cornstalk, decided to attack Lewis and destroy his regiments before he could unite with Lord Dunmore's forces at Fort Gower. On October 9, 1774, a combined force of Shawnee, Mingo, Delaware, and Ottawa warriors approached Camp Point Pleasant under cover of darkness. Hunters from the camp blundered into the native attackers shortly after dawn on October 10, and quickly made a mad dash back to the camp and raised the alarm. Lewis immediately sent out men to meet the Native American attack, and within an hour, a pitched battle had erupted in the surrounding forest.

At first, the Virginians were forced back, but, as more men from the camp reinforced the colonials, they managed to gain a position on high ground nearby. Here they fought off repeated attacks by Cornstalk's warriors, inflicting heavy losses on the Natives. As night fell, both sides were badly bloodied. Lewis withdrew his men into the stockade, but Cornstalk, opting to cut his losses, retreated across the Ohio. Once back at his village, the Shawnee chief held a council with the other tribal leaders, who decided the best path forward would be to make peace with Lord Dunmore.

On October 16 Dunmore marched twelve hundred men westward from Fort Gower to the Pickaway Plains. There he met Matthew Elliott, a white man married to a member of the Shawnee tribe. Elliott carried a flag of truce and conveyed Cornstalk's desire to hold a peace council. In response, the governor sent one of his officers to accompany Elliott back to the Shawnee town to arrange a meeting. The next day, Dunmore camped at a point he named Camp Charlotte in honor of his wife (near present-day Circleville, Ohio). After putting preliminary arrangements in place the day before, the chiefs arrived on October 19 to meet with Lord Dunmore and his officers, William Crawford among them. As they sat down to begin their discussions, William was introduced to a scout and interpreter, a man who would become William's comrade, and later, a formidable foe.

His name was Simon Girty.

Simon Girty

Simon Girty was born in 1741 on the frontier of Lancaster County, Pennsylvania. His father, also named Simon, was an Irish immigrant and fur trader. The elder Girty worked the woodlands between central Pennsylvania and the Ohio River, exchanging English powder, pots, rum, and blankets for the Native Americans' beaver pelts and deerskins. It was a lucrative business but also a dangerous one. The competition with French traders, who posed a greater threat than the Native Americans, was fierce. The Native Americans with whom he dealt, especially the Delaware, considered Girty a friend. As a result, young Simon, his older brother, Thomas, and younger brothers, James and George, grew up with Native Americans of various nations regularly in their midst. Tribal delegations traveling to Fort Duquesne for treaty conferences often stopped at the Girty farm, where they were always welcomed. Simon enjoyed these visits. He would wander among the visitors, fascinated by their clothes and the strange languages they spoke. To him, these were friends, rather than people to be feared.[18]

In 1750, the perilous nature of fur trading on the frontier claimed Girty's father when a drunk man killed him during an altercation. This left Simon's mother, Mary, alone to manage the farm with her four boys. A few years later, John Turner, a neighboring farmer, began calling on Mary Girty, and in 1754, the couple married. John and Mary soon had a child of their own, and he seemed to have been a decent man who treated his stepsons as his own. In spite of all going well, the outbreak of the French and Indian War brought tragedy to the new family. With much of the conflict focused on Pennsylvania, raids by Native Americans and their French allies became common, leading John Turner and the other British settlers to build a refuge fort named Fort Granville.

In late July 1756, as raids increased near the newly built fort, the Girty family and many others in the area fled to it for protection. After a few days, the immediate threat appeared to diminish and most of the settlers returned home to work their fields. John Turner and his family, however, stayed at Fort Granville, along with about twenty-four militiamen. Although most of the British thought the danger had passed, a worse threat was still lurking nearby. On August 2, a force of fifty-five French soldiers and more than one hundred Delaware warriors emerged from the forest to attack the fort. The small militia force held out for twenty-four hours before agreeing to a French demand for surrender in exchange for quarter.[19]

The French took Simon and the other captives to Fort Duquesne, where the French commander rewarded the Delaware by giving them all the white captives. The Delaware marched their prisoners a short distance up the Allegheny River to their village of Kittanning, where they tortured and killed John Turner. Simon's stepfather was burned at the stake as Mary and the boys were forced to watch. The Delaware gave Mary and her infant son to a band of Shawnee, while the four Girty brothers remained with the Delaware. A few weeks after Mary's departure, British forces attacked the Delaware camp and Thomas Girty was rescued, but Simon, James, and George were forced to flee with the surviving Delaware. The Delaware decided to keep George while trading James to a group of Shawnee and giving Simon to the Seneca.[20]

The Seneca elected to adopt fifteen-year-old Simon, a common practice among all the woodland nations. To be accepted into the tribe, Simon was stripped naked and forced to run a gauntlet. He ran past men, women, and boys, all lined up to beat him with sticks and other weapons as he struggled past them. Despite receiving brutal blows, the teenager made it to the end of the line, and he was lifted onto the shoulders of two Seneca warriors amidst the cheers and shouts of the villagers. His new Clan Mothers then washed him, dressed him in Seneca clothing, and sent him to begin his apprenticeship as a Seneca hunter and warrior.

Girty came to love the peaceful, harmonious life of the village. The head of the ruling council, Washington's acquaintance, Guyasuta, became Girty's surrogate father. Over the years, Girty grew to love and respect the elder Seneca sachem. Girty also displayed a natural gift for languages, quickly becoming fluent in Seneca and Delaware, as well as the dialects spoken by the tribes of neighboring nations. Before long, he was sufficiently skilled in these tongues to act as an interpreter for the tribe, but the war between France and Great Britain ended Girty's time with the Seneca.[21]

In the fall of 1764, after eight years of living with the tribe, Girty was returned to British hands at Fort Pitt under the terms of the peace agreement. This change left Girty devastated. He was now a strong and stocky twenty-three-year-old who saw himself as a Seneca warrior, as someone who had earned the right to live with his adopted family. With a heavy heart, Guyasuta took Girty directly to see Sir William Johnson, the British Superintendent of Indian Affairs. Guyasuta introduced Girty to Johnson and then to Johnson's twenty-nine-year-old deputy superintendent, Alexander McKee. McKee, who had lived among the Shawnee and had known Girty when they were both children, would become a close associate of his in the coming years.[22]

Although Girty's sudden departure from life with the Seneca was a jarring experience, he managed his return to the white world better than most captives did. Shortly after his arrival at Fort Pitt, he was reunited with his brothers, James, who had been released by the Shawnee, and Thomas, who had lived near the fort since his rescue from the Delaware. He also found employment.

The infamous American renegade, Simon Girty, is shown in this painting by Cecy Rose, "Simon Girty Scouts the Ambush, Fort Laurens, 1779." (*Courtesy of the artist*)

Alexander McKee hired Girty as an employee of the British Indian Department. McKee knew he could use a man who spoke nine different Native American languages and was "cheerful, energetic, and perceptive." Moreover, Girty also knew and understood the cultural nuances, political structures, spiritual rituals, clan relationships, and daily community lives of most of the Native American nations of the Ohio Country.[23]

At the end of the war with the French, Fort Pitt's value as a trading center had quickly grown. Within months of the Treaty of Paris, ambitious traders flocked to the outpost, anxious to expand their operations down the Ohio and even into the mysterious *Kenhtake* (Kentucky) wilderness. One of these traders was George Morgan, a twenty-four-year-old partner in the Philadelphia mercantile firm of Baynton, Wharton, and Morgan. Morgan had an ambitious plan for expanding the firm's business into the frontier. He would move goods by wagon from Philadelphia for storage at Fort Pitt and then exchange them for furs with the Native American nations downstream on the Ohio and Mississippi. Morgan also planned to have the men he sent downriver hunt buffalo, bringing the salted meat back to Fort Pitt in sealed containers for sale to both the British army and colonial outposts in the Caribbean.[24]

Morgan needed men familiar with the indigenous tribes and capable of surviving in the wilderness. They had to be able to communicate with the Native Americans of various nations and shoot well enough to hunt or fight their way out of confrontations with hostile warriors. The idea of ranging farther west and living the life of a "long hunter" excited Girty. With McKee's approval, Girty left his position in the Indian Department and signed on with George Morgan. Assigned as a boat foreman, Girty left Fort Pitt in June 1768 on a trading and hunting expedition that headed down the Ohio for the Cumberland River in northwestern Kentucky.

Everything went well for Girty's party until they were about two hundred miles up the Cumberland. There the expedition beached their boats on the riverbank, and the long hunters made camp. A few men tended the campsite as the others set off in two groups to hunt, one of which included Girty. Not far from the camp, a party of about thirty Shawnee warriors ambushed Girty and his companions. The hunters were forced to make a run for it. Girty raced into the forest and across a meadow, and took cover in the trees beyond. There he waited. When the first man appeared, Girty killed him with a single shot, convincing the others to give up the chase. As far as anyone knows, this was the first man killed by Simon Girty, and ironically, it was a Native American.[25]

Girty returned to the camp, where he found the rest of the expedition's members dead and the boats smashed. He headed downstream, walking along the river. He was looking for another expedition team led by Joseph Hollingshead that was supposed to have left Fort Pitt a few days after his. After finding the Hollingshead party and warning them about the Shawnee, Girty made his way back to the company's base of operations near Kaskaskia in the Illinois country. His success in alerting Hollingshead and making it possible for them to avoid the Shawnee earned the gratitude of George Morgan. Morgan wrote to his partners in Philadelphia on July 20 saying, "He is a lad who is particularly attached to me otherwise he would not have come here to give me this intelligence but would have proceeded to Fort Pitt. Mr. Hollingshead will give you his character."[26]

After he was almost killed by the Shawnee, Girty decided to abandon his fledgling career as a long hunter. He returned to Alexander McKee at Fort Pitt and resumed his interpreter duties. In the years that followed, Girty proved invaluable to McKee, the Native Americans, and the British government. As Girty's reputation grew, McKee sent him to deliver official messages and diplomatic conference invitations to the council longhouses of the distant indigenous tribes. Girty also developed a reputation as a hard drinker and brawler, which concerned both McKee and his British colonial superiors.

As he aged, Simon Girty grew into the sort of man who was easily bored by the ordinary, and one who became dissatisfied if life was too tranquil. Contemporaries of Girty referred to him as "active, jocular, and outspoken," but he was also a man who quickly resorted to violence, especially if he had been drinking. Simon Girty was a man who dominated a room from the moment he entered, and was someone people never forgot if they encountered him.[27]

With the outbreak of Dunmore's War, Girty had to choose which side to support—Virginia and Dunmore or the Shawnee and the Mingo. During his brief time as a long hunter, Girty had come to see land speculators as a threat to both the frontier life he loved and to his friends, the Seneca. Lord Dunmore operated in close coordination with land speculators and advocated seizing Native American lands, so Girty's choice would seem to have been clear; nevertheless, Girty chose to side with the colonial government at the advice of his surrogate father and mentor, Guyasuta. The immediate target of Lord Dunmore and his army were the Shawnee, an avowed enemy of the Seneca and the other tribes of the Six Nation Confederacy. Guyasuta and his confederates chose to stay out of the actual fighting, but to do all they could to facilitate Lord Dunmore's destruction of the Shawnee.

As McKee and the British Indian Department worked feverishly to prevent a war, McKee's loyal lieutenant, Simon Girty, supported the forces determined to start one. Once the war began, however, the British government felt compelled to support Lord Dunmore, and McKee assigned Girty to Dunmore's forces.[28]

Logan's Lament

To conclude a peace treaty at the Camp Charlotte conference, Lord Dunmore needed Tahgahute to be an active participant in the process. Since the murder of the Mingo leader's family was the flashpoint for the war, the governor desperately wanted Tahgahute to either come to Camp Charlotte or at least send his blessings. Dunmore decided to have Girty go to Tahgahute's village and speak to him. He selected Girty for this important mission not only because of his reputation, but also because he had met Tahgahute during his time with the Seneca.

The journey would be perilous, requiring an extended trip through Shawnee and Mingo lands. Girty chose two men to go with him: Joseph Nicholson, the translator who accompanied William Crawford down the Ohio with Washington in 1770, and Simon Kenton, a nineteen-year-old scout who had been living on his own in the wilderness for three years. The three men successfully made it to Tahgahute's village, and once the chief recognized Girty, he agreed to speak with him. Although Tahgahute would not accept Lord Dunmore's invitation to come to Camp Charlotte, he agreed to send a message to the governor and the other chiefs, slowly and deliberately dictating it to Girty in English. When Girty returned and delivered the message, Lord Dunmore had it transcribed and read several times to those at the conference. Tahgahute's sad, eloquent words had great influence on those assembled at Camp Charlotte and became famous thereafter as "Logan's Lament:"

> I appeal to any white man to say, if ever he entered Logan's cabin hungry, and he gave him not meat; if ever he came cold and naked, and he clothed him not. Such was my love for the whites, that my countrymen pointed as they passed, and said, "Logan is the friend of white men." I had even thought to have lived with you, but for the injuries of one man. Col. Cresap, the last spring, in cold blood, and unprovoked, murdered all the relations of Logan, not sparing even my women and children. There runs not a drop of my blood in the veins of any living creature. This called on me for revenge. I have sought it: I have killed many: I have fully glutted my vengeance. For my country, I rejoice at the beams of peace. But do not harbor a thought that mine is the joy of fear. Logan never felt fear. He will not turn on his heel to save his life. Who is there to mourn for Logan?—Not one.[29]

The talks proceeded without Tahgahute, but his words had an impact. Lord Dunmore put together what he called "The Terms of Our Reconciliation" and presented the document to the conference, and it was adopted as the Treaty of Camp Charlotte. The conditions of the treaty required the Native Americans to surrender all prisoners, return any stolen property, remain north of the Ohio River, and abide by any future trade regulations dictated by His Majesty's government. Dunmore promised to have whites remain south of the river, with the Native Americans receiving a guarantee of protection and good treatment by Virginia. The agreement concluded with a plan to meet the following spring at Pittsburgh to ratify the treaty.[30]

Although most of the Native American delegates agreed to the terms, the Mingo privately grumbled about them and planned to leave the conference. When Lord Dunmore learned this, he ordered William Crawford to take 240 men from his regiment and move against a Mingo town some forty miles up the Scioto River from Camp Charlotte. Fearing the other Mingo in camp might find out about the attack, William spread a rumor that they were merely going to Fort Gower for supplies.

Once away from camp, William moved his men forward quickly. They arrived at the Mingo's Salt Lick Town on the forks of the Scioto (in today's Columbus, Ohio) the following night. Before dawn the next morning, William dispatched half of his men to encircle the village with the rest advancing towards a smaller village about half a mile away.

Whenever a force of British troops or American militia approached a village, the typical Native American response was to fight a delaying action and evacuate the village. Native warriors learned early on in their struggle against the whites that trying to defend a village was a recipe for military disaster. But if they and the villagers retreated to the woods, their enemy would have to be content with burning lodges and food supplies. Although this might often create great hardship, it was better than the alternative, the almost certain slaughter of all the village's inhabitants

As William's men crept forward in the darkness, a Mingo warrior standing guard outside Salt Lick Town discovered their approach. One militiaman shot the warrior down, but the alarm was raised. Most of the young warriors were away from the village, leaving only the elderly, the women, and the children to bear the brunt of William's attack. As his men swept down on the community, the old men defended the village while the rest of the villagers tried to escape. The Virginians pressed into its center, cutting down the elderly warriors. One Mingo woman grabbed her five-year-old daughter in her arms, ran for the river, and crossed to a wooded island. William's men followed her to the riverbank and fired a volley of shots at her. She fell dead on the island's shore, but her little girl was unhurt. The child ran into a thicket and hid in a hollow sycamore tree for two days until returning warriors found her.[31]

The Virginians killed six of the Mingos, wounded several more, and captured fourteen. They also recovered two white prisoners left behind as the Mingo fled. The brief skirmish turned out to be the only fighting William would experience during Lord Dunmore's War. Interestingly, when William wrote Washington about the battle on November 14, he never mentioned the fact that only elderly men opposed his soldiers and that they had killed innocent villagers. Perhaps he did not care what had happened under his orders or, perhaps, there was little in this battle of which to be proud.[32]

Crawford concluded his letter to Washington by returning to matters of land, telling his partner that while he was at Fort Gower he had erected a cabin on Washington's property and cleared about eight acres to make sure there were "improvements" to help solidify his ownership. For now, it appeared that all was back to normal.[33]

However, as the spring of 1775 arrived, tumultuous events in two small villages near a faraway town called Boston altered the course of world history and shaped the dramatic final chapters of William Crawford's life.

Chapter 7

REVOLUTION

Patriot and Soldier

The year 1775 began typically enough for William. He made plans for additional surveying of Washington's lands on the Ohio, and in February, William wrote Washington that he was sending him some new plats and planning for another joint expedition down the Ohio that summer. Then, in March, he wrote him again, discussing supplies for Washington's indentured servants who were living and working at Washington's Bottom and sending additional plat warrants for lands along the Little Kanawha. On April 19, however, shots fired at Lexington and Concord changed both men's world.[1]

Rebellion had been brewing in Massachusetts for more than five years. The source of discontent had been a long series of British taxes and trade policies designed to protect industrial and business interests in the British homeland, all at the expense of American colonists. The core issue with many Americans was not the policies themselves, but the fact that the colonists had no representation in Parliament. Thus, they felt their rights as British citizens were being violated.

With the predominance of the shipping industry in Massachusetts, its residents felt the impact of His Majesty's policies most keenly. Opposition to colonial policy grew stronger each year, and eventually became highly organized. When Britain dispatched troops to Boston in the summer of 1774, many residents of the city fled to the countryside. There the local militias began storing arms and powder.

This open, militarized opposition eventually drew the ire of Whitehall, and in April 1775 His Majesty's government ordered General

Thomas Gage to seize or destroy the militia's weapons and supplies. Gage, the British commander-in-chief in America and the same officer who had been in the lead element during Braddock's defeat, dispatched seven hundred Regulars to the town of Concord with orders to deal with the militia and the small supply depot the New Englanders had been creating there.

On the night of April 18, the Regulars were transported across the Charles River. After marching into the Massachusetts countryside, just after dawn on April 19, they encountered a small group of militia gathered on the village green at Lexington. Upon intercepting Gage's plans, dispatch riders, including Paul Revere and William Dawes, had ridden throughout the area warning the local militia of the Regulars' approach. The Lexington militia, a small group of about seventy men under the command of Captain John Parker, decided to stand their ground despite the overwhelming superiority of the British troops. In their minds they had a right as Englishmen to form on the town green and make a statement of their opposition, but they were not planning to attack Gage's men. Parker had told his men, "Let the troops pass by. Don't molest them, without they being first." When one of the militiamen stated that it was folly to stand there, Parker replied, "Stand your ground. Don't fire unless fired upon. But if they want to have a war let it begin here."[2]

The British officer in charge of the initial detachment ordered Parker and his men to disperse and abandon the green. As the regulars lowered their bayonets and steadily advanced across the green, Parker decided to comply and ordered his men to get off the green, but before the militia could do so, a shot rang out. To this day, no one knows who fired it. British officers tried to restrain their men but the Regulars unleashed a devastating volley of shots at the Americans, who now fled in panic as British soldiers charged forward, bayoneting any American militiaman not fast enough to get away. The Revolutionary War had begun.

The British continued on to Concord, where they searched in vain for the militia's supplies. All they could find to destroy were a few gun carriages that they burned. Meanwhile, a detachment of two hundred Regulars marched north of the town to guard a small bridge over the Concord River and prevent any other militia from crossing. It was not long before a group of militia arrived, but unlike the small group at Lexington, there were over four hundred of them. In fact, unknown to the British, thousands of militiamen had been converging on the area all morning and the men opposing them at the bridge were just the vanguard of a much larger force.

The British fired a volley at the approaching militia, probably expecting them to run away as Parker's men had done at Lexington. Instead, the militia fired back and British troops took their first casualties of the war. The detachment of Regulars beat a hasty retreat back to Concord. Soon, the entire British force began to head back for Boston, but the militia did not go away. Instead, the Americans ran ahead of the British line. They marched down the stone wall-lined road to Boston and ambushed them repeatedly, killing and wounding scores of men. Once the British troops were back in Boston, the militia proceeded to surround the city, cutting it off to any entry or exit, except by sea.

On May 16, only a few weeks after the dramatic events in Massachusetts, the men on the frontier near Fort Pitt held an emergency meeting at the post. The gathering was packed with both Virginians and Pennsylvanians, unified against a potential common foe. This time, however, it was not the Shawnee or the Mingo that threatened them. George III's government was the enemy, the same government many of them, including William, had loyally served during the war against the French.

The meeting resulted in a resolution creating a committee for the defense of the district, and included William as a member. The resolution also established a process for gathering money, arms, and ammunition, and expressed their explicit reasons for doing so:

> The imminent danger that threatens America in general, from Ministerial and Parliamentary denunciations of our ruin, and is now carrying into execution by open acts of unprovoked hostilities in our sister Colony of Massachusetts, as well as the danger to be apprehended to this colony in particular from a domestic enemy, said to be prompted by the wicked minions of power to execute our ruin, added to the menaces of an Indian war, likewise said to be in contemplation, thereby thinking to

engage our attention, and divert it from that still more interesting object of liberty and freedom, that deeply, and with so much justice, hath called forth the attention of all America; for the prevention of all, or any of those impending evils....[3]

William had once again chosen sides. Although he never recorded his feelings about the relationship between the American colonies and Great Britain, the reasons for William's decision to become a "patriot" are not hard to discern. Like many colonists, William probably saw himself as more an American than a British subject. Furthermore, all his associates, particularly George Washington, were aligning themselves against the Crown. More importantly, there was also opportunity for an ambitious man.

William had consistently demonstrated that, above all, he was an opportunist. Although few people were openly using the word "independence" in the spring of 1775, war with Great Britain and the possibility for an independent America was on many minds. What better opportunity for gain than securing a prominent place in a new nation, one with ambitions as great as William's own?

Finally, there was the critical issue of the Native Americans and their lands in the Ohio Country. The resolution produced at the Fort Pitt meeting made it clear that, even now, frontier colonists believed the Crown was complicit in the Indian raiding that threatened them. They felt Britain's policies appeased the Native Americans too much and encouraged Native American attacks. Furthermore, most frontier colonists believed whites had a right and even a moral obligation to expand their particular brand of civilization into the Ohio Country and all the territory west of the Alleghenies. Given William's land speculation efforts with Washington and his participation in Lord Dunmore's War, he was likely in agreement with those who felt the Native Americans must give way for American expansion, even if that meant war.

The rebellion against Great Britain escalated on June 17, 1775 when a force of New England militia fought the first major battle of the Revolutionary War on the heights of Breed's Hill, overlooking Boston Harbor. In what became known as the Battle of Bunker Hill, American colonists defended fixed positions against attacking British Regulars. To the great shock of the British generals on the scene, the Americans did not flee at the sight of massed bayonets coming towards them. Instead, they held their positions, fought, and inflicted horrific casualties on the Regulars. Had the New Englanders not run out of powder, they might have never left their positions, but they did run out, and the British overwhelmed them. Still, the colonists had made a profound statement to His Majesty's government: they would fight British Regulars head-on and do so with resolve and bravery. Although the formal break with Great Britain would not take place for over a year, there would be no turning back now.

On June 14, three days before Bunker Hill, the Second Continental Congress had adopted the New England militia of fifteen thousand men based outside Boston as the foundation for "the American continental army." They also appointed a committee that included George Washington to draft rules and regulations for this new army and proposed to raise ten additional companies of riflemen. Two days later, Congress unanimously appointed William's friend and business partner, George Washington, as the Continental Army's general and commander in chief.[4]

As Washington traveled from Philadelphia to take command of the army, word of Congress' action spread throughout the colonies. Within a month, Congress nearly doubled the number of men authorized for the army. In Virginia, the newly elected and radical assembly overwhelmed Lord Dunmore's attempts to stop any military actions. Despite Dunmore's objections, on August 21, 1775 the assembly created sixteen regional military districts, each of which was required to raise one company of troops for one year of service. By October 21 fifteen of these companies, totaling 1,020 men, had reported for duty at Williamsburg. These companies were organized into two regiments, the First and Second Virginia. Within weeks, the two new regiments were skirmishing with Lord Dunmore's Loyalist units. Nine months later, in July 1776, Dunmore would flee Virginia for Great Britain.[5]

In the midst of these momentous events, something happened to William and his half-brother, John Stephenson, for which the historical record is incomplete. On an undetermined date in late 1775, someone

In this painting, Lord Dunmore flees the rebellious colony of Virginia, ending almost 170 years of British rule. (*Library of Congress*)

publicly impugned their reputations, accusing both men of secretly being Tory sympathizers. The charges were apparently very strong and were published in an unknown but widespread manner. William and John felt compelled to respond. They submitted a letter to Virginia's most widely circulated and well-read journal, Purdie and Dixon's *Virginia Gazette* of Williamsburg. It was printed on the third page of the January 26, 1776 edition and again on the front page of the January 27, 1776 edition:

To The Printers:

Gentlemen,

It is with great reluctance we are drawn into this publication: Had our enemies meditated their attacks against our persons or property, we had been silent; but they have, in violation of truth, of the duties of society, and of every principle of generality, practiced very cruel and insidious arts to deprive us of what is of much higher value than our characters as men, and the esteem of our fellow citizens. They have reported us to our brethren as traitors to the American cause, and consequently inimical to their dearest and invaluable rights. We are accused of holding connections with the avowed enemies to this greatly injured country. It is therefore incumbent on us to challenge those wicked men into open light, that we may have the opportunity of evincing our innocence to the world in the most public manner. In the interim, we set them at the utmost defiance, and are,

Yours, etc.

West Augusta

WILLIAM CRAWFORD.

Jan. 3, 1776.

JOHN STEPHENSON.[6]

On December 28, 1775, Congress authorized six Virginia regiments, and the Virginia Assembly soon increased this number to nine. On February 13, 1776, Virginia commissioned William as a lieutenant colonel and second-in-command of one of the new regiments, the Fifth Virginia. In March, he said goodbye to Hannah as he left for the third war he had served in since enlisting to fight the French in 1754.

He also may have bid farewell to Ann Connell. Given that Hannah was Ann's aunt, and they lived in such close proximity, Hannah must have known or at least suspected Ann's relationship with her husband. One can only wonder what Hannah and Ann's relationship must have been like. Under other circumstances, their relationship should have been one of mutual support, but it is hard to imagine that was possible. With William leaving again, Hannah prepared for a lonely life at Spring Garden. During her husband's absence, she remained a vital force in her family and community. She maintained a "faithful watch and ward" over her children and their families, and she took on a central role in the education of her grandchildren. "(T)o her they were largely indebted for their education, and what measure of life they entered upon."[7]

William traveled to Richmond, where the Fifth Virginia had formally organized on February 28. The regiment consisted of ten companies commanded by Colonel William Peachy, who was subsequently replaced by Colonel Charles Scott in May. The regiment remained in Williamsburg into the summer, training and organizing itself into something that resembled a disciplined military unit.[8]

Following Congress' action to declare American independence in July 1776 and Washington's initial attempt to defend New York in August, the Fourth, Fifth, and Sixth Virginia Regiments were ordered to move north to join the main army outside New York City. William did not accompany them, for he was promoted to colonel and commander of the Seventh Virginia Regiment in Williamsburg.[9]

Once he was with his new regiment, William wrote Washington on September 23 saying, "I should have been glad to have the honor of being with you at New York." At the same time, he communicated more mundane news. While traveling to Williamsburg, he had had the opportunity to visit the site of a new mill on Washington's lands along the Youghiogheny, calling it "the best mill I ever saw anywhere."[10]

A New Command

In November 1776, William was again transferred to a new regiment, the Thirteenth Virginia. Congress authorized this new command on September 16, 1776, and it included nine companies of men enlisted from the district surrounding Fort Pitt. William said goodbye to the officers of the Seventh Virginia, who published a farewell message to their commander in the *Virginia Gazette* on November 22:[11]

> The address of the officers of the 7th regiment
> to col. WILLIAM CRAWFORD.
>
> WE beg leave to take this method of expressing our sense of the warmest attachment to you, and at the same time our sorrow in the loss of a commander who has always been influenced by motives that deservedly gain the unfeigned esteem and respect of all those who have the honor of serving under them. Both officers and soldiers, retain the strongest remembrance of the regard and affection you have ever discovered towards them; but

as we are well assured that you have the interest of your country ever in view, we should not regret, however sensibly we may feel the loss of your, that you have military talents. Permit us, therefore, to express our most cordial wish, that you may ever find a regiment no less attached to you than the 7th, and that your services may ever be productive of benefit to your country, and honor to yourself.[12]

In fielding the Thirteenth Virginia, the Virginia government's intent was that the regiment remain on the frontier to defend against any campaign by the Native Americans against American settlements. William wrote Washington that, "The conditions were that the soldiers were enlisted during the war; and if an Indian war should come on this spring, they were to be continued there, as their interest was on the spot; but if there should be no Indian War in that quarter, then they were to go wherever called. On these conditions many cheerfully enlisted."[13]

On December 27, 1776, just after Washington's victory at Trenton, the Thirteenth Virginia was ordered to leave the frontier and join the main army in New Jersey. In early January 1777, before they began the march east, William's brother, Valentine, and his half-brother, Hugh Stephenson, passed away within days of one another. Because Valentine had died without a will, William had no choice but to return home and sort out the estate. Writing Washington from Fredericktown, Maryland on February 12, William explained the situation and his need for absence from duty. "The loss of Hugh Stephenson and Valentine Crawford, who died...without any will, is very hard on me," he wrote, "as the affairs of the latter and mine are so blended together that no man can settle them but myself." "If I can have some little time to administer and settle the estate," he added, "I can then appoint a man to act for me, and then I am ready to obey your commands."[14]

William requested that his regiment's assignment to the main army also be delayed. He wrote "The regiment, I believe, by this time, is nearly made up, as five hundred and odd were made up before I came away, and the officers were recruiting very fast." William added that, as with many new regiments, there were also problems obtaining equipment. Therefore, it might take time before the regiment was ready for action. William told Washington that "should they be ordered away before they get blankets and other necessaries, I do not see how they are to be moved.... There are no arms...the place very bare; but let me be ordered anywhere and I will go if possible." Crawford concluded the letter saying that he was traveling to meet with Congress "to see how my regiment is to be armed, and to get necessaries." The process of equipping his men proved very challenging, and he wrote Washington again on April 22, reporting that two-thirds of his men still had no weapons.[15]

Up to now, William had been in the Continental Army for more than a year, but he had yet to hear a single shot fired. That would soon change. Despite their lack of proper equipment and supplies, on May 22, 1777 the Thirteenth Virginia was ordered to march east over the mountains and join the main army that was trying to block General Sir William Howe's army in New York from reaching and seizing Philadelphia. Upon arrival, the Thirteenth Virginia was assigned to the First Virginia Brigade under the command of General Peter Muhlenberg, part of General Nathanael Greene's division.[16]

Muhlenberg was a thirty-one-year-old Pennsylvanian and son of a Lutheran minister. Educated at Pennsylvania University and in England, he became a Lutheran pastor upon his return to America. He moved to Virginia in 1772 and became an active leader in the patriot cause, despite intense criticism from local clergy. When war broke out, Virginia appointed him as colonel and commander of the Eighth Virginia Regiment. In February 1776, Muhlenberg and his regiment fought under General Charles Lee in Georgia and South Carolina. Although Lee's campaigns ultimately failed, he commended Muhlenberg for his bravery and noted him as an outstanding commander. This praise led to his promotion to brigadier general and command of the First Virginia Brigade in April 1777.[17]

Nathanael Greene, William's division commander, stood out among Washington's generals. In an army that was led by relative amateurs, the thirty-five-year-old Greene was a gifted amateur. A native of Rhode Island and the son of a Quaker, Greene joined the Patriot cause after the Royal Navy seized one of his ships, the *Fortune*, as an alleged smuggling vessel in 1772. He began the war as a private but suddenly found himself pulled from the ranks by the Rhode Island General Assembly, who appointed him as a colonel commanding Rhode Island's Army of Observation. He and his men joined Washington's army outside Cambridge, Massachusetts shortly after Bunker Hill, and by April 1776, Greene was commanding a brigade of five regiments. Greene caught Washington's eye because he was an uncompromising disciplinarian who served with distinction at Trenton and Princeton. He was eventually awarded his own independent command in the southern theater; after an encounter with Greene, British General Cornwallis said of him, "Greene is as dangerous as Washington. I never feel secure when encamped in his neighborhood."[18]

William Crawford's men may not have been completely ready for active service, but the reason for their transfer was clear—the Continental Army was in desperate straits. After the American victory at Princeton in January 1777, Washington had withdrawn his army to winter quarters at Morristown, New Jersey. When spring arrived, he moved his army forward towards Howe in New York, but it could barely be called an army. More than ninety percent, or almost twenty thousand men, who had opposed Howe in New York the previous summer were gone—either dead, wounded, sick, or prisoner—and a large number had deserted. The euphoria felt by the army after Trenton quickly evaporated during their gloomy winter in Morristown. Desertions became rampant. Washington wrote John Hancock saying, "Our Army is shamefully reduced by desertion, and except the people in the country can be forced to give information when deserters return to their old neighborhoods, we shall be obliged to detach one half of the army to bring back the other."[19]

Congress called for more troops while Washington shifted units like William's from other districts. Time was working against Washington, and the new American states were slow to respond to this renewed call for troops. Meanwhile, General Howe sat in New York planning his next move. The British commander had Washington significantly outclassed in terms of numbers, weapons, training, and logistics. With spring now arrived and summer on its way, Howe wanted to take the offensive soon. The only question left was where to strike—the answer: Philadelphia, the *de facto* capital of the rebellion against George III.[20]

In June, Howe sent General Burgoyne up the Hudson, hoping to draw Washington away from Philadelphia or at least split his forces, a maneuver which almost worked. When Burgoyne captured Fort Ticonderoga in northern New York in July, Washington moved his forces to the Clove, a position above Manhattan along the Hudson River, hoping to stop Howe from joining with Burgoyne. Luckily, Washington suspected Howe's true intentions, telling John Hancock on July 2, "Things should be examined with all possible certainty. I shall not be surprised, to hear of several ships appearing in or off Delaware."[21]

While Washington's spies in New York watched the British army closely, Howe debated on the best approach to Philadelphia. With Washington's army at the Clove, the American general had ably positioned his forces to either cut off a move north by Howe to support Burgoyne or quickly march back into New Jersey before Howe could take Philadelphia. Therefore, the British commander analyzed whether it was better to march overland or to use the Royal Navy to move his army closer to his objective. In July, he concluded the latter was the best strategy. An overland march would expose him to attack, but once his army sailed, Washington would have no way of knowing where it would land; the initiative and the element of surprise would be all Howe's.

On July 23 Howe and his army of over sixteen thousand men set sail from New York harbor in a fleet of 267 ships. Washington's well-informed intelligence network informed him of Howe's departure within hours of the sailing of the first British ship, so he immediately issued orders to begin marching toward New Jersey. Of course, Washington did not know precisely where Howe's army was going. He confessed to Hancock that, "The amazing advantage the enemy derive from their ships and the command of the water, keeps us in a state of constant perplexity and the most anxious conjecture. We are not yet informed of their destination, nor can any plausible conclusions be drawn respecting it—at least, not such as appear satisfactory."[22]

At 9:15 a.m. on July 31, as Washington's army camped at Coryell's Ferry on the Delaware River north of Philadelphia, Washington received word that Howe's fleet had been sighted off the Delaware Capes. He had no doubt that Philadelphia was the target.[23]

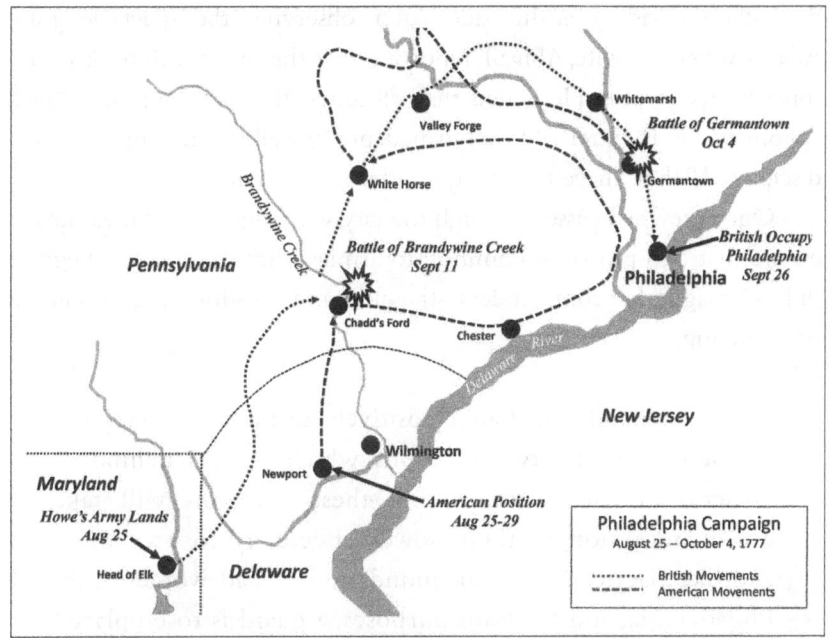

Map depicting the movements of the British and American armies during the Philadelphia Campaign of 1777. (*Drawn by the Author*)

Unfavorable winds delayed Howe's progress and the voyage from New York took thirty-two days instead of the planned eight. Washington continued to press southward despite the hot and humid weather. One soldier wrote that he "never endured more with the heat."[24]

On August 24, William and his regiment paraded through the streets of Philadelphia along with the rest of the army. In fact, they were among the lead element, as Muhlenberg's First Virginia Brigade was ordered to be at the head of the army as it marched through the city's streets. To make sure they would make an impression on both Patriot and Tory onlookers, Washington had the soldiers spruce up their appearance. He told his officers to "see that the men carry their arms well, and are made to appear as decent as circumstances will admit" and that the "drums and fifes of each brigade are to be collected in the center of it," playing a "tune for the quick step."[25]

As they entered the city, Washington rode at the head of the army on his great, gray horse, with the young French volunteer, the Marquis de Lafayette, riding at his side. After observing the spectacle, John Adams wrote his wife, Abigail, reporting that the procession took nearly three hours to pass. He added that, although the army appeared "well appointed" and "extremely well-armed, pretty well clothed, and tolerably disciplined," they "have not yet, quite the air of soldiers."[26]

Once they had passed through the city, Washington took measures to ensure that two problems common to armies since the Roman Legions did not plague his commanders: stragglers and prostitutes. He issued an order stating:

> The Commander in Chief positively forbids the straggling of soldiers of the two divisions which remain behind.... General Officers commanding these divisions will take every precaution in their power effectually to prevent it; and likewise to prevent an inundation of bad women from Philadelphia; and for both purposes, a guard is to be placed on the road between the camp and the city, with particular orders to stop and properly deal with both.[27]

The next morning, with the Royal Navy's ships *Vigilant* and *Roebuck* in the lead, the British fleet carrying Howe's army arrived at Elk Ferry in northeastern Maryland where Turkey Point juts into the mouth of the Elk River. The ships immediately began disembarking their cargo of troops, horses, artillery, and supplies. Because Washington could not be sure where the British army might make landfall, he chose not to oppose any landing. The British and Hessian troops came ashore without a fight and began to move inland.[28]

Brandywine Creek

On August 28, the vanguard of British forces arrived at Head of Elk (present-day Elkton, Maryland), while the Continental Army awaited them some twenty miles to the northeast outside Wilmington,

Delaware. Washington was determined to make a stand and thought Wilmington was the best place to position his men.[29]

At 4:00 a.m. the next day, Crawford and his regiment, along with the rest of Greene's division, moved out of their positions near Wilmington to the southeast, just past Newport, Delaware. Not long after the division camped, the general issued orders for his two Virginia brigades each to detach one hundred men to act as a reconnaissance force, placed under William's command. Crawford then gathered his men and moved them toward Iron Hill. From there, they could clearly see Howe's forces in the distance and provide intelligence on their activities. Soon after, William's men were joined by a much larger force consisting of a light infantry brigade under the command of Brigadier General William "Scotch Willie" Maxwell. Maxwell's assignment was to block the Wilmington Road via Cooch's Mill and Christiana Creek, and William was to support him.[30]

On the morning of September 3 William and his men saw signs that the British were breaking camp. A few hours later, they observed Howe's army start its general advance. Howe had decided to move towards New Castle, Delaware, where he hoped he would finally confront Washington. General Knyphausen, commander of the Hessians in Howe's army, and four hundred of his jaeger[31] led the march down the Old Baltimore Pike. It did not take long before they ran into Maxwell's light infantry and William's small scouting unit. The Americans proceeded to set up and execute a series of ambushes in a running fight over the four miles to Cooch's Mill and the Christiana Creek bridge. Once the Americans were forced to the far side of the creek, the jaeger made a concerted charge. The Hessians drove the Americans back into the woods, where one Hessian officer reported that William and Maxwell's men "defended themselves obstinately." Once night fell, Maxwell fell back to rejoin the main army, and William and his men returned to their Virginia brigades.[32]

Howe paused at Cooch's Mill, spending five days weighing his options. Washington pulled his army forward and built entrenchments along nearby Red Bank Creek outside Newport. Finally, on September 8, Howe decided to turn his army north toward Newark, Delaware.

In the early morning darkness, the British troops struck their tents and began the march. Washington's scouts reported a stirring in the British camps, and Washington assumed Howe's attack was finally coming. At 3:00 a.m., the sound of drums beating the call to arms awakened William, and his regiment began striking their tents. After the men gathered their weapons and formed up with every officer at the head of his platoon, William wheeled his regiment into line and awaited orders.

At 9:00 a.m., alarm guns sounded and the entire army moved into the line of battle in the entrenchments they had dug along the creek. After a while, William and his men, who were on the far right of the American line, watched as General Weedon's Second Virginia Brigade advanced in an attempt to bring on a fight with the British. All they got for their trouble was some minor skirmishing with enemy pickets, whom Washington said, "were only meant to amuse us in front." The Continental Army remained under arms for the entire day awaiting an attack that never came.[33]

That night, scouts brought word that Howe was heading north on the main road from Wilmington towards Lancaster, Pennsylvania. Washington realized his right flank had been turned. To effectively screen Philadelphia and ensure he did not end up out of position, Washington had to immediately turn his army north. He ordered the army to pull out of its defenses and move into Chester County, Pennsylvania, where he hoped he might pick the right ground and force Howe to battle.[34]

The orders to march came to William at 4:00 a.m., and he placed his men on the road, where Greene's division took the lead. William's regiment marched northeast to the Crooked Billet on the same road as Howe, before turning towards Kennett Township, and crossing Brandywine Creek at Chadd's Ford. Here, William's exhausted men were ordered to halt, camp, and prepare for an upcoming battle. Washington had received intelligence indicating Howe was going to turn his army toward Brandywine Creek and Chadd's Ford, so he decided to make his fight there.[35]

The next day, September 10, Washington deployed his army on the high ground above the creek. William's Thirteenth Virginia, along with the rest of Greene's division of twenty-five hundred men, took positions near Chadd's Ferry as the left-center of the American line. General Anthony Wayne's division was placed on their right with the rest of the

REVOLUTION

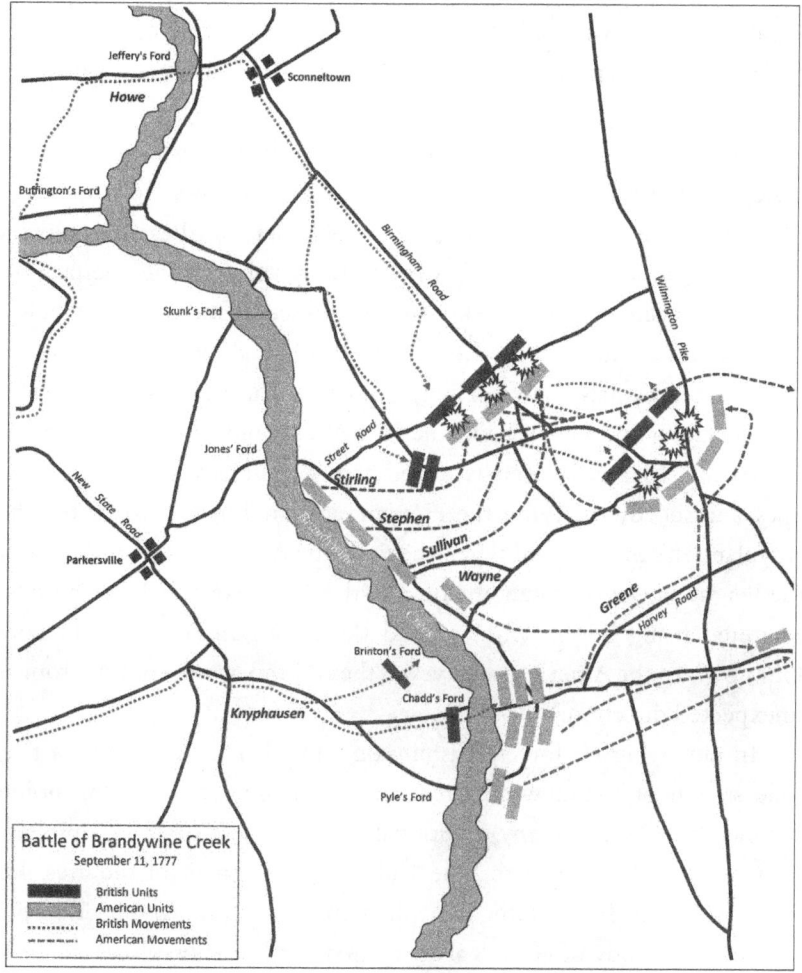

Map depicting the movements of the American and British armies at Brandywine Creek. (*Drawn by the Author*)

army further upstream. About a mile above Chadd's Ford, General John Sullivan's Maryland Division covered the approach to Brinton's Ford, and the general detached two units from his division to guard the next three fords upstream to the right. Then they waited for Howe's army to appear.[36]

September 11 dawned with the kind of weather that portends a hot, humid, late summer day. As Crawford peered across the buckwheat field towards Brandywine Creek and the woods beyond, a thick fog lay above the water that began to burn away slowly as the sun climbed in

125

the sky. Howe's army was only five miles away beyond the trees and Washington sent Maxwell's light infantry across the creek. Maxwell's men ventured forward, looking for opportunities to ambush the enemy as they approached the creek.

Howe began advancing at 5:00 a.m., with Knyphausen's Hessians marching toward Chadd's Ford. It did not take long for Maxwell's men to see the Hessians coming, and the Americans began employing "shoot and scoot tactics." They would blast a volley at the enemy from concealed positions, then quickly fall back to set up another attack before the Hessians could react. As the fighting intensified, William and the rest of the Continentals waited. They could hear the bursts of musket fire coming closer and knew their wait for battle would not be long. Around 10:00 a.m., Maxwell's men retreated across the creek to the American lines, and shortly thereafter the Hessians appeared in the woods beyond. Knyphausen's men paused when they saw the American forces dug in on the heights above the Brandywine, and they took cover behind the trees. Scattered firing began, with isolated skirmishes around Chadd's Ford. Unknown to the Americans, however, the real threat was coming from an unexpected direction.[37]

In deploying his forces, Washington had taken care to cover a five-mile stretch of Brandywine Creek and eight potential crossing points, but he did not order any additional reconnaissance farther upstream, a surprising move given that he had no decent maps of the area. His decision proved his undoing. Knyphausen moved against Chadd's Ford, and the main body of Howe's army turned north to cross above the forks of Brandywine Creek at Jeffrey's Ford, where there were no American forces.

Although the early morning fog helped conceal Howe's movement, some American scouts did encounter the main British column. Word soon began trickling into Washington's headquarters that Howe's army was marching north, but for the balance of the morning, Washington assumed this meant Howe would attack across one of the defended northern fords, either Jones or Skunks. No one, including Washington, imagined the British would cross three miles further to the north, allowing the enemy to march unobstructed against a totally exposed American right flank.

Around noon, reports from American dragoons scouting above the forks of the creek, as well as local patriot supporters, came into Washington's headquarters. All of them said that Howe was moving against the American right. Although this news was still unconfirmed, it initially made Washington believe that an opportunity might exist to attack and defeat the enemy piecemeal while their forces were divided. He immediately ordered Greene to advance his division across the creek to engage Knyphausen.

When Washington's orders arrived at Chadd's Ferry, William placed his men in line and began advancing towards the creek, but before they could get across and attack the Hessians on the far side, Washington changed his mind. He issued orders to fall back while he waited for more intelligence on Howe's location. The Hessians, who had begun to move forward to meet William and the rest of Greene's division, also pulled back, poised to strike as soon as Knyphausen received word that Howe was attacking the American right flank.

Just before 2:00 p.m., as William and the Thirteenth Virginia waited in the muggy heat above Chadd's Ferry, General Sullivan, whose division was deployed the furthest to the right at Bristol Ford, received a message from Virginia cavalry that Howe was across Jeffery's Ford. This news shocked Sullivan. He grabbed some paper and quickly scratched out an urgent dispatch to Washington: "Colo. Bland has this moment sent me word that the enemy are in the rear of my right about two miles coming down. There is he says about two brigades of them." Sullivan signed his name and then added an ominous postscript: "He also says he saw a dust rise back in the country for above an hour." There was now no doubt that the bulk of Howe's army had flanked the Americans.[38]

When Washington received Sullivan's message, he leaped into action, knowing Howe had once again out-maneuvered and out-generaled him. He ordered Stirling's and Stephen's divisions to take a position across the road on Birmingham Hill. The two divisions quickly marched through Sconneltown to Dilworth, where they halted and deployed for battle in a line perpendicular to the road. Washington realized these two divisions would not be enough to stop Howe, so he ordered Sullivan to join the line on Stirling's left. Still, this meant there were only four thousand American troops trying to halt Howe's force of eight thousand.[39]

At around 4:00 p.m., Howe's men, under the command of General Cornwallis, collided with the hastily formed American line on Birmingham Hill. The fighting was furious, with constant volleys of musket fire, punctuated by artillery blasts, filling the late summer afternoon. One American on the scene wrote his father, "We had been there but a short time when they appeared, and the heaviest firing I ever heard began, continuing a long time, every inch of ground being disputed." The carnage was appalling. The British took terrific losses, but their superior numbers, training, and experience began to tell. The Americans steadily gave ground before completely collapsing around 5:00 p.m. Washington now needed to act quickly if he was going to save his army from complete destruction.[40]

As Crawford remained facing Brandywine Creek and Knyphausen's Hessians, the sounds of pitched battle to his right rear must have concerned him. The rumble of artillery and rattle of musketry had been echoing from upstream for over an hour. He almost certainly knew that hearing fighting behind you when the enemy was supposed to be to your front

This drawing depicts the heavy fighting during the defense against Howe's flank attack. (*Library of Congress*)

was not a good sign. Thus it was no surprise when William received word to pull back from the creek and make a rapid march to the rear. General Weedon's Second Virginia Brigade led the way, and Muhlenberg's First Virginia Brigade followed close behind.

In the dusk William's regiment marched onto the Great Post Road, at first heading east and then turning northeast up Harvey Road toward Dilworth. Great clouds of choking dust rose as the men strode quickly forward with a sense of desperate urgency. They covered the three to four miles in less than forty-five minutes, quite a feat for men carrying packs and weapons. When William's regiment arrived, he and his men saw the signs of a panicked retreat, as men streamed past them "in the most broken and confused manner," their faces covered in black powder, some bleeding from wounds, others staring ahead, their eyes wild with fear.[41]

Greene quickly deployed his division on heavily wooded, rising terrain that would make it almost invisible to the advancing British Fourth Brigade and Second Grenadiers Battalion. Weedon's brigade, along with those survivors from Stirling's and Stephen's divisions still able to fight, made up the right wing of this new defensive line. They formed up just to the east of the Birmingham Road in an L-shaped formation. Meanwhile, William's Thirteenth Virginia and the rest of Muhlenberg's First Virginia Brigade took a position on the west side of the road with the survivors from Sullivan's division. William and the others in the left wing formed a defensive line that stretched along a wide, concave, tree-lined front generally facing northwest. The combination of Greene's deployment pattern, terrain, woods, and the oncoming dusk meant that the advancing British troops would march straight into a deadly crossfire before they realized what was happening.[42]

A few minutes before 7:00 p.m., as the dusk deepened, William could hear the sounds of drums. Steadily and ominously, the sound came closer, beating the two-step rhythm used to keep marching soldiers in step. Then he spied the bright red uniforms of the British as the Second Grenadiers advanced across the open ground to William's front. As he peered into the distance off to his right, he could also just make out the British Fourth Brigade moving towards the Second Virginia Brigade's position.

Although the British were bloodied from the fighting on Birmingham

Hill, they still came on. The Grenadiers approached in the standard two-parallel line formation, their muskets and bayonets at the shoulder arms position. Flush with the prospect of certain victory, the British officers and men thought they were about to put the finishing blows on a routed rebel army. They had no idea what awaited them in the dark woods ahead.

When the Grenadiers were about one hundred yards away, William prepared his men. He went down the line quietly ordering them to "Prime and Load." Once their muskets were loaded and the flints were in place, William directed them saying, "Make Ready." His soldiers raised their muskets vertically in front of their faces and cocked the hammer, and William told them, "Present." His men lowered their muskets and took aim on the advancing Grenadiers. While William awaited the general order to open fire, he could see that the Grenadiers were very close. His men could clearly hear their officers' commands and even make out their smoke-stained faces. The order to fire had to come soon or a massacre might take place.

Just then there was an explosion of artillery and musket fire as the American right wing opened fire on the British Fourth Brigade. Many of the advancing Grenadiers turned their heads to their left at the sound. Within seconds, William and the left wing were ordered to open fire, and they blasted the Grenadiers with a deadly fusillade. The Grenadiers halted in disbelief, their men dropping by the dozens. After a few moments of confusion, the British officers gained control of their troops and began trading volleys with the Americans. William urged his men to fire as fast as they could, pouring a steady stream of musket fire into the Grenadiers. Standing in the open, the British troops on both sides of the road did not fare well, and within minutes, two British regiments lost virtually every officer.

The fighting continued, "without giving way on either side until dark." Finally, as one soldier remembered, "Our ammunition almost expended, firing ceased on both sides." By 8:00 p.m., it was over, and Greene ordered his division to retreat. William quickly pulled his men back, formed them up on the road, and began to march away. Although the battle at Brandywine Creek had been lost, William and his men fought as part of a defensive stand that saved Washington's army from what might have been total annihilation.[43]

Howe decided to halt and regroup while Washington moved his men toward Chester. One soldier remembered the retreat being nearly as horrible as the battle. "Our way was over the dead and dying," he recalled, "and I saw many bodies crushed to pieces beneath the wagons, and we were bespattered with blood."[44]

The next day, Washington's exhausted army marched through Chester, on to Derby, and then moved around Philadelphia, arriving in Germantown on the afternoon of September 13. Here William and his men slept in tents for the first time in over a week. Unfortunately, their rest would be short-lived. Washington had them moving again the next day, and they marched on to Reading, and then finally Paoli on September 15. The weather soon added to the misery with torrential rain falling for nearly eighteen hours straight. "This march for excessive fatigue," one soldier in Greene's division wrote, "surpassed all I ever experienced." Given everything that Washington's men had faced up until now, that said quite a lot.[45]

On September 25, as Washington's army camped at Pennybecker's Mill, Howe and his army marched triumphantly into Philadelphia. Hundreds fled the city in panic, including the Continental Congress, which relocated first to Lancaster before finally settling in York. Two days before the British capture of the city, Crawford's regiment was positioned to harass a British crossing on the Schuylkill River. While he was there, Colonel Joseph Reed, one of Washington's aides-de-camp, arrived on his way to his home along the river. Reed needed to evacuate his family and William offered to accompany him. They were just in time, getting Reed's wife and children away only fifteen minutes before British troops arrived. With Reed's family safe, the two men proceeded to a nearby Presbyterian meetinghouse. There they collected a group of fifty volunteers and returned to the Reed home, where they drove the British away and captured two prisoners for interrogation. Reed quickly scribbled the intelligence they gathered from their prisoners on a page torn from a child's copybook. Apologizing for using "such paper as I can get," Reed added, "I have a Colonel Crawford with me—a very good officer."[46]

Germantown

As humiliating as the fall of Philadelphia might have been, it seemed to have steeled Washington's resolve. Rather than limping away from the city to lick his wounds, he decided to strike back immediately at a time when Howe would least expect it. At first, Washington's generals balked at such an audacious move. During several late September councils of war, they all voted against the idea. Then, Washington learned through intercepted dispatches that Howe had placed half his army in Philadelphia, with the remainder camped in and around Germantown, less than ten miles north of the city. This meant that the Americans would have almost equal numbers. They would also have the element of surprise because, in the minds of many British officers and soldiers, the rebellion was as much as over. In fact, Howe's men did almost nothing to fortify their camps or the town itself.

Washington spent two days making plans for his upcoming attack on Howe. He developed a strategy that was thorough and complex, perhaps too much so. It called for a synchronized attack by four different columns to begin at precisely 5:00 a.m. on October 4, 1777. Maryland and New Jersey militias would move far to the left to attack Howe's right flank while two units of Pennsylvania militia moved against the British left. Meanwhile, the bulk of the army under Sullivan and Greene would advance to strike directly at the left and right, respectively, of Howe's main line. The combined effect was that of a gigantic pincer assault, conducted using surprise in the early hours of a Saturday morning.[47]

Washington's plan also meant that, in order to remain undetected until the attack, his troops would have to travel in darkness over unfamiliar terrain while observing complete silence, covering distances of fourteen to twenty-five miles. Asking any army to carry out such a plan was perhaps unrealistic, and for an army made up of inexperienced officers and men this kind of maneuver was foolhardy. Despite the risk Washington's generals all agreed to the plan, and at about 7:00 p.m. on the evening of October 3 the army began to move forward.

From the beginning, things did not go as planned. After a warm

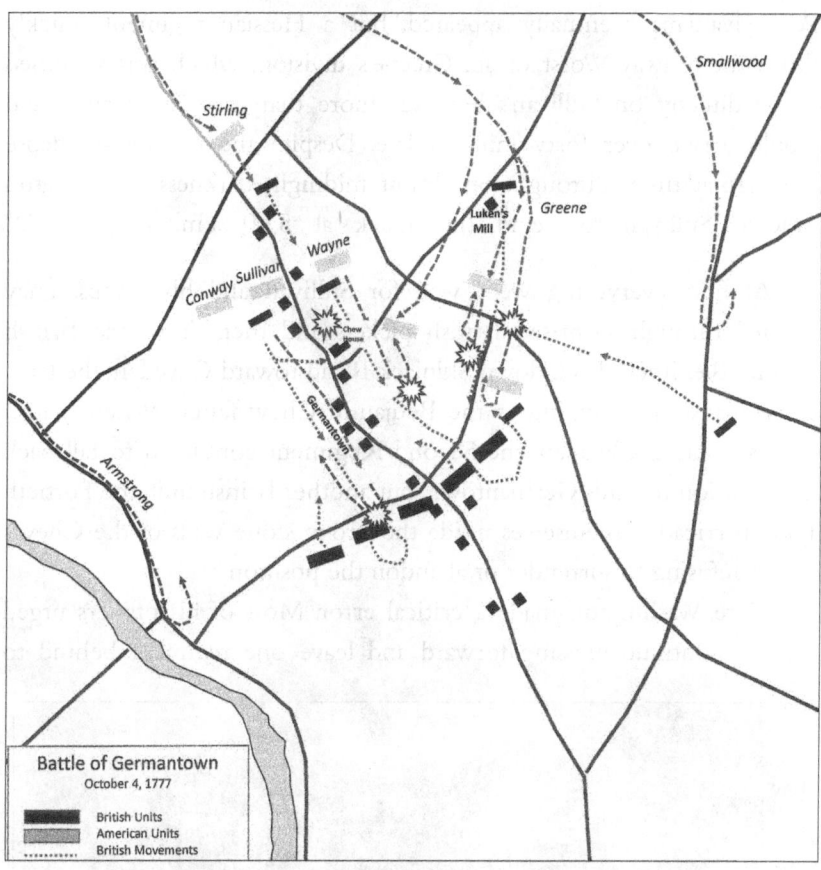

Map illustrating the execution of Washington's ambitious plan to attack British forces at Germantown. *(Drawn by the Author)*

day, the temperatures dropped rapidly and dense fog formed over the countryside. One soldier remembered it as the "thickest fog known in the memory of man." Now, an army that was trying to find its way forward in darkness had to grope through the fog as well. The impact of the fog and darkness had its greatest effect on Greene's division where William's regiment marched. Their guide, a local man supposedly familiar with the area, became confused and led them down the wrong road, going more than a mile too far to the left of the intended route.[48] When 5:00 a.m. arrived only Sullivan's men were in line for the attack and they had no idea where the rest of the army was. The Maryland and New Jersey militias never made it to Germantown. The

Pennsylvanians eventually appeared, but a Hessian regiment quickly drove them away. Worst of all, Greene's division, which was supposed to be directly on Sullivan's left, was more than two miles away and would arrive over forty minutes late. Despite the continuing dense fog that, at times, "brought on almost midnight darkness," Washington ordered Sullivan to begin the attack at 5:00 a.m. as planned.[49]

At first, everything went well for Sullivan and his troops. They crashed through surprised British pickets and then drove the British Second Regiment back down Skipjack Road toward Cliveden, the large stone mansion belonging to the Benjamin Chew family. When British troops reached Cliveden, the Second Regiment continued to fall back in confusion towards Germantown, but another British unit, the Fortieth Foot, barricaded themselves inside the strong stone walls of the Chew's house, refusing to surrender or abandon the position.

Here, Washington made a critical error. Most of his officers urged him to continue pressing forward and leave one regiment behind to

In this drawing, American forces make repeated attacks against the stubborn British defenders at the Chew House. (*New York Public Library*)

deal with the Fortieth Foot at Cliveden. Instead, Washington listened to Henry Knox's advice and ordered the house to be subdued before continuing the advance. Wave after wave of American troops attacked the mansion, but the stubborn British defenders would not yield, delaying the main American attack for over an hour.

On the far left of the American line, William and the rest of Greene's men heard the firing begin in the distance at 5:00 a.m. The fog muffled the sound, making it difficult to gauge the direction of the shooting. William's men and the rest of Greene's division continued to wander to the southeast in the fog. At times, one could see about fifty yards ahead. Then, the fog swirled about them, making it impossible to see even five yards out. Finally, just after 7:00 a.m., Greene began to deploy his men into battle formation just north of Luken's Mill.

The Connecticut Brigade moved into line on the far left with the Second Virginia Brigade positioned to their right. William's regiment and the First Virginia Brigade swung into line next to the Second Virginia, and the Third Virginia Brigade lined up on their immediate right. All this was accomplished with great difficulty since even the relatively simple task of moving formation was complicated by the fog and by the numerous fences and low stone walls in the area. Frustrated officers and soldiers stumbled and cursed as they struggled to get organized. Finally, at Greene's order, they all fixed their bayonets and staggered down Limekiln Road toward Luken's Mill.

Around 7:30 a.m., the Connecticut Brigade made contact with the enemy, driving in the British pickets at Luken's Mill. At the same time, the Third Virginia Brigade became lost in the fog and veered off to the right, away from the rest of Greene's division, attracted by the sound of battle on Skipjack Road. As the advance continued, William and the Thirteenth Virginia Regiment found themselves alone on the right, their flank hanging out in the air. As the smoke from gunfire and burning field stubble added to the fog, two nearby American units collided and opened fire on one another before realizing it was not the enemy in their front.

Meanwhile, Howe moved his men up from the main British camp in response to the attack. As Greene continued to advance, the first of

Howe's counterattacks hit his left, but the men from Connecticut drove the British back. At 8:15 a.m., the main weight of Howe's advance ran into Greene, and the real fight was on. As men fired blindly into the heavy mist, the Ninth Virginia Regiment moved forward out of the First Virginia Brigade's line directly into the British forces. Suddenly, things in William's regiment went very wrong.

Perhaps it was the combination of fear, confusion, and poor visibility, but William's men simply refused to obey orders and move forward. William shouted at them to advance, and his officers swatted men with the broad side of their swords, but it did no good. A few ran away, and none would step into the swirling fog towards the sounds of musket fire ahead. This exposed the left flank of the Pennsylvania State Regiment from Sullivan's column, which had arrived on William's right only moments before. Consequently, the Pennsylvanians advanced alone and were immediately hit with a relentless attack on their exposed left flank. William's regiment could have prevented this if they had continued the advance. A Pennsylvania officer later wrote, "…the cowardice of the 13th Virginia Regiment, gave the enemy an opportunity of coming round our left flank" and this forced the Pennsylvanians to retreat. "It was disagreeable to have to leave the field," he added, "when we had almost made a conquest if the Virginians had stood to our aid."[50]

Greene finally ordered his men to retreat in the face of Howe's counterattack. By 9:00 a.m. the entire American army was moving back towards Whitemarsh Church with the British following in cautious pursuit. Even with their meticulous plan and the element of surprise, the Americans had still failed, leaving behind over twelve hundred comrades who "lay as thick as the stones in a stony plowfield." With their refusal to advance and fight, William's Thirteenth Virginia had played their own sad part in the defeat.[51]

About a week after Germantown, when the army camped at Towamensing, Pennsylvania, Washington called Crawford to his headquarters. Washington asked him to take command of a new brigade made up of militia from the Virginia counties of Prince William, Culpepper, Loudoun, and Berkeley. Given William's militia experience, this assignment made great sense, and on October 11 Washington formally issued William's appointment. The Quartermaster General and Commissariat were directed to assign personnel directly to William's brigade, and William was urged to use his "utmost skill and industry" in arming and supplying his new command. A few days later, William proposed that John Lawson, the adjutant from the Prince William County militia, be commissioned a brigade major. Washington, who knew Lawson well, approved the selection immediately. For the next five weeks, Crawford worked diligently to organize, train, and equip his new brigade.[52]

In mid-November of 1777, Washington repositioned his army closer to Philadelphia, briefly encamping at Whitemarsh Church before the final trek to Valley Forge for the winter. While there, the commander in chief received word from Congress that William's services were urgently needed back at Fort Pitt. Soon Crawford was headed for York, where he would meet with Congress before returning to Spring Garden, Fort Pitt, and a new war on the frontier.

Chapter 8

WAR ON THE FRONTIER

William's sudden departure from Washington's main army was the result of a special committee report that had been submitted to Congress. This committee investigated a new series of Native American raids, and their report claimed that Colonel Henry Hamilton, British Lieutenant Governor and Superintendent of Indian Affairs at Fort Detroit, was orchestrating a campaign of terror by tribes along the American frontier. Hamilton, they wrote, was also threatening neutral Native American nations such as the Shawnee and Delaware with reprisals if they did not join the British cause. The committee concluded "so long as that post [Fort Detroit] continues to be garrisoned by British troops who are restrained by no laws of humanity from using every means to accomplish their purpose of subjugating these states, those frontiers will be incessantly exposed to the barbarous ravages of the Native American tribes under their influence."[1]

The committee resolved that three commissioners should be dispatched to Fort Pitt "to investigate the rise, progress, and extent of the disaffection in that quarter, and take measures for suppressing the same." They also proposed that General Edward Hand, currently in command at Fort Pitt, work with the commissioners to develop a plan to take the war to "the British garrison at Detroit and its dependencies" and effect the "reduction of that fortress" with a force of two thousand men. The committee also agreed that "General Washington be requested to send Colonel William Crawford to Pittsburg, to take command, under Brigadier General Hand, of the Continental troops and militia in the western department." The report and resolutions were placed to vote and approved by the Congress on November 20, 1777.[2]

Five days later, on November 25, Washington received a copy of the Congressional report. With it was a request from Henry Laurens, the new president of the Congress, to detach William from the main army and assign him to duties at Fort Pitt. Washington gave William the news that afternoon, and by evening William had packed his horse and started the ride to York. There he would meet with the congressional committee before moving on to Fort Pitt. The directive had come just as he was training his new brigade and it meant going to what was clearly a less important theater of the war. Crawford may have interpreted this as a demotion, but he never openly complained to anyone about it.[3]

At the time General Hand was not a happy man. He found himself pressured to take action against the Native Americans in the Ohio Country, while he was also under constant political scrutiny. Hand's biggest problem was that he was a Pennsylvanian, and as a result he was constantly battling local Virginians. They suspected him of supporting his native state's interests in the ongoing border dispute with Virginia. The demands to take action against the Native American nations were particularly difficult to deal with. The forces Hand had at his disposal were poorly trained and ill equipped. Worse, they were mostly local militia, and therefore unreliable.

General Edward Hand, the Pennsylvanian who commanded the Western Department in 1777 when William Crawford was reassigned to Fort Pitt. (*New York Public Library*)

There was also the matter of the enemy they faced. The majority of the Native American tribes allied themselves with Britain in the war against the colonies. Their reasons were simple. Although the woodland nations had no great love for the British, they realized the Crown had at least tried to restrain American colonists from moving west of the Alleghenies, so it seemed their interests would more likely be served if the British were victorious. The Americans, on the other hand, were clearly determined to take every acre of land that they could grab. In the process, the colonists would rape, pillage, and murder innocent Native Americans, fulfilling the definition of white men uttered by the Shawnee chief, Chiksika, who proclaimed, "The whole white race is a monster who is always hungry and what he eats is land."4

Only the Shawnee and Delaware considered themselves American allies. However, as Congress was voting to send William to Fort Pitt, a group of Virginians at Fort Randolph murdered Cornstalk, one of the key leaders of the Shawnee nation. Despite American condemnation of the murder, most of the Shawnee immediately realigned themselves with the British side. This left just the Delaware to support the American cause. If one asked the Delaware about their loyalties, however, they would not have described the Americans as allies. The Delaware saw themselves as a neutral party at peace with everyone. They did not believe they had made any commitment to support the colonies' fight against the British.

Originally, the Delaware had lived along the Atlantic coast, occupying an area that stretched from New York to New Jersey and Delaware. Their tribal name was Woapanachke, which meant "the People from the Rising Sun." In the days before the Europeans arrived, the Delaware were seen as a powerful tribe among the Native American nations, and they took pride from being known as a Lenni-Lenape tribe, which meant "the real or original people."5

The Dutch and Swedes drove the Delaware away from the Atlantic coast in the early seventeenth century, and the nation moved into eastern Pennsylvania after they sold their land to William Penn in 1682. By 1742, colonial expansion and attacks by the Iroquois had forced the Delaware into central Pennsylvania. Following the French and Indian

War, the once proud and powerful tribe was pushed farther west into the Ohio Country, where they settled along the Muskingum River.[6]

As Hand met with the three commissioners from Congress to develop a plan for subduing Fort Detroit, pressure from the local populace grew for the general to strike somewhere, anywhere, and to do so soon. In late December 1777, an opportunity to strike a blow against the British and their Native American allies appeared. Moreover, someone whom William knew well came to deliver the plan to General Hand—Simon Girty.

The Squaw Campaign

Girty had been working for American officials since the beginning of the war but was considered suspect because of his close relationship with Alexander McKee, the former British Indian Agent. McKee was still residing at Fort Pitt but was living under virtual house arrest. He privately maintained his loyalty to the Crown, and despite efforts to keep a close watch on him, McKee continued to communicate with British officials at Fort Niagara and Fort Detroit.

Girty, meanwhile, worked hard to ingratiate himself with the American officials. He actively sought work in support of the patriot cause while also pursuing a commission in the American forces. During this time, he stayed at William's Spring Garden home, and William supported awarding a commission to Girty.[7]

In April 1776, Girty's old friend and former employer, Daniel Morgan, was appointed to lead the West Augusta Committee of Safety, the civil organization tasked with overseeing the defenses in the area around Fort Pitt. Morgan hired Girty and sent him to Onondaga, New York, to present the Great Peace Belt of the United Colonies to the Grand Council of the Six Nations and to urge their neutrality. Girty's mission was a resounding success, as five of the nations agreed to stay out of the war. The sole exceptions were the Mohawks, who had concluded a separate alliance with the British.[8]

Yet, Girty's reputation among the Americans was still not secure. On

August 1, 1776, a month after Girty returned from New York, Morgan removed him from his post, officially stating "ill-behavior" as the reason. Beyond that, there is no record of Girty's offense. Some believe the dismissal was due to Girty's drunken brawling, but that was nothing new to Morgan. Given Girty and Morgan's long friendly association, something more serious must have happened. Girty may have gotten wind of Morgan's ongoing work with land speculators, who were planning to carve up the Ohio Country once the war concluded. This meant that Morgan was secretly working against Girty, which would have infuriated him since he had spent the last two years assuring his Indian brethren that the Americans had no desire to take their lands. He may have confronted Morgan, who then fired him from his post.[9]

Throughout 1777 and into early 1778, Girty tried to regain the good graces of Morgan and the other American officials in Pittsburgh. He recruited men to a militia company and raised his quota of 150 enlistees. Girty hoped to get the captaincy of the company, but all he was offered was a lieutenancy. Worse, as soon as the company was mustered for duty in South Carolina, Girty was ordered to remain behind. When General Hand arrived in Pittsburgh, Girty initially supported the new commander by working with the local Native American tribes. In August 1777, however, Girty resigned his commission, frustrated that his services seemed so unappreciated.[10]

In the early fall of 1777, General Hand convinced Girty to go on a mission to visit his old family, the Seneca. At this point in the war the Seneca remained neutral, but now intelligence was coming in indicating they might ally themselves with Britain. Hand wanted Girty to determine if that information was true. In return, the general told Girty he would be awarded a captaincy. In mid-November Girty arrived at the Seneca village of Connewago on the Allegheny River. He met with the council led by his aging surrogate father, Guyasuta. Girty presented his case that the Seneca should continue their neutrality, but he did not get the reception he hoped for. In fact, what happened was far beyond anything he might have imagined.

Guyasuta told his adopted son that he no longer considered him a Seneca and accused him of being an American spy. From other statements made in the council house, it became clear to Girty that his former people had already decided to make war on the Americans. Guyasuta informed Girty that warriors would take him to Fort Niagara the next day, where they would turn him over to British authorities who would likely hang him. That night, a badly shaken Simon Girty made his escape and returned to Fort Pitt. He told General Hand what he had learned, giving valuable intelligence for the American cause. Even with this mark on Girty's credit, Hand decided to not even restore Girty's commission, much less provide the captaincy he had promised.[11]

Hand then sent a discontented, reluctant Girty on a scouting mission into northeastern Ohio to search for signs of British activity. He particularly wanted intelligence on how the British were moving weapons and supplies to the Native Americans. Girty left Fort Pitt and headed for the forested hills near the mouth of the Cuyahoga River on Lake Erie. Within a few days he sighted numerous boats arriving from Fort Detroit filled with powder, rifles, food, clothing, and trade goods. He also saw other boats leaving for the British fort with captive settlers to be sold to Colonel Hamilton for ransom. The British supplies were stored onshore in a depot and staging area for the raids occurring along the frontier. On December 20, 1777, Girty arrived back at Fort Pitt with the intelligence he had gathered. The excited General Hand now had a target to attack.[12]

Hand decided that a winter expedition certainly presented numerous challenges, but it also had an increased chance for success. At this time of year, the Native Americans would be at home in their villages or isolated winter hunting camps. Since they would not expect an attack in this season, surprise would be on the Americans' side. As a result, the Cuyahoga depot might be very vulnerable.

On December 28 Hand wrote to William, who was resting at Spring Garden while recovering from a severe bout with "the itch," the eighteenth century term for both scabies and psoriasis. Hand's letter was brief but filled with obvious enthusiasm. "There are at Cuyahoga about one hundred miles from here," he wrote, "a magazine of arms and provisions, sent from Detroit, and fifteen bateaux [flat-bottomed boats] lie there. You may guess the rest." William replied on January 4, assuring Hand that he would be at Fort Pitt within a week. But despite his assurance William's recovery was delayed, and he was still at Spring Garden on February 5 when Hand wrote him with more details:

Col. Wm. Crawford
Yohogania [sic] County, February 5, 1778.

Dear Sir: As I am credibly informed that the English have lodged a quantity of arms, ammunition, provision, and clothing at a small Indian town, about one hundred miles from Fort Pitt to support the savages in their excursions against the inhabitants of this and the adjacent counties, I ardently wish to collect as many brave, active lads as are willing to turn out, to destroy this magazine. Every man must be provided with a horse, and every article necessary to equip them for the expedition, except ammunition, which, with some arms, I can furnish.

It may be necessary to assure them that everything they are able to bring away shall be sold at public venue for the sole benefit of the captors, and the money equally distributed though I am certain that a sense of the service they will render to their country will operate more strongly than the expectation of gain. I, therefore, expect that you will use your influence on this occasion, and bring all the volunteers you can raise to Fort Pitt by the 15th of this month.

I am, dear sir,
Your obedient, humble servant,
Edward Hand[13]

William arrived at Fort Pitt a few days later. Given the sentiments of the local population, he had no trouble finding five hundred men to join him on the expedition. This was not necessarily a good thing. As angry as most settlers were towards the Indians, having five hundred militia volunteers who were relatively untrained and undisciplined meant that they might quickly turn into a bloodthirsty mob. Having dealt with militia troops for many years, William undoubtedly harbored doubts about the men's potential conduct. Moreover, Hand decided that he would lead the expedition himself, with Crawford serving as an advisor. As it would turn out, this was the first indication that William's supposed assignment as commander of all troops in the Western Department was nothing more than a mirage.

William posed a problem for Hand, the same problem Hand's successors would also face. The general knew about William's close relationship with Washington. He also realized that he was popular and respected by both the Congress and the local population around Fort Pitt. If Hand gave him command of all the department's troops and William achieved some military success, then William might be promoted to the command of the Western Department. That would leave General Hand without a post, and he could potentially end up somewhere worse than Fort Pitt. Therefore the general chose to follow a strategy that allowed him to tap William's knowledge, while at the same time assuring himself that he got all the credit for any success which might follow.

On February 15 the expedition marched out of Fort Pitt. Hand estimated the operation would last no more than two weeks, an estimate based on a march conducted over hard, snow-packed ground. What Hand got instead was a cold, steady rain that melted the winter snows and turned the ground into a slippery, boggy mire, making every stream a raging torrent that blocked the path ahead. Worse, for some unknown reason, Hand decided to only use Simon Girty as an interpreter. This was very odd, for Girty knew the woods better than anyone at Fort Pitt and he knew the exact location of the British depot. Instead, the general hired a man named William Brady to act as guide. It quickly became clear that Brady did not know the best route to the Cuyahoga. Between the weather and Brady's incompetence, it took the expedition several days to go just a few miles.[14]

As the men marched onward, many grew sick and the rest became discouraged. Progress was so slow that it became clear their supplies would not last until they reached the Cuyahoga. Girty counseled Hand to turn back. William agreed with him, but the intractable Hand refused to listen. He was determined that the expedition accomplish its goal. By the time the men reached the Forks of the Beaver River near

Lancaster County, Pennsylvania, even Hand could see that continuing the expedition was pointless.[15]

The next morning, as the Americans prepared to turn back for Fort Pitt, excited militia scouts ran into camp reporting they had sighted a large Indian village only three miles away. According to them there were at least sixty warriors present. Hand immediately decided to form up and attack. That way, he could take all the credit for striking a blow against the Native Americans.

When the inexperienced militia scouts arrived with their news, both Brady and Girty were away from camp, trying to round up some horses that had wandered off during the night. Had he been present, Girty almost certainly would have urged caution and gone out himself to reconnoiter the village. What Girty would have found was a small winter hunting camp occupied by an elderly man, a few women and some children, without a warrior in sight. More important, Girty likely would have realized that this was not a hostile camp, but one occupied by friendly Delaware. What no one would have known, not even Girty, was that the old man in the camp was Bull, the brother of the Delaware chief Hopocan, known to the whites as Captain Pipe. One of the women was Hopocan's mother, and another was Bull's wife, Michikapeche.[16]

Bull was working outside his lodge when the first Americans attacked the camp and fired a volley at the old man. He immediately grabbed his musket and fired back, hitting one officer and breaking his arm. As Bull tried to reload his weapon, another officer rode up and drove a tomahawk into the elderly warrior's skull, killing him instantly. Hearing the sound of shooting, Bull's mother emerged from the lodge and saw her son being scalped. She ran forward, holding her arms out, begging the militia to stop, trying to let them know this was a friendly Delaware camp. By now, Hand's men had turned into the mob William had feared they might become. The old woman was shot down and scalped by a soldier, who placed the bloody prize into his food pouch beside a chunk of bread.[17]

Terrified women and children now emerged from another lodge and scattered into the woods. The troops fired at them as well, but missed. The militia quickly turned their attention to the other lodges where the imaginary warriors might be hiding. As Hand and William arrived in the camp, the militia poured volleys of musket fire into the empty huts, but the firing quickly subsided as soon as the volunteers realized there was no one inside the lodges to kill. Girty galloped into camp in time to see Bull's wife, Michikapeche, run from a lodge in an attempt to flee into the woods. The soldiers turned and fired at her, with one bullet striking her in the hand, cutting off a finger.[18]

Bleeding profusely, she continued to run until a soldier overtook her, wrestling her to the ground. He was about to scalp her when William ran up, grabbed the soldier's arm, and roughly pushed him down. Crawford ordered that Michikapeche's wound be attended to while Girty interrogated her. She told them that they had attacked a friendly Delaware village and that she was a relative of Hopocan. William arranged to have her taken to Fort Pitt, whence she would be sent back to the Delaware, an act of compassion that would return to haunt him later on.

While the attack at Bull's hunting camp was going on, another detachment from the expedition found a small camp a few miles away on the Mahoning. It also had no warriors, only five women, four of whom escaped while another was taken prisoner. On their return, the detachment spotted a Native American boy out in the woods hunting birds with his bow and arrow. The militiamen immediately shot and killed him.[19]

Hand marched the expedition back to Fort Pitt, with the two women prisoners and a couple of scalps to show as their trophies. The general was ridiculed what became known as the "Squaw Campaign," but no one attacked him for his men's wanton killing of the innocent Delaware. Instead, they criticized him not finding and killing more of them. The worst repercussion of the Squaw Campaign occurred when Michikapeche returned to her people and told Hopocan about the killing of his mother and brother by the militia. The Delaware chief was justifiably angered.

Hopocan was a very influential war chief among the woodland nations. One missionary who knew Hopocan well described him as "an artful, cunning man. Ambitious and fond of power." Hopocan's name meant "pipe," so the whites called him Captain Pipe. He was born in Pennsylvania around 1724 and was a member of the Delaware Wolf Clan. He was the son of the chief Nutimus and became a war chief upon his father's death in 1757. He was an able warrior who fought with the French against Braddock and with the Shawnee at Point Pleasant during Lord Dunmore's War.[20]

Among the woodland nations Hand's actions were viewed as murder, and the attack on Hopocan's family constituted the foundation for a traditional blood feud. For a Delaware, there could be no more compelling reason for war. Hopocan ordered his people to move their villages west to the Sandusky River, where they would cement a new alliance with the British and wage a war of revenge on the Americans.[21]

Although there is no record of William's feelings about the expedition, this campaign seemed to have been the event that triggered Simon Girty's decision to abandon the American cause forever. Girty was repulsed by what he saw as the Americans' bloodthirsty desire to slaughter Indians, no matter their position in the war with Great Britain. This, combined with their intense desire to take Native American lands after the war, and the disdain they seemed to hold for him, moved Girty to change allegiances for good.[22]

The Renegade Traitors

The Squaw Campaign served as a seminal event in the war. This was because, in addition to pushing Hopocan's Delaware over to the British, it caused Simon Girty and Alexander McKee to take a more active role on the British frontier. On his return from Hand's expedition, Girty went to see McKee, who told him that he planned to escape from Fort Pitt. Since late December, McKee had resisted an order from General Hand to report to York, where he was to testify before the Continental Congress Board of War about his activities. McKee did not intend to do this since it would undoubtedly lead to a death sentence. Although he had been quietly supporting the British war effort, he worked hard to appear ambivalent about the conflict to the public at large. Moreover, McKee had much to lose if he defected. He had acquired considerable wealth and property while developing good business relationships with many leading men in Pennsylvania. Even so, Hand's insistence that he turn himself over to American officials forced the former British Indian Agent to take action.

Girty and McKee planned their escape along with Matthew Elliot, the friend and business associate of McKee who had orchestrated the peace conference at Camp Charlotte in 1774. Girty shared his plans with his brothers; Thomas chose to remain in Pittsburgh and would quietly live out his life as a loyal American citizen, while George would eventually make his way to Fort Detroit and serve the British. James Girty, who had also been working with American officials, planned to be out of the city when Girty and McKee planned to flee. Once they all were safely away, James would also join the British cause. On the night of March 28, 1778, McKee, Elliott, and Girty with McKee's cousin Robert Surphlitt, his servant John Higgins, and two of his African slaves mounted their horses, rode out of Pittsburgh, and began their journey to Fort Detroit. Their timing was impeccable. Just a few hours later, General Hand sent a group of armed men to McKee's house to arrest him. Finding the house empty, an embarrassed Hand said that he was "mortified."[23]

The defectors made a slow trip across the Ohio Country, meeting with many Native American leaders along the way. As they traveled, news of their defection spread. There was great excitement among the woodland nations as it was learned that two men long considered friends and able leaders had come over to the side of George III. McKee, Elliott, and Girty finally arrived at Fort Detroit in early June 1778. Meanwhile, back in Pennsylvania and along the frontier, there was a corresponding sense of fear and dread. One man wrote about what he observed, saying,

> As we drew nearer to Pittsburgh, the unfavorable account of the elopement of McKee, Elliott, Girty, and others, from [Pittsburgh] to the Indian country, for the purpose of instigating the Indians to murder [caused great excitement]... Indeed, the gloomy countenances of all men, women, and children, that we passed, bespoke fear—nay, some families even spoke of leaving their farms and moving off.[24]

Even General Hand was fearful of what McKee and Girty might

accomplish as agents of the British. Only two days after the escape, Hand sent an urgent message to William, who was back at Spring Garden, requesting help. "Your assistance may be necessary towards preventing the evils that may arise from the information of these runaways," he wrote, "I beg you may return here as soon as possible."[25]

McKee's and Girty's defections could not have come at a worse time for Hand and the Americans along the frontier. So far, the war in the wilderness region had been a series of raids and counter-raids. British leaders feared that the Americans might gather sufficient strength to not only penetrate the Ohio Country but also threaten Fort Detroit itself. Because such a defeat might topple the entire British war effort along the frontier, Colonel Hamilton and other British officials at Fort Detroit felt they needed to rally their Native American allies and conduct a campaign that would keep the Americans both fearful and off-balance. Hamilton saw McKee as the key to his plans, writing Lord George Germain, the British Secretary of State for America, "I shall place great dependencies on his knowledge of the country and of these people employed for its defense." He immediately commissioned McKee as a captain in the British Indian Department and appointed Girty to an interpreter's post.[26]

The American authorities accused and convicted McKee, Elliott, and Girty of treason *in absentia* in a Lancaster, Pennsylvania court. From this point on, they would be considered outlaws and traitors, subject to execution without further trial if captured, and any man who brought them in would receive a reward of $800.[27]

Both Hamilton and his successor, Major Arent DePeyster, made good use of McKee and Girty. McKee traveled among the Ohio Country tribes, consulting with their village councils, gathering intelligence, arranging for the exchange of captives, and conducting diplomacy aimed at maintaining the Crown's alliance with the woodland nations. On occasion, McKee organized raids against American military and civilian objectives along the frontier, but for the most part, he left this work to Simon Girty, who proved more adept than McKee might ever have imagined possible.[28]

Girty spent much of his time working with the Wyandot, the most powerful and influential nation in the Ohio Country. He also organized raids by Shawnee and Mingo warriors that ranged into northern Kentucky, as well as western Pennsylvania and Virginia. Usually, these raids involved a few dozen warriors who burned farmhouses, ambushed supply wagons, and most importantly, spread fear and panic among American settlers. Militarily, these attacks were minor compared to the highly organized campaigns being fought east of the Alleghenies. Congress considered them an annoying irritant, but the persistent attacks were a matter of great significance for citizens and leaders on the frontier who clamored for increased military assistance.[29]

The incursions also allowed Girty's reputation to grow beyond the reality of his actual capabilities. His ability to mount raids all along the frontier gave the impression that he was everywhere at once. The Americans believed Girty was capable of suddenly appearing to inflict deadly harm, and then disappearing into the dense forest only to appear and strike elsewhere with stunning speed. The Native Americans he led often scalped, burned, and tortured settlers. Although there is no record of Girty participating in these activities, he did not seem moved to stop them either. As a result, he gained a reputation, perhaps unwarranted, for cruelty and barbarism.

Feelings against Girty ran especially high around Fort Pitt. Girty did not feel he was doing anything dishonorable, and when he heard about the bounty placed on his head, he sent word to Fort Pitt that he "expected no mercy from the Americans and would give none." Girty's notoriety also had some military value for the British. American soldiers and their commanders grew to fear his abilities. On one occasion, a force of two hundred and sixty militia besieging a Shawnee town near Chillicothe received a false report that Girty was approaching with one hundred Mingo warriors. Rather than stay and fight, the militia chose to burn a few buildings and hastily retreat, even though they outnumbered Girty and his phantom Mingo army. Later, when the American general, William Irvine, was contemplating a new campaign against the Wyandot and British forces at Fort Detroit, he cancelled the attack because of Girty's presence. One officer wrote in a letter to a comrade, "The chance is now against General Irvine's succeeding...and, it is said, [he] set out with only 1,200 men. Simon Girty can outnumber him; and, flushed with so many victories, to his natural boldness, he will be confident."[30]

Fort Laurens

Girty and McKee's departure, combined with the shameful Squaw Campaign, caused Washington to recall General Hand from Fort Pitt in April 1778. On May 12 Washington notified Henry Laurens that he was replacing Hand with General Lachlan McIntosh. McIntosh, the son of a captain in the Scottish Highlanders, was a protégé of Laurens. McIntosh initially commanded Continental forces in Georgia, but after he had killed another officer in a duel, he was transferred to the main army at Valley Forge in late 1777. On May 26, Washington informed McIntosh that Congress had approved the appointment, and after a brief stop in York, the new commander journeyed to Fort Pitt.[31]

General Lachlan McIntosh, who replaced Edward Hand as commander of the Western Department. (*Library of Congress*)

Upon arrival at the fort, McIntosh immediately became consumed with planning an expedition against Fort Detroit. The Congressional mandate for this expedition was still a matter of intense interest back in York. While McIntosh planned his strategy to approach the British garrison, there was also an issue of the troops required for such an expedition. Congress had estimated that twenty-five hundred men would be needed, but McIntosh did not have anywhere near that number available. Washington tried to help by ordering the remnants of the Thirteenth Virginia and Eighth Pennsylvania back to Fort Pitt. Both units included men from that region, and he hoped that their transfer might cause deserters from both regiments to return to duty.

As soon as the Thirteenth Virginia returned to Fort Pitt, a dispute arose as to who should be the regiment's commander. Since William Crawford had been sent west without being formally relieved of command of the regiment, he felt that he had a rightful claim to the position. Colonel William Russell, who had led the regiment since William's departure, argued the command was his. Although Washington acknowledged he "would recommend Col. Crawford to the command," he apparently felt that he needed to make sure it did not appear that he was favoring William, his business partner and friend. Washington resolved the issue by appointing Colonel John Gibson to command the Thirteenth Virginia.[32]

This meant that any chance William had of being commander of all troops on the frontier was likely gone, despite the fact it had been requested by Congress. Perhaps worse, it also meant that he would no longer be an officer of the Continental Line, an issue he would dispute for several years with McIntosh, Washington, and Congress. In May 1778, William was assigned to locate and erect a small stockade outpost for supplies a short distance above the mouth of Puckerty Creek, about sixteen miles north of Fort Pitt. Over the next four years, the fort, named Fort Crawford, would be garrisoned only on occasion, and William would act as its tacit "commander" each time troops were present. In September, McIntosh appointed William as commander of the militia troops from Youghiogheny, Monongalia, and Ohio counties, and asked him to form them into a brigade. In all this, William became little more than a volunteer officer serving at the discretion of General McIntosh and anyone who might succeed him later as Western Department commander. Given William's long relationship with Washington and his service to date, this had to be a bitter pill for him to swallow.[33]

As the summer of 1778 arrived, Congress again pushed for a campaign against Fort Detroit. On June 11, they resolved "That an expedition be immediately undertaken, whose object shall be, to reduce, if practicable, the garrison of Detroit, and to compel to terms of peace such of the

Indian nations now in arms against these states." The force was to consist of three thousand men, including twenty-five hundred from Virginia. The Virginia Executive Council initially withdrew their support for the campaign but then reversed themselves. Their support, however, was contingent on the campaign beginning before September 1, 1778. The Thirteenth Virginia did not arrive at Fort Pitt until August 10 and there were no supplies available for them, making the September date for the start of the campaign problematic.[34]

It was October 17 before McIntosh was at last ready to move. He marched out of Fort Pitt with thirteen hundred men, heading southwest for a new fort located thirty miles downriver where the Beaver River entered the Ohio. The new fort, named Fort McIntosh in honor of the commanding general, was a quadrangular structure enclosing nearly two acres. Its long side faced to the Ohio, and it had earth-filled bastions on each corner to support six pieces of artillery. When McIntosh arrived on October 18, William's militia brigade and Colonel Daniel Brodhead's brigade, which included the Thirteenth Virginia and Eighth Pennsylvania, were waiting for him.[35]

Once the entire army was gathered at Fort McIntosh the general paused to supply, train, and discipline his troops. The latter task seems

In this nineteenth-century lithograph, Fort McIntosh is shown along the banks of the Ohio River. (*Ohio History Connection*)

to have been a particularly acute problem. The men were sloppy, slow to report to formations, and guilty of every possible infraction. From the time the men arrived at Fort McIntosh until their return from the expedition eight weeks later, General McIntosh convened no fewer than ten courts martial.[36]

As the troops languished at the fort awaiting supplies they sought ways to entertain themselves. One of their favorite diversions was carving their names on trees in the nearby forest, a practice that offended the spiritual beliefs of the local Delaware. McIntosh issued stern orders that this practice stop, stating that it caused "great uneasiness to our good friends and allies" from the Delaware nation. He even offered a reward of "five pounds to any person who shall made information of such who in contempt of orders have acted."[37]

The other diversion that caused McIntosh some irritation was the random firing of weapons. The first instances began to occur within days of his arrival at Fort McIntosh. The general issued warnings to stop what he referred to as an "unmilitary practice," but as the expedition got underway, the problem continued to plague the army. McIntosh and the other officers were concerned that they would be unable to tell if an Indian attack was underway or if some miscreant was merely playing with his musket.[38]

Despite William's loss of Continental Line officer status, General McIntosh recognized his experience commanding militia troops. On October 27, McIntosh ordered that newly arrived troops from Berkley and Augusta counties be attached to William's brigade with two regiments of men from Hampshire and Rockingham counties. McIntosh also requested that William handpick fifty officers and men from these groups to act as the army's light infantry company.[39]

On November 4, McIntosh realized that the command was as ready as circumstances were going to allow. Despite concerns about the coming weather and inadequate supplies, he ordered his men to move west, but he altered the objective of the campaign. Given their late fall start and the lack of supplies, the goal of destroying Fort Detroit was deemed unattainable. The army would likely run into rain and snow, slowing their progress so much that they would run out of food long before they reached the

British garrison. McIntosh decided instead to try to reach the Native American towns along the Sandusky River. There, they would destroy the sources of Indian raiding parties and "chastise" the Native Americans.[40]

Within a few days, it became obvious that even reaching the Sandusky towns might be impossible. The first day, he saw the army march less than seven miles before making camp, a figure repeated the following day. It would turn out that these two days were the best the army would see on the trail, with the men averaging less than five miles a day for the rest of

Uniform of a soldier in the Thirteenth Virginia, as displayed in the Fort Laurens Museum. (*Author photo*)

the expedition. Most of the officers and men were very inexperienced. Therefore, the process of gathering up cattle and horses, repacking supplies and tents every morning, and then setting up a secure, defendable camp in the evening, took much longer than it should have. Moreover, the constant need for disciplinary activities, including the recurring courts martial, did not help.

On November 13 snow began to fall, causing the army to remain in camp until conditions improved, which they did on November 15. The day before breaking camp, friendly Delaware messengers arrived to tell the Americans that a group of their warriors would join the army before they reached the Tuscarawas River. To prevent a friendly-fire incident, McIntosh ordered that no one was to go very far ahead of the main column. He also ordered his men to be cautious about firing on any party of Indians until they could be certain they were not friendly Delaware. To aid in this recognition process, McIntosh asked that the men collect and save "all the deer's tails they can get and wear them in their hats which may induce our friend Indians to do the same & distinguish ourselves and them from our enemies."[41]

Late in the day on November 18, the column crossed the Tuscarawas and camped on a broad plain about two miles south of what was called the Great Crossing (near present-day Bolivar, Ohio). There, a group of Delaware converted to Christianity by Moravian missionaries enthusiastically greeted them. These Christian Delaware, who were often referred to simply as the "Moravian Indians," lived at the Lichtenau Moravian mission farther south on the Muskingum River. They were dedicated pacifists who had renounced the warrior culture of their tribes. They dressed in European clothing and maintained a peaceful, friendly relationship with white settlers. It is tragic that many of the friendly Delaware that William met that day would later be victims of a massacre that would have a great impact on his own life.[42]

It was mid-November, and the Americans had only covered about half the distance to the Sandusky, so McIntosh paused to consider his options. No follow-up supplies had reached the army since November 11, and the weather was almost certain to get worse. Although his army was intact, McIntosh's men were tired and sick. Also, he was now forced to reduce their daily rations to only one pound of flour per man per day. He decided to abandon the idea of reaching the Sandusky. Instead, McIntosh would have his men build a fort on the campsite that would serve as a forward outpost and supply depot for a future expedition against Fort Detroit.[43]

McIntosh ordered that anyone not on guard duty be assigned construction duties on the new fort, a garrison soon to be called Fort

Laurens in honor of Henry Laurens. William's brigade participated in its construction. On November 23, he issued brigade orders detailing how he wanted the brigade organized for construction tasks:

B O [Brigade Orders] Head Quarters November 23d 1778

A fatigue to be got ready by 8 of the clock tomorrow morning of One third of the whole militia to set up pickets then each company of the different battalions of militia are to bring in pickets agreeable to a detail which will be given or delivered agreeable to the proportion of the several companies.
    Wm Crawford
    An Officer from each company is to attend and see the above duty performed and make a report to me of the same.[44]

One private from William's brigade, John Cuppy of the Hampshire County militia, recalled the work on the fort:

Where Fort Laurens was built, was no timber, on a high bank, and a barren back for half a mile or more; and the men had to carry in the timber, four, or five to a stick. Made mostly of large, hardwood timber, split, some six inches thick, bullet-proof, planted in trenches three feet deep, solidly packed around, and extending fifteen feet above ground…the fort, which was on the west bank

Called "Fort Nonsense" by many soldiers, this drawing depicts the fully constructed Fort Laurens. (*Ohio History Connection*)

of the Tuscarawas, enclosed about an acre of ground, and was the longest on the river....The gate was on the west side of the fort, no spring; relied upon the river for supply of water. There was one block-house, about 20 feet square, which was directly to the right of the gate, and next to it, and formed a part of the outside in place of picketing: the block-house, about six feet above the ground, the block-house was made a foot wider on the wall side, and made to over-jut, so if Indians came up, the garrison could shoot down through this open jut directly upon an enemy below; and the floor of puncheons on a level with the over-jut; and the timbers built up some eight feet, so as completely to protect those within from the enemy without, and port-holes all around about five feet from the floor, and some two or three feet apart, through to which for the garrison to fire in case of an attack, with a rude roof slanting one way, and that within the fort...There were also about 2 cabins built on each end of the fort, not quite together and in a line with the picketing, and helped to form the enclosure, and also had over-jutting, and with port-holes; but smaller than the block-house; and these were for shelter for provisions and baggage."[45]

By December 1, the fort was well on its way to completion. McIntosh was anxious to march the bulk of the army back to Fort McIntosh. Then he could return to the comfort of his quarters at Fort Pitt and spend the winter in front of a warm fire. McIntosh held a council of war with his officers, who overwhelmingly voted to go home. They would leave a garrison of 150 men behind at Fort Laurens, a place many of the men were now calling "Fort Nonsense."[46]

Troop morale, particularly among the militia under William's command, provided another compelling reason to begin the march back to Fort McIntosh. On December 1, the general announced his plans to return the army to Fort McIntosh. He used his message to the troops to assure the militia that they would not be held for service beyond their current enlistments. He added that he would personally accompany them to Fort McIntosh "in order to see them paid off for their services." When

The outline seen in the cut grass marks the location of one of Fort Laurens' blockhouses at Fort Laurens Historic Site. (*Author photo*)

the council of war voted to return, part of the plan was to build four blockhouses along the seventy-mile trail back to western Pennsylvania. Within two days, however, McIntosh promised his grumbling militia that, if they finished construction at Fort Laurens promptly, they would only have to build one blockhouse. As it turned out, they did not even build that one.[47]

Some members of the militia had pushed their bad behavior far enough to warrant punishment. A few of the men in William's brigade from Ohio County had acted with such insubordination that they were referred to as "mutineers." On December 3, McIntosh authorized William to dismiss these men, "who laid such bad examples to the whole army," from service once the army reached Fort McIntosh and to do so without pay.[48]

On December 9, the fort was complete and the garrison in place, and the army began the return march. They only had two days' rations, and McIntosh ordered the men to proceed "without any stope or delay" to Fort McIntosh. There were six inches of damp snow on the ground as they left Fort Laurens, but it did not seem to impede their progress. The return march became even less disciplined than the one that had brought them to the Tuscarawas. Although individual companies generally stayed together, that was the only cohesion. The army eventually became so spread out that it covered almost half the distance between the two forts.[49]

The march quickly took on an "every man for himself" character, especially among Crawford's militia. Most of them ate their two days' rations immediately and almost starved before they reached Fort McIntosh. While some begged for food from hunters and Native Americans they met along the trail, others scavenged the cattle carcasses the column had butchered on their outbound march, roasting the dried hides before devouring them.[50]

The militia also continued to demonstrate their increasing disdain for authority. A few days after work had begun on Fort Laurens, McIntosh sent two companies of Continental troops and one company of militia back to Fort McIntosh with all the army's packhorses. Their assignment was to load the horses with fresh supplies and then return with these provisions for the new garrison at Fort Laurens. When the three companies encountered the army on its way back to Fort McIntosh, the men in the militia company chose to abandon their packhorses, turn around, and go home, leaving the Continental troops with the job of supplying Fort Laurens.[51]

Most of the army arrived at Fort McIntosh after a four-day march, where each man was issued two full days' of rations and a half-pint of whiskey, the latter of which William's militia immediately drank. Given their physical condition and lack of nourishment, this made many of them very sick. The general ordered the Eighth Pennsylvania to remain as a garrison for Fort McIntosh while the Thirteenth Virginia returned with him to Fort Pitt. Not surprisingly, the undisciplined mob that had once been William's militia brigade was paid off and sent home. He was glad to see them go, but, once more, he was left with no command and no real position.[52]

Although William returned to Fort Laurens with General McIntosh as part of a relief expedition to resupply the garrison in March 1779, his part in the frontier war seemed to be at an end. Following this expedition, General McIntosh requested a transfer to another post. Washington agreed, and McIntosh was replaced by Daniel Brodhead. Brodhead was a surveyor like William, but he was also a staunch Pennsylvanian. This combination set the two men at odds from the start; William neither trusted nor respected Brodhead, and apparently the feelings were mutual.

In July 1779, William wrote Washington, barely able to conceal his bitterness. First, he mentioned the issue of his status as a Continental Line officer. "Sometime last summer," he penned, "I wrote you in regard to my being left out of the Virginia Line, as it put it out of my power to serve as an officer with the Continental army with my proper rank; but I do not know whether my letter came to your hands or not." He added that when General McIntosh went to Washington's headquarters en route to his new assignment, "he told me he would acquaint you with my case." William expressed his frustration when Washington informed McIntosh that this was an issue William would have to handle himself with army auditors.[53]

In his letter Crawford also proposed an expedition against the Shawnee towns near the Scioto River, which he clearly hoped to lead. Noting recent reports of a good trail sufficient for carrying "two field pieces, four to six pounders, that would batter down block-houses which the Shawanese have built to defend themselves in their towns," he suggested that fall, "when the corn is in roasting ears," would be a good time for such an expedition. "I only mention this, Sir, for your consideration," he added diplomatically, "in case matters should not be otherwise settled." Finally, he added that Colonel Brodhead had asked him to join a campaign up the Allegheny. He agreed to do this, saying, "as I would not wish to hurt the service, or leave it in the power of him to say I did not do everything I could to serve my country; which is the only motive I have for serving one moment."[54]

William accompanied Brodhead on the Allegheny campaign with some of the Virginia militia, but not in any significant command capacity. The expedition burned a few Seneca villages that had been left undefended because the warriors were away with others from the Six Nations trying to counter an American expedition into central New York. The Allegheny campaign accomplished little, although Brodhead hailed it as a major success in a report to Washington. Interestingly, in this same report, Brodhead never mentioned Crawford's presence during the expedition.[55]

William gradually faded from the center of military operations at Fort Pitt. In May 1781, he wrote Washington what would be his final letter to his friend and business partner. It was a short note, discussing the possible sale of some of Washington's land. William concluded the letter by mentioning that he might join a new campaign with Colonel George Rogers Clark. However, at almost sixty years of age, William admitted that he would do so only "if my health will permit." Apparently, his health did not allow him to go, and he remained at Spring Garden with Hannah. Washington never responded to this final letter. In the end, William's business partner, friend, and a man he had known for over thirty years simply ignored him. Washington had gone on to greater things, and William Crawford was apparently no longer someone the general had either the time or inclination to support.[56]

In late October, William heard of Cornwallis' surrender to Washington at Yorktown. The Revolutionary War was over in the eastern theater of operations, and American independence was now assured. With that turn of events, William retired from the army, determined to focus on his work as surveyor and Justice of the Peace for Youghiogheny County, as well as tend to his farm at Spring Garden.

From the tone of his final letter to Washington, it seems clear that William had become a changed man. Although only two brief paragraphs long, it reflects an underlying sense of deep fatigue, frustration, and the need for relative peace in his life. William had seen much death during the war and far too much stupidity from officers such as Hand, McIntosh, and Brodhead. They had denied him his rightful position in the Western Department, and the main army had refused to recognize his status as a Continental Line officer. His friend Washington had abandoned him and left his hopes of a military career dashed. William was thoroughly fed up with commanding undisciplined, insubordinate militia who ignored their duties and acted as unruly mobs instead of soldiers. It was not surprising that the military no longer had any attraction for him. In addition, although peace would almost certainly bring with it renewed land speculation activity, William no longer seemed very interested in pursuing it.

The time had come for him to set aside the ambitions of his younger years and turn his attention to personal business matters. He had not attended these while he was surveying for Washington and soldiering on the frontier, and this had resulted in numerous debts. Many former customers owed him payment for surveys, and to pay off his debts he needed to collect on those accounts. William Crawford would finally forsake the warrior's path and be done with a soldier's duties.

Or so he thought.

Chapter 9

EXPEDITION TO THE SANDUSKY

Americans greeted the new year of 1782 with hope. After Washington's victory at Yorktown, the British realized that they could not stop American independence by use of force. In February, the opposition party in Parliament's House of Commons successfully passed a motion stating, "...this House will consider as enemies to his Majesty and this country, all those who shall endeavor...the farther prosecution of the offensive war on the continent of North America, for the purpose of reducing the revolted colonies to obedience by force." By fall, formal peace negotiations between British and American delegations had begun in Paris.[1]

Despite this outbreak of peace on the eastern front of the war, the conflict on the American frontier continued. Directives from London to cease hostilities were slow in reaching Fort Detroit, and when they did finally arrive the Native American nations saw little need to heed Whitehall's orders. The Indians did not consider themselves as subordinate to the Crown. They were fighting for their way of life, and their very survival as a people.

Not long after William resigned and departed from Fort Pitt for Spring Garden, Washington fired Brodhead as commander of the Western Department, replacing him with General William Irvine. Irvine, commander of the Sixth Pennsylvania Regiment, was captured during fighting in Canada, but the British later paroled and exchanged him. When he returned, Washington appointed him to command the Second Pennsylvania Brigade of the main army, which Irvine had led at the Battle of Monmouth. After several mutinies in the brigade, Washington transferred Irvine to recruiting duties. He languished there until he reported to Fort Pitt in November 1781.

General William Irvine, who replaced Daniel Brodhead as commander of the Western Department. *(New York Public Library)*

At first, things went well for Irvine. He injected new energy into his command, making repairs and improvements to the fort his first priority. As a result, morale among the Continental troops improved, along with a renewed sense of command cohesion among the officers. However, things changed when Irvine left Pittsburgh in January 1782 to attend to pressing issues at his home in Carlisle, leaving Colonel John Gibson in command. By the time he returned to Fort Pitt on March 25, the fort and surrounding region were in turmoil due to a sudden spike in Indian raiding activity along the frontier. The fort's garrison was in a state of near mutiny, and local civilian leaders were calling for Indian blood. Irvine reported to Washington that things were so bad that a "number of wrongheaded men" believed Colonel Gibson was too friendly to the Indians, and that "he must be killed also." The worst news Irvine conveyed was the story of "an outrage" committed by militia troops while he was absent—the massacre at Gnadenhutten.[2]

Gnadenhutten

Late in 1781, Major Arent DePeyster, the British commander at Fort Detroit, ordered several groups of Christian Delaware living along the Tuscarawas to move west to the Sandusky River for their protection. In reality, DePeyster wanted to move the converted Delaware away from the Americans, with whom they were friendly and to whom they often provided intelligence about British and Indian raiding activities. DePeyster's plan was to place the Christian Delaware under the watchful eye of his most reliable ally, the Wyandot chief Dunquat.

Dunquat, the most powerful of all the Native American leaders in the Ohio Country, was an accomplished Wyandot warrior. He was also an intractable foe of the Americans, and had long sought to remove the Christian Delaware from their mission villages because he despised them for forsaking their native warrior culture. He had once proposed to use force to bring them to the Sandusky, but DePeyster and Alexander McKee urged him into pretending friendship to accomplish his goal. Dunquat journeyed to their villages on the Tuscarawas and addressed their council elders as an ally and protector:

> My cousins, ye believing Indians, in Gnadenhutten, Schoenbrun, and Salem, I am no little troubled about you, for I see you live in a dangerous place. Two powerful and mighty spirits or gods are standing and opening wide their jaws toward each other to swallow, and between the two angry spirits, who thus open their jaws, are you placed; you are in danger, from one or from the other, or even from both, of being bruised and mangled by their teeth; therefore, it is not advisable for you to remain here longer, but bethink ye to keep alive your wives, and children and young people, for here must you all die. Therefore, I take you by the hand, raise you up and settle you there where I dwell, or at least nearby me, where you will be safe and will live in quiet. Make not here your plantations and settlements, but arise and come with me, take with you also your teachers, and hold there, whither you shall come, your worship of God forever, as has been your wont.

Ye will at once find food there, and will suffer no want, for on this account am I come to say this to you, and to bring you to safety.[3]

Despite Dunquat's assurances, the Christian Delaware interpreted his speech and DePeyster's orders as an implicit threat; nevertheless, they saw it as one to obey. Given the short notice, they were forced to leave behind many of their possessions and the crops that would be needed for food during the upcoming winter. By February 1782, the Delaware's plight in their new village on the Sandusky River had become dire due to inadequate food supplies. Fearing starvation, the Delaware begged Dunquat to allow them to return to their villages and harvest the remaining corn standing in their fields. Although reluctant to agree, he allowed them to go out of pity.

The next day, about 150 hungry men, women, and children began their trek across central Ohio, leaving a one-hundred-mile trail through the deep snow that covered the wooded hills and open prairie. Upon reaching the Tuscarawas, they split into three groups of about fifty each, with one group going to Gnadenhutten, another to Salem Village, approximately twelve miles upriver, and a third to heading Schoenbrun, which was about the same distance down the Tuscarawas.

As the Christian Delaware were arriving in Gnadenhutten, a Wyandot raiding party made an unusual, late winter attack on isolated homesteads in western Pennsylvania. The raiders returned to the Sandusky, and they left the mutilated remains of two settlers along the trail for any pursuing militia to find. The Wyandot also stopped to trade at Gnadenhutten. The elder of the Christian Delaware, a man named Abraham, told them, "You should not have come here! We have troubles enough already. You are not welcome and we wish you to go." The warriors responded that they would leave when they felt like doing so. They soon departed but not before trading a few of the goods stolen from the ransacked settlers' farms with the Delaware in the village.

As soon as the warriors left for the Sandusky, Abraham and the leaders from the other two villages met to discuss their situation. They all expressed concern that American militia might soon arrive in pursuit of the hostile

Indians, but Abraham assured the other leaders they had nothing to fear. After all, they had long been good friends with the Americans who knew and understood their "peaceable ways" and their "innocence in any of those bad things that may have occurred."[4]

The Delaware leaders were right to have been worried. Shortly after the attacks on the settlers, a group of one hundred militiamen from Washington County under the leadership of Colonel David Williamson, the thirty-year-old commander of the Washington County, Pennsylvania militia, set out after the raiding party. From the moment the militia was on the move, Williamson, a devoted Indian hater, indicated his belief that the Christian Delaware were somehow complicit in the attacks. It did not matter that the converted Delaware were dedicated pacifists, posed no threat to anyone, and had maintained a long, friendly relationship with the region's white settlers. To Williamson and many of his men, they were Indians, and that was enough to prove their guilt.

Some of the militia, including Williamson, were members of an odd Pennsylvania Presbyterian vigilante sect known as the "Paxton Boys," a group that had operated on the frontier since Pontiac's War in 1763. Their goal was the extermination of all Native Americans. They believed "the Indians were the Canaanites, who by God's commandment were to be destroyed; and that this not having been done by them at that time, the present war might be considered as a just punishment from God for their disobedience." The Moravian missionaries' conversion of the Delaware to Christianity deeply offended the Paxton Boys. The Wyandot raid gave them an excuse to eliminate this particular group of "Canaanites."[5]

Late in the afternoon of March 6, 1782, Williamson and his militia arrived at Gnadenhutten and encircled the town. As they approached, they came upon six Delaware men and women working in the fields, and immediately killed and scalped them, despite the fact that they were all dressed like Europeans and were clearly not warriors.

When the remainder of the village saw Williamson's men approaching, they did not attempt to flee, believing they had nothing to fear. Some of the Delaware recognized a few militiamen as neighbors with whom they had shared food and shelter in the past. Williamson told them that he and his men had come to take them to Fort Pitt, where they would be given food, shelter, and protection. The Delaware had no reason to distrust the militia commander and they willingly handed over their hunting weapons when Williamson asked them to do so. Indeed, some thought this was a good offer. Given their long friendship with the Americans, they believed they would receive far better treatment at Fort Pitt than the British had provided on the Sandusky. What they received in return for their honest friendship and faith was instead a savage betrayal.

When the militia heard about the other Christian Delaware at Salem, Williamson appointed a group of the natives to accompany the militia there to urge their tribespeople to come to Gnadenhutten before returning to Fort Pitt. Once they made it to Salem, the militiamen repeated Williamson's offer of food and shelter, encouraging them to come by saying, "you are indeed good Christians." As the Delaware left, however, they saw the soldiers set fire to their community, an action the militia claimed was necessary to deprive hostile Indians of a harboring place.[6]

When all the Delaware were gathered at Gnadenhutten, Williamson proceeded to herd the men and older boys into one cabin, and he locked up the women and children in another. He then announced to their leaders that he was certain they had perpetrated the attacks in Pennsylvania. As a result, he would execute every member of the village. The Delaware protested their innocence and pleaded for their lives, but to no avail. Williamson held a council with his officers to decide how best to carry out the execution process. Some men protested and refused to partake in the killings. As one militiaman recalled, "They wrung their hands—and calling God to witness that they were innocent of the blood of these harmless Christian Indians, they withdrew to some distance from the scene of slaughter." When told of their impending deaths, the Delaware asked for time to prepare themselves, a request Williamson granted. The air was soon filled with wailing and prayers, a mixture of Delaware death songs and Christian hymns. The tearful goodbyes that echoed in the chilly night air were the saddest of all, as husbands, wives, and children called out to one another between the two buildings.[7]

At dawn on March 8, the killing began. Abraham turned to the

This nineteenth-century drawing depicts the brutal massacre at Gnadenhutten.
(*Ohio History Connection*)

other men and told them, "Dear brethren, according to appearances we shall all very soon come to the Savior, for as it seems they have so resolved about us." The militia first dragged the women and girls out into the snow and raped them. Then they began a cold, methodical process of brutal murder, using two additional cabins that they called "slaughterhouses." Members of the militia hauled two or three captives at a time into one of the cabins, where another man crushed their skulls with a large, wooden cooper's mallet. One of the Paxton Boys, having murdered fourteen of the Christian Delaware with a mallet, handed the blood-stained weapon to a fellow militiaman saying, "My arm fails me, go on with the work. I think I have done pretty well." Soon, the slaughter became so appalling that one militiaman remembered "the blood flowed in streams" from the slaughterhouses.[8]

None of the Delaware resisted, but a few tried to run away. They were shot in the back, pitching forward dead into the snow. Meanwhile, the rape and murder continued unabated until ninety-six of the Indians were dead, some thirty-five of them children. Williamson's men piled the corpses high in the slaughterhouses and set the entire mission village afire. Within a few hours, the village of Gnadenhutten, whose

This quiet, pastoral grove in a small park in Gnadenhutten, Ohio, was the site of the horrific massacre of March 8, 1782. (*Author photo*)

name meant "Houses of Grace," had been reduced to ashes along with the remains of its peaceful residents.

Some nineteenth century apologists would later claim that Williamson honestly intended to take the Christian Delaware to Fort Pitt. They argued that he only changed his mind when his men found the Delaware in possession of items taken from the ransacked settlements in Pennsylvania, and the events that resulted were the consequence of a tragic misunderstanding. Williamson's men, however, shot down the first Christian Delaware they saw, men and women working peacefully in a cornfield, long before they allegedly found the stolen items. There is little doubt that, from the start, Williamson planned to kill these innocent people.

Ironically, a war chief of the Delaware, Pachgantschihilas, had warned the Christian Delaware that this fate might befall them. Addressing the converted Delaware, he said:

> I admit that there are good white men, but they bear no proportion to the bad; the bad must be the strongest, for they rule. They do what they please. They enslave those who are not

of their color, although created by the same Great Spirit who created us. They would make slaves of us if they could, but as they cannot do it, they kill us! There is no faith to be placed in their words. They are not like the Indians, who are only enemies, while at war, and are friends in peace. They will say to an Indian, my friend! my brother! They will take him by the hand, and at the same moment destroy him. And so you will also be treated by them before long. Remember that this day I have warned you to beware of such friends as these. I know the long knives; they are not to be trusted.[9]

Even when compared to other atrocities committed by whites in the long history of frontier warfare, the Gnadenhutten massacre stands out as one of the most horrific. There were the victims: Christian converts and sincere pacifists who knew and trusted their white neighbors and posed no threat to them. Worst of all, though, was the cold-blooded, systematic nature of the killing. Williamson's men did not kill the Delaware in the heat of battle, as would happen on the plains of western America. Instead, their murderers carefully planned, and after calculated discussion of the most efficient method of execution, they killed without hesitation or remorse. As such, it stands out as one of the most tragic examples in American history of racially motivated brutality against Native Americans.

Unknown to the militia, two of the Delaware boys they scalped and left for dead survived and fled to spread the news of what had happened. The outrage it produced throughout the Indian nations was without precedent. Native Americans had seen similar depredations by the settlers and their soldiers over the decades since the first Englishmen arrived in North America, but this was different. These Indians had believed in the European's Christian god, and had renounced the warrior culture and made permanent peace with the settlers. If the Christian Delaware could not trust the whites, then no Native could. The woodland nations believed the only recourse was to continue their war against the Americans and respond to white atrocities with the same brand of brutality demonstrated at Gnadenhutten.

The Sandusky Expedition Forms

As General Irvine's letter about Gnadenhutten made its way to Washington, the Native American raids on the frontier increased. On March 27, a raiding party captured a woman living on Buffalo Creek, about forty miles north of Fort Pitt, but she managed to escape unharmed. Five days later, a family of eight disappeared after Indians visited their farm, and the next day, the Indians killed and scalped a man near the Washington County courthouse. On Easter Sunday, a force of seventy Shawnee attacked the Miller blockhouse on the Dutch Fork of Buffalo Creek in Washington County, killing two men. The worst of the renewed attacks occurred a few weeks later, on a Sunday morning, May 12. A raiding party ambushed a Baptist minister named John Corbley, his wife, and their children on their way to Sunday services. The warriors killed Mrs. Corbley and three of the children and left a badly wounded Reverend Corbley for dead.[10]

Leading citizens of the region began to clamor for action against the Indian towns on the Sandusky. The loudest of these men were David Williamson, the same Washington County militia colonel who had led the attack on Gnadenhutten, and James Marshal, the Lieutenant of Washington County. They campaigned for a militia expedition to attack and destroy the villages that served as the base of operations for raids by the Wyandot, Shawnee, Mingo, and Delaware. General Irvine was not immune to the pressure, but he was determined that any such operation be conducted with the highest chance of success while ensuring there was no repeat of Gnadenhutten.[11]

To help achieve his goals, Irvine listened to the counsel provided by experienced frontier soldiers such as John Gibson and Daniel Morgan. These veteran frontiersmen believed that attacking the Indian towns was futile, and perhaps even counterproductive. They argued that such an attack was meaningless unless the American forces could provoke and win a major battle against Indian warriors. If such an expedition was to take place, the strength of such a detachment must be adequate, it had to move quickly, and it must avoid detection during a trip of over two hundred miles across the Ohio Country. Based on what little intelligence

Irvine could gather about the combined Indian strength on the Sandusky, he decided that the force should consist of at least three hundred men, all on horseback.[12]

The general also wanted to be certain that the expedition's purpose was perfectly clear. At the time that Williamson, Marshal, and others were promoting the campaign, there was much talk in the nearby settlements of a mass emigration west, beyond the Ohio, where settlers might create a new state. Irvine considered the idea mad, as anyone attempting it "will either be cut to pieces, or they will be obliged to take protection from, and join the British." Irvine also believed this scheme was an attempt by speculators to acquire large tracts of lands at the expense of endangering settlers. Since the talk of this emigration was gaining momentum, the general did not want anyone to think a military expedition to the Sandusky was a part of this dangerous idea.[13]

Irvine also decided not to exercise his authority to call out the local militia for the expedition. Instead, he chose to call for volunteers who agreed to place themselves under military authority and be liable to the rules and articles of war of regular troops. He hoped this condition would mean only the best men from the militia would enlist for the expedition. Irvine thought that, if only the top men volunteered, then perhaps he could prevent David Williamson's election as commander and lessen the likelihood of another Gnadenhutten. Still, since these volunteers would elect their commanding officer, Irvine must find someone to go on the expedition and run in the election against Williamson, someone he could trust. That someone was William Crawford.[14]

Irvine sent a message to William in early May requesting that he volunteer to lead the expedition. At the time, William was planning future surveying projects and working with his slaves to finish the spring planting. Neither Irvine's plans for the expedition nor his request that William make himself available as a candidate for command were met with any enthusiasm. Given the nature of the campaign and the volunteer militia force, William saw the entire enterprise as bordering on insanity.

More than anyone in the Western Department, William knew the unreliability of volunteers drawn from the militia ranks. Asking anyone to take such men on a march two hundred miles deep into enemy territory, a march requiring speed, discipline, and stealth, was unrealistic. He also knew that the expedition would likely face a large, combined Indian force supplemented by British Rangers, who could move quickly by water from Roche de Bout on Lake Erie and then upriver to the Sandusky villages.

Just months before, William had committed to putting down the sword and living the rest of his life in peaceful pursuits, sleeping soundly every night in his bed at Spring Garden. The offer to command such a risky enterprise was not something he desired. Despite this and his issues with the army and Congress, William still technically held the rank of colonel in the Continental Army. Moreover, Irvine was requesting that he accept command of what was clearly an important expedition. Both his son, John, and his son-in-law, William Harrison, were volunteering for the campaign, and William felt that duty was calling one last time, offering a chance to complete his military career on a high note. After much reflection, William accepted Irvine's request, but he did so with reluctance and a sense of deep foreboding that he expressed only to Hannah.[15]

William had never before taken any extra measures to put his house in order before leaving to fight. The fact that he set about doing so speaks loudly about his feelings regarding the coming expedition. On May 14, he conveyed sixty-eight acres of land along the river adjoining his own farm to his son-in-law. Then, on May 16, William executed his final will and testament, in which he laid out a series of bequests designed to ensure that he provided for all of his family.

For his "much beloved wife, Hannah Crawford," he provided all of Spring Garden, as well as "one negro man named Dick, and one mulatto man Daniel," and all the furniture and livestock. To his son, John, he bequeathed five hundred acres of the lands he had acquired down the Ohio, as well as the Spring Garden farm upon Hannah's death. To John's sons, Moses and Richard, he left four hundred acres, each from the same Ohio River lands. He also bequeathed another four hundred acres of those lands to his granddaughter, Anne McCormick.

To Hannah's niece, Ann Connell, his supposed lover, William provided the lands where she lived along the Youghiogheny and Braddock's Road and all the livestock and farming equipment there. He also directed that, upon Ann's death, all the property be divided equally among her four children. In addition, he directed that Ann's sons, William and James, receive five hundred acres of the Ohio River lands as soon as they reached the age of majority, while her two daughters, Nancy and Polly, would equally divide a six hundred-acre tract on the Ohio. The nature of these bequests would seem to confirm his relationship with Ann and that he likely believed he had fathered at least some of her children.[16]

On the morning of May 18, William finished packing his horse and said goodbye to his daughters, as John Crawford and William Harrison had already left for the rendezvous point at Mingo Bottom. After saying his farewells, he and Hannah mounted their horses and rode across the Youghiogheny together, dismounting in a small clearing near an old, moss-covered, white oak log. They sat down on the log and chatted, before sharing a final, tearful embrace. As William rode away, Hannah found herself filled with a sense of intense apprehension and dreadful finality.[17]

Crawford arrived at Fort Pitt that afternoon and initiated discussions with General Irvine that lasted through the next day. William expressed all his doubts about the expedition and urged Irvine to provide him with some trustworthy Continental officers to help corral what he expected to be an unruly volunteer mob. All Irvine could do was assign his aide, Major John Rose, to William's staff. Rose, who served as Crawford's aide for the campaign, was put in place by Irvine to insure against a repeat of Gnadenhutten.

Irvine knew he could count on Rose to keep complete records of the expedition and provide a thorough after-action report. The general also made his strong feelings about the importance of avoiding another massacre clear to William. The general left no doubt in William's mind that the events at Gnadenhutten were a major factor in his request that William go to Mingo Bottom and seek election as the expedition's commander. Although men under William's command had committed their own atrocities at Salt Lick Town back in 1774, he agreed with Irvine that another such massacre must not happen. Perhaps it was the nature of Williamson's brutality that caused him to feel this way, or maybe he had concluded that such barbaric tactics were immoral.

Whatever the reason, William pledged on his honor to Irvine that he would prevent a repeat of Gnadenhutten.[18]

As for William's new aide, Major Rose was an unique individual. He was actually a Russian nobleman, the Baron Gustav Heinrich de Rosenthal. He was born in 1753 in the Russian Baltic province of Livonia and attended two German universities in preparation for a diplomatic career. Shortly after finishing his education, he killed a man in a duel in Russia and had to flee the country. He traveled first to England, but then sailed to in America just before the start of the revolution. Assuming the name of John Rose, he trained as a hospital steward and joined the Sixth Pennsylvania Battalion at Fort Ticonderoga. There, he met and became a favorite of General Irvine. Unfortunately for Rose, the army found him incompetent as a surgeon, reduced him in rank to a surgeon's mate, and sent him to a hospital at Valley Forge.

In 1780, Rose left the army and went to Philadelphia in search of a ship's surgeon position, likely figuring that the Continental Navy might be less discriminating. He took a post on the privateer *Revenge*, but the Royal Navy captured the ship and took him prisoner. He was exchanged and released from a British prison in New York in April 1781, and soon joined Irvine again as his aide-de-camp. He followed Irvine to Fort Pitt, where he became a respected and well-liked member of the command staff. The fact the general selected him to go with Crawford says much about the trust Irvine placed in him.[19]

On May 20, William and Major Rose left Fort Pitt for Mingo Bottom. The next day Irvine wrote to Washington about the expedition saying, "I have taken some pains to get Colonel Crawford appointed to command, and hope he will be." Before William departed, Irvine provided him with written orders detailing the campaign's goals and guidelines for its conduct. The objective was to "destroy with fire and sword (if practicable) the Indian town and settlements at Sandusky," and if that could not be accomplished, William was to "perform such other services in your power as will, in their consequences, have a tendency to answer this great end."[20]

As for the officers and men under his command, Irvine reiterated his plan that the volunteers elect all officers. The general also ordered William to define and communicate a clear command structure to the volunteer soldiers. The volunteers would receive full credit for their military service, understanding and accepting that they were subject to the rules and regulations of the Continental Army during the upcoming expedition. Irvine also restated that the operation must be a complete surprise. This, he wrote, would demand "forced and rapid marches" and an arrival at the towns at or before dawn.[21]

About the expansionist "new state" scheme, the general made it very clear that the expedition must not be seen as supporting that effort. He wrote William that, though the main goal of the campaign was "the protection of this country," William was to consider himself and his command as "acting on the behalf and for the interest of the United States." Irvine added that "it will be incumbent on you especially who will have the command, and on every individual, to act, in every instance, in such a manner as will reflect honor on, and add reputation to, the American arms." Before all this could happen, the volunteers would have to elect William as commander to make sure Irvine's orders had any chance of execution, let alone success.[22]

On May 21, William and Major Rose arrived at Mingo Bottom, the same place where William had camped with Washington on the third day of their 1770 expedition down the Ohio. They found that some of the more eager men had been camped there since May 15, but many volunteers had yet to arrive. The rendezvous location was the product of careful planning by General Irvine. Several advisors had suggested Fort McIntosh, but Irvine believed that the fort was too exposed to Indian observation. Should one of the Indian scouting parties that routinely ranged east of the Muskingum see the force gathering, they would spread the alarm and the expedition would be over before it began. Mingo Bottom, on the other hand, was further downriver on the Ohio, far from the usual paths of Indian raiding or scouting parties.

Mingo Bottom was a low plateau of about 250 acres along the river on the Ohio side. At that time, there was a small, twenty-acre island lying just offshore called Mingo Island. There, the riders could ford the waterway from the Virginia side during low waters. Unfortunately, as volunteers from Virginia and Pennsylvania reached the Ohio, the river was high. With only four small canoes to ferry men and baggage across the river, the pace of arrivals slowed significantly. As a result, not all the volunteers reached the rendezvous site until the morning of May 24.[23]

The first order of business that afternoon was the election of officers. The men were divided into eighteen small companies, each of which was to elect a leader. Following those elections, the most important vote would take place—the vote to choose the expedition's commander. As Irvine had anticipated, William's opponent was Colonel David Williamson. More than two-thirds of the volunteers came from the Washington County militia that Williamson commanded. Not surprisingly, he had many ardent supporters among the volunteers, some of whom had helped him slaughter the Christian Delaware just over eight weeks earlier. Should the men elect Williamson, General Irvine's worst fear might come to pass. However, William's reputation and his experience as a Continental Line officer carried great weight with many of the volunteers. The ballots were cast, and when counted William defeated Williamson by only five votes, 235-230. Williamson then offered to act as second-in-command, and William accepted his offer, one he would soon come to regret.[24]

In reporting the election results to General Irvine, Rose gave Williamson great credit for urging unanimity after the election results were known and "cheerfully" accepting the second-in-command position. Rose added that, in his opinion, if the results had been different, William would have "pushed home and very likely we should have dispersed." This seemed to indicate a low opinion of William and later entries in Rose's journal suggest that although he liked William personally, he had little professional regard for him.

Crawford, he said, was "a man of sixty and upwards. Blessed with a constitution that may be called robust for his age. Inured to fatigue from his childhood, and by repeated campaigns against the Indians acquainted with their manner of engaging." Rose noted his personal regard for William by adding, "In his private life, kind and exceedingly affectionate, in his military character, personally brave, and patient of hardships."[25]

Rose's view of William's professional characteristics was more of a mixed bag. "As a partisan," he said, "too cautious, & frightened at appearances; always calculating the chances against. Consequently, by no means, calculated for its hazardous enterprises." Rose felt William was "cool in danger," but he lacked any "systematical approach" to command. He also felt William tried to do too much on his own and did not properly delegate his authority. This meant "everything was but half done, and everybody was disgusted."[26]

Rose's harshest comments came regarding William's lack of leadership "charisma." Rose said that, during councils of war, William "speaks incoherent, proposes matters confusedly, and is incapable of persuading people into his opinion, or making use of their weak sides for his purposes." Worse, he characterized William as "a mere quack in the profession of a soldier. No military genius; & no man of letters." Some of these criticisms could be dismissed as reflecting the prejudices of an educated Russian aristocrat, but as one of the few surviving eyewitness accounts of William's abilities as a commanding officer, they must be taken seriously. Unfortunately, history would reveal the truth in Rose's comments.[27]

With the voting concluded, Crawford prepared the small army to march the next morning. He first assigned Dr. John Knight to act as the expedition's surgeon. Knight, also a member of Irvine's staff, was born in Scotland in 1751 and made the journey to America in 1770. He originally enlisted as a private in the Thirteenth Virginia and served as a sergeant under William, fighting with him at Brandywine Creek and Germantown. Given the medical training he received as a young man in England, he was eventually appointed as a surgeon's mate at Fort Pitt.[28]

Next, William exercised the command in the formation they would use to cross the two hundred miles of woods and prairie between Mingo Bottom and the Sandusky. The 480 volunteers would align themselves as an advance guard, advanced body, main body, rear body, and rear guard. The advance, main, and rear bodies would march in four parallel columns, with the advance and rear guards in two parallel columns. It was a compact formation designed to move fast, while providing a quick defense if required.[29]

As for the volunteers who would make the journey across the Ohio Country, they came in all ages, and the majority showed great enthusiasm for their upcoming endeavor. Since it was clear the army would move quickly over a great distance each day, one would expect that the

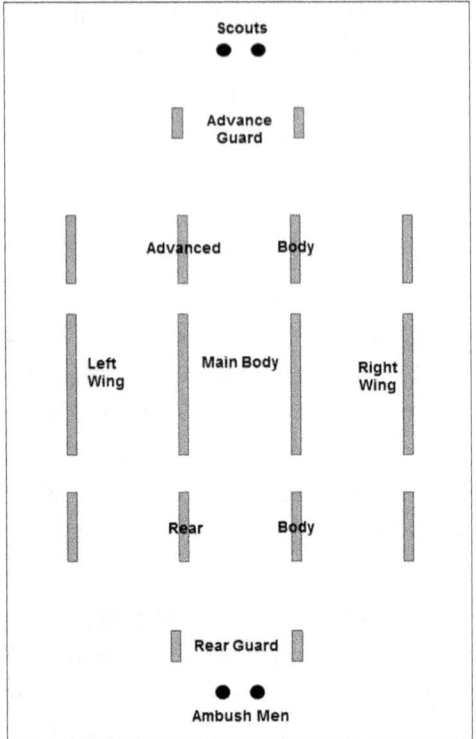

This diagram depicts the planned column formation to be used by Crawford's small army as it moved across the Ohio Country. (*Drawn by the Author*)

volunteers had carefully selected their horses. Instead, it seems that the opposite occurred, or at least so thought Major Rose, who was appalled at their selection. Rose wrote that the typical volunteer "takes care to mount the very worst horse he has upon his farm." On top of this poor animal, he "loads with at least as much provisions as he is well able to carry," not bothering to calculate "the distance he is going, or how long he can possibly be absent." Rose went on to state that each soldier "has provisions enough to maintain at least three men on the campaign, he does not stint himself to a certain allowance."[30]

Still, most of the men wore very practical clothes and came well equipped. Many wore long hunting shirts that went halfway down their thighs and were belted at the waist, a style typically favored by the long hunters of the time. On the belt, there was usually a tomahawk on the right side and a scalping knife on the left. Each man had a knapsack made of coarse cloth tied to his saddle, usually carrying a few small articles placed there by a wife or mother. They tied a canteen to the pommel of the saddle, which rested on top of a blanket that doubled as a sleeping cover at night. Most men relied on a rifle as their primary weapon and carried a powder horn, as well as a bag with bullets, bullet patches, and extra flints.[31]

On the evening of May 24, William wrote a final dispatch to General Irvine. He told the general that the army would set off at 8:00 a.m. the next morning. "I shall endeavor to do all in my power for the good of my country," he wrote, "but, as those whom I command are volunteers and subject to alter their minds, I can only say I will do all I can for the best, and as far as I can." He followed his statement about the reliability of his men by trying to strike a more confident note writing, "The whole at present seem determined to fight; and I am resolved they shall have an opportunity if I can [give them one] with a color of success." He concluded by thanking Irvine for providing Major Rose, adding, "…he will be of great service to me." As a rider galloped off to Fort Pitt with this dispatch, William laid down for the night.[32]

Tomorrow, he and his small army would head for the Sandusky.

The Advance

The morning of May 25 dawned bright and clear. Volunteer militia being what they were, William did not get his army moving at 8:00 a.m., as planned. It was after 10:00 a.m. before the four columns of horses and men began to move forward. William's goal was to arrive on the Sandusky in a week. This meant that the army needed to advance approximately twenty-five miles per day. From the very beginning, the rate of advance was much slower than needed. The expedition only went ten miles the first day, and seldom did any better. Moreover, the hilly, wooded terrain between Mingo Bottom and the Muskingum River required the army to move in two columns, rather than the four intended. This caused the length of the army to stretch to twice the distance calculated. This not only made the force less defendable, but it also slowed progress every time they had to ford a stream.³³

The army initially moved due west towards the Tuscarawas River. Captain John Biggs' company acted as the advance guard, with the two scouts, or pilots as those on the march called them, leading the way. The two pilots, John Slover and Jonathan Zane, were well qualified for their roles in the expedition. Slover, age twenty-nine, was taken captive by the Miami when he was eight-years-old. The Miami adopted him into the tribe, naming him Mannucothe. He lived with them until they sold him to the Delaware at age fourteen, who then passed him along to a white trader. The trader did not keep him very long before selling him to the Shawnee living along the Scioto River. Finally, in 1773, when Slover was twenty-years-old, the Shawnee brought him to Fort Pitt, and he reluctantly returned to live in white society. Having spent much of his twelve years among the Miami and Shawnee on the Sandusky Plains, Slover knew the area well. As such, he was a perfect choice to serve as one of the expedition's pilots.³⁴

Jonathan Zane, the other pilot, was also well-suited to work with Slover in guiding William's command. Zane, who was about thirty-two-years-old and lived in the Wheeling area, was renowned as one of the best hunters on the frontier. An expert sharpshooter, in the 1770s he made

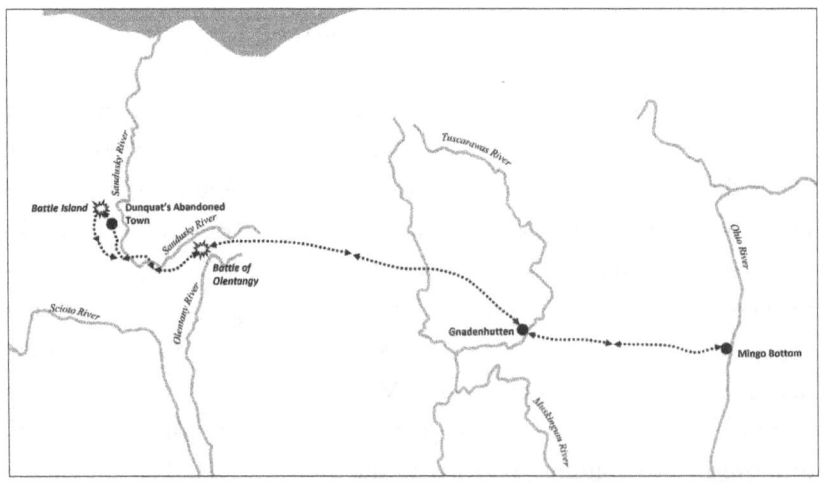

Map of the army's route to the Sandusky. (*Drawn by the Author*)

numerous explorations down the Ohio and further west into the wilderness that would later become the state of Indiana. He also served as a scout during Lord Dunmore's War and led Colonel Brodhead's expedition up the Allegheny in 1779.[35]

When the army camped on the night of May 25, William personally walked the perimeter and felt that it was secure so long as sentries were properly placed. That very first night demonstrated the type of undisciplined behavior among both men and officers that made the expedition so dangerous. On making his rounds after dark, Major Rose discovered that several companies had decided to make camp outside the sentries' picket line and were completely unprotected. From then on, Rose made certain that he was present for the posting of sentries. Of course, even though sentry duty was an obvious necessity for the safety of the army, many of the volunteers grumbled and complained at how unfair it was to stand guard at night after a long day of traveling. More than once, men returned to the warmth of their campfires after only a few hours on watch, often because they saw their officers do the same.[36]

Normally, such dereliction of duty would result in harsh punishment. Often, soldiers serving during this era were executed for failing to carry out sentry duties properly. The elected officers were as unmanageable as the men, and William found himself unable to do much more than issue stern warnings via his daily orders. These orders required that officers make rounds every other half-hour and perform a "Grand Round" of the entire picket line twice a night. He and Rose also decided to rise early every morning and personally drive the men to their alarm posts an hour before dawn.[37]

On the second day of the expedition, the army's departure was delayed once more, this time because some of the volunteers had not properly secured their mounts for the night. The horses had wandered away, a repeat of what William had experienced on the Fort Laurens expedition. Within two days, several men lost their horses completely, causing William to order those without mounts to turn around and return home on foot. The horses themselves posed even more problems for the expedition. First among these was providing food for over five hundred animals. There were no supply wagons carrying fodder, so the expedition's mounts had to eat whatever grass was available at the campsite. Within the small boundaries of the camp's picket line, it took the horses less than an hour to devour most of the edible grass. Searching for more pasturage, the horses would wander away from camp, and their riders would have to search for them in the morning. As a result, the men began to stake their horses all night. This practice was only practical at a campsite where there was sufficient grass nearby for the horses to eat, and this was almost never the case. Between Mingo Bottom and the Tuscarawas, the horses had very little food. By the time the army had marched three or four days, many of the mounts were on the verge of collapsing.[38]

Then, there was the way the horses were handled tactically. Although they were required to move the army quickly, the horses actually limited military efficiency. At the first sign of potential danger, rather than being ready to defend themselves, every soldier's first action upon dismounting was to see to his horse. This was not surprising. Without his mount, each soldier would have no means of escape and no supplies. This behavior concerned Major Rose so much that he proposed a tactic that allowed the horses to be gathered while the army defended itself. Since the army traveled in four columns, Rose thought it made sense to have the men in the two outer columns immediately jump from their horses and engage the enemy, while the men from the inner columns tended to all the horses. Once the animals were tied down, the men from the inner columns would join in the fight.

Rose presented this practical concept to the officers' council on the third day of the expedition. They firmly rejected the idea. The officers from the inner columns objected to the suggestion of their men being hostlers for the outer columns. Instead, the army would rely on a system sure to leave them defenseless in the face of an attack. As Rose later pointed out, this same system provided every coward "an excuse for skulking—the care of his horse and provisions." "Such a man," Rose noted, "once out of the ranks, will never reappear there," a sad fact proven in the days to come.[39]

On the night of May 27, the army neared the Tuscarawas River and the abandoned Christian Delaware villages. They veered their course slightly south before camping eight miles from Gnadenhutten. Here, William needed to decide which path to follow the next day. The most direct course crossed ground that included numerous hills and swamps. With the horses so worn down already, some officers advised they take a course across level and firm ground, a route that went through Gnadenhutten. Both Slover and Zane pointed out that the path via Gnadenhutten crossed heavily used Indian trails that would potentially expose them to a roving enemy hunting party. William listened to the arguments and reluctantly chose the plan offered by his officers—they would march through Gnadenhutten. He ordered that an advance force of 112 men under Colonel Williamson go ahead the next morning in case the village was not as empty as anticipated. This would be another decision that William would regret.

Major Rose rode with Williamson the next morning as they approached Gnadenhutten. When they were about two miles away, Williamson halted his men while he, Rose, and another officer rode closer to see if there were any warriors in the area. All they found were the sad remnants of destruction, what Rose described as "ruins of the lowest house in town... mixed with the...bones of the burnt bodies of the Indians."[40]

The entire army soon caught up, and they advanced several more miles before settling for the night. While camp was being set up, two officers went forward to look for any signs of Indian activity. They did not have far to go. When only about a quarter of a mile from the main camp, they sighted two Indians and exchanged shots with them. The entire army dashed to their alarm posts, but soon the officers returned to say that the Indians had run off after they traded volleys. There was no indication of any larger body of warriors nearby, but William realized his worst fear—they had been discovered. Nevertheless, there was no thought of turning back now. William would try to push the men to move more quickly, hoping to reach the Sandusky towns before any resistance could organize.

The terrain finally allowed the army to move in four columns, but it was rough. Every crossing of a creek or path into a steep defile caused confusion and further delay. The companies or columns should have methodically approached these obstacles, each choosing a crossing point. Instead, every man would rush helter-skelter forward until the entire body of the army was packed into a small space. The resulting delay made the columns stretch to four times their proper length. Again, this slowed the army down and made it more vulnerable to attack.[41]

As the army moved deeper into the Ohio Country, they found increasing signs of Indian activity. On May 29, a day after leaving Gnadenhutten, they came to a fork in the trail, where they discovered a tree painted to mark the killing of prisoners, with three scalps hanging nearby. There were also signs of a recent encampment, and fresh tracks. The next day, they reached a warriors' path, onto which Zane turned them, heading northwest. From the tracks on the trail, Slover and Zane calculated at least sixty warriors had traveled the path only two days before. More ominous, however, were the horse tracks indicating at least two warriors had been observing the army and moving ahead of them towards the Sandusky.[42]

The army continued northwest along Killbuck Creek, and then turned west again. By now, more horses had been lost, and at least sixty men were on foot. Since the army had now advanced very far into hostile territory, William could not send them back. Instead, they marched on foot, keeping up as best as they could.

On June 1, the army advanced into a large river bottom area, where the pilots found a wide Indian trail running off to the right. William sent a detachment forward down the path that quickly ran into two Indians. As before, the men exchanged shots, and the warriors made their escape. Upon hearing the firing, the army moved into a square defensive formation to await a possible attack. When no attack came, William called for another council meeting with his officers.

At this meeting, William made his concerns very clear. He stated that many of the men were down to only a ten-day supply of food, which was not enough to continue forward and then support a return march. Worse, he added, the army had been sighted for the second time, and it was very likely that the enemy knew of their approach. This meant the Indians would be gathering every warrior within fifty miles of the Sandusky towns to thwart any attack. They also would call for assistance from British Rangers. William had no doubt the army could reach the Sandusky and make a fight of it, but at the same time he told the officers that he also had to consider the prospects for a safe retreat. Given the lack of food, the condition of the horses, and the potential size of the enemy force that might be gathering, the prospects for a successful withdrawal were not good.

William proposed to follow these large Indian trails to the north, where there was certain to be an Indian town. Zane confirmed that he knew of such a town about thirty miles away. William said the army could attack and destroy it, and then withdraw towards Mingo Bottom. Despite the urgency of his appeal, the officers rejected his plan and voted to continue toward the original objectives on the Sandusky. At this critical moment, William should have exercised his command authority and rejected the council's vote. Once again, he demurred to the opinion of his volunteer officers. William's inability to trust his own good judgment and considerable experience clearly confirmed Major Rose's concerns about his leadership abilities.[43]

On the morning of June 3, the army finally emerged from the hilly, wooded terrain and entered the Sandusky Plains. Spread out ahead of them was a broad expanse of high, coarse grass, much of it over three feet tall, spanning from horizon to horizon. Here and there, small islands of trees punctuated the high grass and undulating terrain. Wildlife, including prairie hens, sand hill cranes, prairie owls, geese, fox squirrels, and numerous rattlesnakes filled the land. The more experienced fighters among the army looked about them and realized there would be no hiding their presence in this sea of grass, and there would be little cover in a fight. It made a bad situation worse.[44]

At 6:00 p.m., the command halted for the night. William called another officers' meeting to discuss the options for their final approach to the Sandusky towns. He told the assembled group that they could march through the night to the main Wyandot town, where Dunquat held council, and make an assault before dawn. Alternatively, they could wait until morning, when they could move forward, conduct a reconnaissance, and plan the attack accordingly. All agreed the latter option made the most sense because a night advance might result in confusion. With the meeting concluded, everyone went to rest after preparing for the day they hoped would bring the victorious climax of the expedition.[45]

Unknown to them, the enemy was very close, and had been preparing for their arrival.

Chapter 10

BATTLE ISLAND

Given the need for surprise, William and his officers were concerned about the warriors that had sighted them outside Gnadenhutten on May 28 and again on June 1. One wonders how they would have reacted if they had known that a Wyandot scouting party had been monitoring the initial arrival of volunteers at Mingo Bottom. Within a day of the first volunteers appearing on the Ohio, runners arrived at Sandusky to tell the Wyandot chief Dunquat that an American invasion force was gathering.

The scouts watched William's army depart and followed them along the trail towards the Muskingum, waiting to see which way the Americans would turn at that key juncture. As soon as the army crossed the river and continued west, the scouts realized that the Sandusky was the invaders' objective and additional runners soon carried the word to Dunquat.

The news surprised no one on the Sandusky, especially Simon Girty. On April 12, more than a month before the first volunteers arrived at Mingo Bottom, Girty had warned the British commander at Fort Detroit, Major Arent DePeyster, about an impending expedition. In a letter to DePeyster he explained that an American prisoner taken captive by one of Girty's raiding parties had told him General Irvine planned to gather a force "of about 500 foot and 300 horse" along the Ohio to move against the Sandusky towns. In this same letter, Girty also told DePeyster about the tragic events that had occurred at Gnadenhutten.[1]

Of course, the news about Gnadenhutten had already reached the Sandusky, causing profound grief and anger among all the Native American towns. The same scouts watching developments at Mingo Bottom also relayed news which ignited fear and hatred among the woodland nations.

After the Americans had left, the scouts slipped into the abandoned camp to see if the volunteers might have left behind any useful items. Instead, what they found enraged them. Several of William's men, probably some of the Paxton Boys, had peeled back the bark on trees to leave messages written with coal. The scouts made impressions of these messages to carry back to the Sandusky. Once in Dunquat's hands, interpreters translated the messages, which said the volunteers in William's army would give no quarter to any Indian, be they warrior, the elderly, woman, or child. To the Native Americans, it seemed that William Crawford and his men were in the process of planning yet another massacre.[2]

When DePeyster received Girty's dispatch in mid-April, he began preparations to counter any coming American expedition. He ordered his men to make ready a small ship, the *Faith*, which could carry British Rangers who were mounted troops highly experienced in frontier warfare to the Sandusky as soon as further intelligence on a potential invasion force was available. When Dunquat received word from his scouts that the Americans were definitely headed for the Sandusky, he sent messengers to Fort Detroit via canoe. They carried an urgent request from the Wyandot chief asking for British assistance, to which DePeyster responded by dispatching his Rangers. They also loaded two pieces of field artillery and a mortar onboard the *Faith*. If these weapons made it to the Sandusky, the Rangers would greatly outgun William's volunteers. The horses were sent overland around the lake, taking longer to reach the Lower Sandusky than the ship. By the morning of June 4, the Rangers and their horses were reunited and the British troops mounted and began moving towards Dunquat's town. Meanwhile, the Native Americans had begun rounding up their own fighting force.[3]

The Wyandot numbered about seven hundred people in the area near the Sandusky, making them the most numerous local tribal group. They had lived in the region since the late seventeenth century after their arrival from their traditional homeland in the area between Lake Simcoe and Georgian Bay in present day Ontario, Canada. The Wyandot had lived in Ontario since the early fourteenth century, and they called this lush land of forests and lakes Wendake, which meant "the island" in the Wyandot language. They called themselves the Wendat, which meant "the people of the island," the basis for the word Wyandot. Located between two bodies of water and surrounded by dense woods and wetlands, Wendake probably did feel like an island world unto itself.[4]

In the forest on this island, the Wyandot created a great four-nation confederacy that became a dominant force among the Native American nations. Their power came from trade rather than from military force. When the French first encountered the Wyandot in 1535, the nation was the most prominent in the political and economic hierarchy of the northern woodlands nations. As such, they held sway over what was the most widespread and unified trading network in North America. Also, the Wyandot language served as the *lingua franca* for trade and diplomacy among at least fifty Native American nations.[5]

When the French arrived in force along with their Jesuit priests in 1615, there were between 22,500 and 25,000 Wyandot spread out among twenty-five villages in Wendake. As with the other Native American nations along the east coast of America, the European diseases devastated the Wyandot. By 1640, recurring waves of European illnesses had killed almost sixty percent of the Wyandot population in Wendake, leaving only about 10,000 survivors. Moreover, as the Jesuits converted many of the Wyandot to the Christian faith, they created deep rifts in what had been a society bonded by their own belief system. These events fractured the Wyandot Confederacy, making it vulnerable to outside attack. That attack arrived in the form of an invasion by the Iroquois Confederation.[6]

Because of their growing fur trade and the over-trapping of the beaver population in their territory, the Iroquois began to covet the beaver living in the hunting grounds of neighboring nations. This desire became even stronger when the Iroquois looked west to the Wendake. The Wyandot were master traders, and as a result, their success drew the Iroquois' jealousy. What began as a series of small raids in 1640 exploded into open warfare in 1648. The Iroquois attacked the village of Teanaostaiae and the mission of St. Joseph. In the resulting fighting, the Iroquois killed almost seven hundred Wyandot.[7]

The Iroquois attacks continued, and by 1653, the great Wyandot Confederacy was destroyed, and its people driven from their beautiful Wendake forever. The nation wandered for decades in search of a new home. Some would go to Quebec and place themselves under the protection of the French garrison, while others fled to the Neutrals, the Erie, the Tionontati, and other non-Wyandot nations. When the Iroquois attacked some of these tribes, such as the Tionontati, they and their Wyandot guests took refuge on the islands of Lake Huron. For the remainder of the surviving Wyandot, their wandering led them to Michilimackinac, Manitoulin Island, Green Bay, Chequamigon Bay, and the south shore of Lake Superior. By the late seventeenth century, they had finally settled along the Sandusky River.[8]

Long after the Wyandot were driven from Wendake, the other nations still looked up to them and allowed them to be the keeper of the sacred council fires. In 1721, the Jesuit historian Pierre Francois Xavier de Charlevoix wrote, "The [Wyandot] nation is almost defunct, and they are reduced to two mediocre villages that are very distant from one another, yet they continue to be the moving spirit in all the councils when matters of general concern are being discussed."[9]

There were several Wyandot towns scattered about the Sandusky region. The largest was the village where Dunquat lived and held council, the Americans' primary target. Both Slover and Zane had visited the town, located on the west bank of the Sandusky River about five miles downriver from the current city of Upper Sandusky, Ohio.

Simon Girty was visiting Dunquat when runners arrived with word of the American advance beyond the Muskingum. He soon played a critical role in rallying and organizing the Native American forces. Furthermore, the Native American intelligence system was excellent. They knew how many Americans were coming, and they realized that David Williamson and William Crawford were among them. Girty immediately began gathering warriors, with Dunquat's town serving as the rendezvous point. He was not only a valued advisor to the Wyandot; he also had a close relationship with the Delaware living along the Sandusky. He sent runners to the large Delaware town on Tymochtee Creek where the sachem, Hopocan, held council.[10]

Having moved his people to the Sandusky after General Hand's army blundered into his brother's hunting camp, Hopocan had waged war ever since, becoming a reliable British ally and an intractable foe to the Americans. His village eleven miles from Dunquat's town was unknown to William or his pilots, Slover and Zane. Hopocan rallied over two hundred warriors as soon as he heard of the American approach, and marched his men directly to the Wyandot village.

Once there, Hopocan's men merged with nearly four hundred Wyandot warriors under Dunquat, creating a force that greatly outnumbered William's army of 480 men. Girty also sent runners to more distant Mingo and Shawnee villages with word that the Wyandot were threatened. Although it would take longer for these warriors to arrive, both nations responded with messages that they would march for the Sandusky as quickly as possible.[11]

Girty also sent runners to gather warriors from a smaller Delaware village (near present-day Crestline, Ohio) led by the warrior chief Wingenund. The missionary John Heckewelder wrote of Wingenund, "This great and good man was not only one of the bravest and most celebrated warriors, but one of the most amiable men of the Delaware nation. To a firm undaunted mind, he joined humanity, kindness and universal benevolence; the excellent qualities of his heart had obtained for him the name of Wingenund, which in the Lenape language means "the well beloved.""[12]

While Hopocan relished the chance to confront the Americans, Wingenund's reaction was almost certainly less enthusiastic. Unlike the other Native American leaders of the Sandusky region, Wingenund actually knew William Crawford personally. The two men had met during several conferences at Fort Pitt, and the two liked and respected one another. Wingenund, who spoke English and French, had even visited William and Hannah at Spring Garden on more than one occasion and appreciated the friendship and hospitality he had been shown. Although William was now coming to visit him, his reasons were far from friendly.[13]

As word of the American approach reached the Sandusky, British traders also reacted to the news. These men bought furs from the Native Americans and sold everything from trinkets to food and ammunition in the Sandusky towns. They immediately began to pack up their goods and prepare for a hasty retreat to the safety of Fort Detroit. One of the traders, John Leith, was a former Delaware captive who worked as the agent for a firm at the fort. He had a network of personal spies among the populations of the various towns who fed him regular reports on the progress of the American army as it made its way across the Ohio Country. When his spies reported that the Americans were only fifteen miles away, Leith began to gather his horses and pack his goods—about £1,500 worth of silver, furs, powder, and lead shot.

The next morning, Leith and most of the other traders were headed north, away from the coming battle. Leith took his goods and horses with him, as well as all the cattle owned by his company. He had only gone three miles when he met Captain Matthew Elliott, who was coming in advance of the force of British Rangers. Elliott, the same man who escaped Pittsburgh with Simon Girty and Alexander McKee in 1778, promptly seized sixteen head of his cattle before letting him pass. Leith finally camped fourteen miles away, hoping it was far enough to be out of the path of any fighting.[14]

Captain William Caldwell, an Irish-born Loyalist, accompanied Elliott. Caldwell was to command the combined Native American-British force, while Elliott would be second-in-command, responsible for coordinating the movements of the Native American warriors led by their tribal war chiefs. Given Elliot's many years among the Indians and his ability to speak multiple woodland nation languages, he was an ideal selection for the task. Dunquat led the Wyandot warriors, with Wingenund and Hopocan commanding the respective groups of Delaware fighters. Finally, Simon Girty would fight alongside the Wyandot, while his brother, George, would accompany the Delaware.[15]

On the night of June 3, a small party of Wyandot warriors waited outside the Americans' final encampment, watching them closely, eager to dispatch a message once the invaders broke camp. The strategy devised to counter William and his men was simple. First, Dunquat abandoned his town, moving all the Wyandot women and children seven miles farther down the Sandusky, where they would be safe in a newly built town. This meant that the Americans would find an empty village devoid of both people and possessions when they arrived. Believing that William's men would not be satisfied with burning an empty village, the Native Americans thought that the American army would advance further north down the river. This would allow the Native Americans to overwhelm William's men with an army of warriors—warriors determined to destroy the Americans before their families met the same fate as the Christian Delaware of Gnadenhutten.[16]

The stage for a climactic battle had been set.

The Army's Approach

Before dawn on June 4, after what was likely a sleepless night for many of the volunteers, Crawford's army began to stir. Amid the sounds of chirping crickets and birdsong, the men made coffee, filled canteens at the nearby spring, and prepared for what they expected to be an eventful day.

Late afternoon showers from the previous day dampened the air, and a heavy fog was clinging to the ground as the sun rose above the eastern horizon. Because of the rain, many of the men's rifles were wet, and around 7:00 a.m. companies test-fired their weapons into the air to ensure they were not fouled. It was a strange and poorly conceived act for an army attempting to surprise its enemy. Not long after that, the booming sound of several cannons firing in the distance to the north startled William and his men. This deeply concerned both the volunteer soldiers and the officers. Meeting an enemy armed with rifles and tomahawks was one thing, but artillery was something entirely different. It meant that there were British units with the Indians.[17]

Soon after clearing their weapons, the men began dousing campfires and packing up their horses. The rising sun burned off the fog, and William ordered his men to mount. The army advanced north in company order, sliding quietly through the waist-high grass on the Sandusky Plains.

As the temperature warmed, the sky took on a clear, bright blue hue, portending a hot, humid day ahead. Seven miles up the trail, the column came upon the ruins of a village. Scouts scoured the burned out remains of about twenty buildings but found nothing, since it was obvious that it had been destroyed some months before. From there, the army crossed a creek and moved up a steep, lightly wooded ravine. The path they had been following soon met the main road leading to the Dunquat's town.

The men could see it a short distance ahead, lying along the banks of the Sandusky.

Anticipation ran high as William formed his men for their attack, dispersing them into a line formation that stretched across both sides of the road. At that moment, it appeared that the element of surprise might be on their side after all. There was no sign of enemy scouts or even lookouts on the stockade surrounding the town. William raised his arm above his head, waved his men forward, and the army swept into the settlement.

As soon as they cleared the gates, everyone pulled to a halt—the town was completely deserted, with no sign of anyone or anything. The volunteers quickly dismounted and searched the village. The longhouses were completely empty—no people, no animals, not even blankets or cooking implements. It was clear that the Wyandot had only recently abandoned the village, and that the Indians had gotten advance warning that they were coming.[18]

With this ominous discovery, a "murmur arose among the men" and a group of about one hundred volunteers began shouting that they wanted to abandon the expedition and head home as quickly as possible. William convened yet another officers' council to discuss the situation. Several of the officers agreed with the volunteers clamoring for a prompt withdrawal. However, both Slover and Zane believed that a new town might only be a couple of miles farther downriver. Colonel Williamson proposed that he take a detachment of fifty handpicked men to gallop ahead and burn the new town. William dismissed this idea out of hand, pointing out to Williamson that this would mean dividing the army at a point when it was most likely to meet determined opposition. He and Williamson argued for several minutes until Crawford forcefully ended the dispute, but Williamson's anger was clear. As the expedition moved west, he had become increasingly strident at every council meeting, stating his opposing views to most of William's orders. At this point, Williamson bordered on being openly mutinous.[19]

William ordered the army to re-form and move down the road to see if they could discover the new town the pilots believed might exist. But there was no new town on the Sandusky, much less a single cow, horse, or

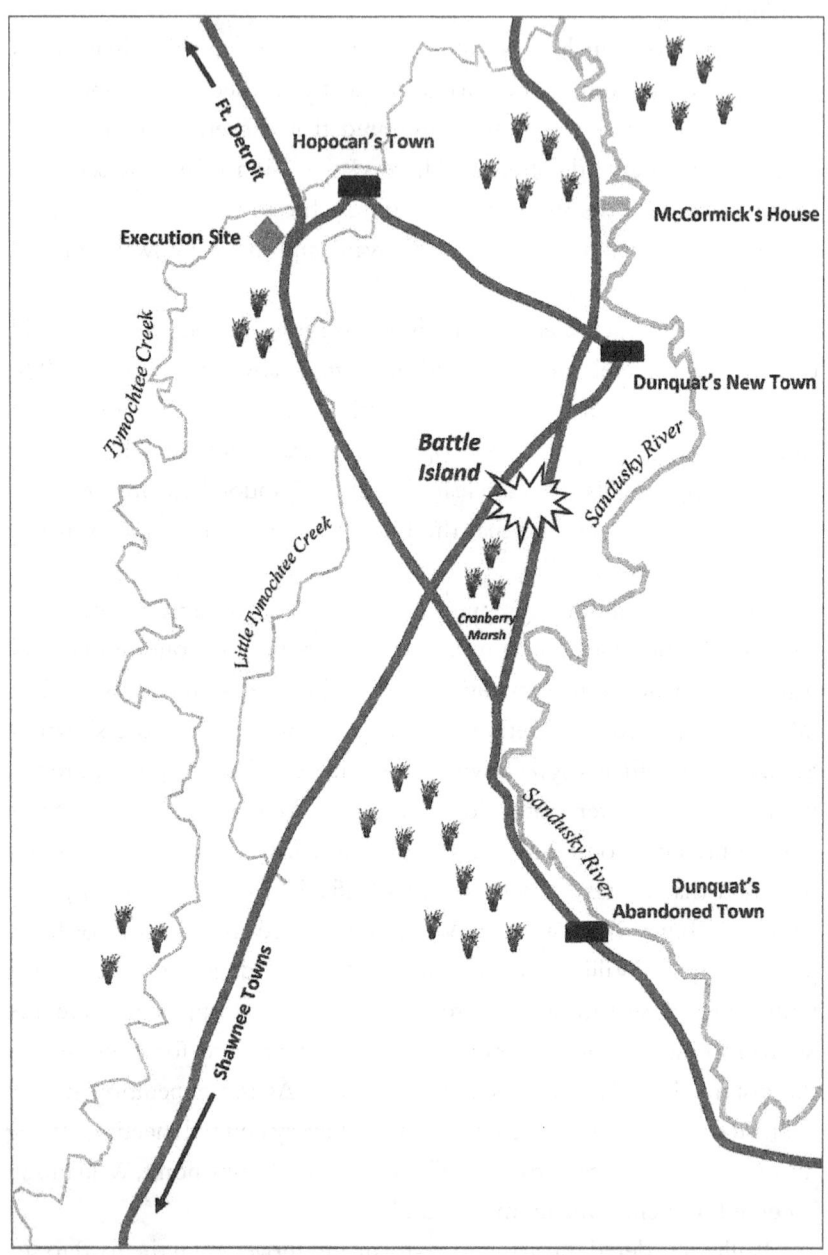

Map depicting the army's positions in and around Battle Island. (*Drawn by the Author*)

Indian. William brought the army to a halt near a shady grove of trees. The men dismounted to take their noon meal while William convened the second officers' council of the day. Before the meeting began, he pulled Major Rose aside and told him to take forty men mounted on the best horses and scout ahead. In the meantime, he would meet with the officers and determine how to proceed.

As Rose's detachment rode away, William took the measure of his officers' opinions. Zane spoke first, making it clear that he was convinced a significant Indian force was nearby, lying in wait. Given Zane's experience as a scout and Indian fighter, everyone took his views very seriously. Zane argued that the fact no Indians had been found in an area where hundreds were known to live was convincing evidence that they were concentrating nearby, preparing for battle. William agreed, having feared this possibility for some time. He ordered that, upon Rose's return with whatever news he might have, the army would begin the return march home. This decision received the overwhelming support of the majority of the officers. Only a few, such as David Williamson, still argued for offensive action.[20]

While Crawford was meeting with his officers, Major Rose and his scouting party were moving north along the road. It soon became clear that many of the horses were too loaded down with provisions to move as quickly as needed, so Rose directed his men to a wooded hill just a few hundred yards to the left of the road. The forested glade seemed an island of cool green rising from the tall prairie grass, making it a good spot to take a brief rest while they unloaded their horses and hid the supplies among the trees.

As the men cared for their animals in the grove of trees, Rose surveyed the area. The spot was only slightly elevated above the adjacent terrain, but it was raised enough to make it a defensible position should they need one. The oak trees had dense foliage, providing good shade, but the surrounding prairie grass still grew quite high. To the north and west of the hill, a broad, open expanse of grass spread out with small groves of trees here and there. A mile to the east, Rose could see a long line of trees marking the banks of the Sandusky. Halfway between the trees and the grove where he stood was the road they had just covered; it might

The slight rise seen on the horizon of this quiet field marks the site of Battle Island (*Author photo*)

still lead to a Wyandot town further to the north. Hidden from view a few hundred yards to the southwest was a large cranberry marsh, one so deep that no horseman could possibly cross it. This bog would later prove deadly to some of the volunteers.[21]

After hiding their provisions, Rose and his men returned to the road and continued to scout downriver. They had gone about three miles when the road ascended up a low rise in the prairie. As they cleared the small hill, Rose could see a stockade wall and the roofs of several longhouses in the distance—they had found the new Wyandot town! But within minutes his excitement was dashed as dozens of painted, screaming warriors arose from the tall grass and charged toward the Americans.

The trap had been sprung.

The Fight for Battle Island: June 4, 1782

Hopocan was leading the Delaware warriors at Rose's front. They had laid in wait in a deep ravine surrounded by heavy underbrush. This ravine ran perpendicular to the road with the open prairie to the right and the trees along the Sandusky River about three-quarters of a mile to the left.

It was a perfect location for an ambush. As they leapt from the cover of the ravine and the tall grass, the warriors immediately began extending their lines to the left and right in a large V-shaped formation, intending to envelop the American detachment.[22]

The warriors' sudden appearance startled Major Rose and his men. In spite of this, Rose calculated a series of actions within seconds, after ordering two of his best riders to speed back to the main column and get the army moving forward as quickly as possible. As the riders wheeled about and galloped off, Rose executed a fighting withdrawal, attempting to delay the enemy advance as long as possible. Given the confusion and discord he left behind at the army camp, Rose feared it might take longer than usual for William to get the soldiers organized for a counterattack.

He commanded his men to dismount and engage the warriors with rifle fire, while the Americans steadily withdrew towards the grove of trees where their supplies were hidden. In a series of shifting movements the volunteers would fire volleys, remount, move to the next small piece of high ground on the prairie, and dismount to fire again. For more than an hour, Rose and his men stayed just ahead of the Indian advance, edging closer and closer to the grove of trees. Mounted warriors began to overtake the small group of Americans—at one point, several of the warriors closed in on Major Rose, coming near enough to hurl tomahawks at him. Only Rose's skill and horsemanship saved him as he expertly dodged the attack.

More Indians joined the fight, pursuing Rose's detachment. These were Dunquat's Wyandot, with Simon Girty among them. They moved rapidly over the prairie in an attempt to gain the Americans' rear and cut them off from the island of trees Rose was so desperately trying to reach. As the Americans finally made it to the grove with the warriors in close pursuit, Rose and his men took cover in the trees, turning to engage the warriors. The Indians had such overwhelming strength and were so close that some warriors quickly overran the eastern end of the grove, threatening to trap and destroy Rose's command.

Meanwhile, Rose's riders had reached the main army and told William what had happened. William quickly ordered the officers to get the men mounted and ready to advance. As Rose had anticipated, this process did not happen rapidly or without some dissension in the ranks. Eventually the army was ready to move, and William led them down the road in four columns at a gallop.

They arrived just as the attacking warriors had taken the eastern end of the grove. The army crashed headlong into the trees, dismounting and driving the Indians out with a determined charge, killing and scalping eleven warriors in the process. Realizing he had possession of the only favorable fighting ground in sight, William deployed the army, choosing to make a stand among the trees. In local lore, the site would later become known as "Battle Island." He extended his lines along the borders of the grove, but the Indians tried again to gain the American rear. Colonel Gaddis, who commanded the rear guard, drove the Indians back, despite the difficulty he had getting his men to fight in the open. After deploying the defensive line, Major Benton found he had extended his men too far to the left. The warriors quickly took advantage of this with a counterattack that threatened the American flank. William hastily corrected the situation by ordering Benton to shorten his line.[23]

By 4:00 p.m., the battle became a general engagement. The rattle of musketry filled the air until it became one continuous roar. Clouds of choking smoke formed around Battle Island as the late afternoon sun burned down relentlessly on the combatants. Waves of new warriors continued to pour onto the battlefield, extending the Native American line across the northern approach while almost completely enveloping William's position.

Artist Frank Halbedel's painting of the fighting at Battle Island.
(*Wyandot County Historical Society*)

At this point, Captain Caldwell of the British Rangers arrived on horseback. Wearing the Rangers' eye-catching green uniform, he rode in clear view of William's men. As he directed the movement of the warriors, an American rifleman took aim, fired, and brought him down. Caldwell had been hit in one leg, and the ball had passed cleanly through and lodged in his other leg. Before being evacuated to the rear, Caldwell turned command over to Captain Elliott, who immediately ordered Hopocan to flank his Delaware warriors to the right, trying once more to seal off the American rear and any potential escape path.[24]

William walked the length of his defensive line, and he observed his men fighting independently. Captain James Munn had crept forward from the trees attempting to get a better view of the enemy through the smoke. A musket ball broke his leg and as he turned to crawl back to the trees, a warrior hurled a tomahawk, striking him in the head and laying open one side of his face. As Munn lay helpless in the grass, several warriors began crawling towards him. One of Munn's men, William Brady, saw what was happening, mounted his horse, and rode forward to rescue his wounded commander. Reaching Munn, Brady hoisted him up on the horse and galloped back into the grove. At the same time, an Indian rifle shot ripped into Captain Ezekiel Rose's breast, sending him to the surgeon, and another soldier had his lip shot away by a warrior's musket ball. Even William was not immune to the rifle fire, as a random shot shattered the powder horn slung on his hip.[25]

The fighting intensified, and Crawford watched as more of the volunteers and enemy's warriors were crawling out into the tall prairie grass. They would pop up, quickly shoot, and then crouch down again amidst the cover of the grass. Angus McCoy, however, chose to stand upright in the grass, daring both fate and Indian rifle fire. Although his coat was riddled with bullet holes McCoy miraculously remained unharmed.

Several other men climbed the tall oak trees, where they could better observe the enemy warriors hiding in the grass. One of these men, Daniel Canon, was widely considered the best sharpshooter in the army. From his place in the tall branches, Canon exacted a heavy toll on the enemy. "I do not know how many Indians I killed," he said afterward, "but I never saw the same head again above the grass after I shot at it."[26]

Private Phillip Smith fired at the warriors on the ground from the cover of the trees. About one hundred feet away, a warrior hid in the grass, jumping up now and again to shoot at him. The shots smacked into the tree right by Smith's face, kicking up bark. Smith figured out the warrior's hiding place and fired several shots in an attempt to bring him down. On the seventh shot, he hit his target, who immediately collapsed in the grass. Smith crawled forward to take his victim's scalp, but there was no body, just a bloody trail.[27]

Mike Myers crawled to a tree just outside the grove. Like Smith, an Indian musket ball hit the tree, blasting bark into his face. He wiped the fragments from his eyes and peered around the tree. His attacker was about twenty feet away behind a white walnut tree. The walnut forked about three feet above the ground and Myers could see the warrior's head every time he rose to shoot. Myers aimed for the fork of the tree and waited, timing his shot for the next time the warrior popped up to fire. After several minutes, Myers' target popped into view, and he fired and killed him. Myers could see a "large number of squaws" to the rear of the attacking warriors, yelling and banging loudly on kettles, in an attempt to intimidate the Americans. Myers watched them search the grass for dead Americans, whom they quickly stripped of their clothing and possessions. The women also looked for their own wounded, and they gathered them up and carried them to the rear.[28]

One of Captain Craig Ritchie's men, Francis Dunleavy, remembered fighting a one-on-one battle with a huge warrior. The warrior, whom Dunleavy described as being almost seven feet tall, crept towards him through the remains of a recently downed tree. He came close enough to hurl his tomahawk, narrowly missed the American private's head. The warrior escaped but Dunleavy met him years later, when the Shawnee, who called himself "Big Captain Johnny," fought alongside the Americans in the War of 1812. Dunleavy remarked that Big Captain Johnny "was as frightfully ugly as he was tall."[29]

The warriors continued to press their attack, and Simon Girty rode among them on his white horse wearing his signature red headscarf, shouting words of encouragement to the Wyandot braves. Several of William's officers and men knew Girty well, having served with him on more than one occasion. They not only recognized his horse and attire, but could also clearly recall his voice. There was no doubt in their minds that the infamous "white savage" was leading the enemy in battle, inspiring dread in many of the Americans.

This nineteenth-century drawing depicts Simon Girty astride his horse, wearing his signature red bandana.
(Ohio History Connection)

However, even Girty could not protect one of his men from his own stupidity. Francis LeVillier, who was a French interpreter serving with the British, sought to demonstrate to his Native American comrades that he possessed a special magic protection. Le Villier had his native wife paint a bright red spot on his ruffled shirt, directly over his heart. "Here," he told the warriors, "is a mark for the Virginia riflemen!" Not long after this boast, he went into battle, and one of William's men shot him dead right through the magic red circle.[30]

As sunset approached, the warriors gradually pulled back, slackening the pace of their firing. By nightfall, the fighting ceased and William took stock of the army's situation. Despite the ferocity of the encounter, he had lost only five dead with nineteen wounded. Of the five killed, two died immediately, and three others succumbed to severe wounds, while the nineteen wounded included six officers. Dr. Knight told William that at least three of the remaining wounded would not survive until morning.[31]

Ammunition and water supplies were now of grave concern. The brisk exchange of musket fire had diminished the store of ammunition to dangerously low levels. If they remained trapped in this position too long, the stock of ball and powder would not hold out. As for the water, most of the men had not filled their canteens since they left camp that morning. With the intense heat of the day and the exertions of battle, many men had drained their canteens dry. The enemy had them bottled up tightly and there was no safe path from the grove to the river. William ordered a search for any water source, and a volunteer named John Sherrard found one.

In the darkness, Sherrard crawled out from the wood and discovered a nearby tree that had blown down in a recent storm. A pool of water had gathered in the hollow where the roots had been. Although it was not clean and there was not much of it, some water was better than no water at all. Sherrard drank from the pool, filled his canteen, and crawled back to safety. Once back in the grove, he collected his comrades' canteens and crept back to the tree to fill them. Nearby warriors heard Sherrard moving through the grass and began firing at him in the gloom. With bullets whizzing past him, he filled the canteens and returned, repeating the process until all the volunteers had water. One man, who was a beneficiary of Sherrard's unselfish courage, later told Sherrard's son that he did not know how his father survived "exposed as he was, when none else along the line would undertake such a dangerous task."[32]

As the night deepened, William ordered his men to build large fires around the perimeter so they could see any attempt at a surprise attack. Interestingly, the Native Americans did the same, lighting huge blazes so they could observe any American effort to escape in the darkness. The bonfires flickered brightly, casting ominous shadows over the prairie, as a deep mist began to form along the ground, giving the scene a macabre, forbidding feeling.

William ordered his men to sleep on their arms in groups of four to "stand guard all night two and two together lest one should fall asleep." Few slept. The moans of the wounded, the occasional war cry from the enemy, and random gunshots echoing out in the dark added to the night's gloom. Most of the volunteers experienced a strong sense of dread about the coming dawn. They believed the army was outnumbered and they doubted there was any way to escape a grim fate. That feeling of trepidation was too much for some men, and during the night fifteen volunteers from Washington County deserted, sneaking past the surrounding warriors. When they reached home safely, the deserters told anyone who would listen that the army had been "cut to pieces."[33]

That night, as William walked the perimeter with Major Rose, he realized that the right flank was very thin and essentially unprotected for a distance of about one-quarter mile. As Rose had feared a few days earlier, this weakness was caused by men taking care of their horses. These volunteers left the line with their mounts when the fighting started and never returned, having skulked into the relative safety of the grove's interior.[34]

It was a long night, and William likely spent much of his time trying to figure out how he might disengage his army from its dire position. Had he known that more warriors were nearby, coming to support the Delaware and Wyandot, and that they would soon be joined by more Rangers with artillery, his night might have felt even longer.

The Battle Continues: June 5, 1782

The firing began again at about 6:00 a.m. the following morning. This time only sporadic rifle shots came from the warriors surrounding the grove. It seemed that the shots were intended to harass more than cause any real damage. As the sun rose, the warriors also let themselves be seen as they maneuvered in small groups, moving left and right through the prairie grass. This served two purposes: it made their numbers seem larger than they were, and it caused William's men to waste ammunition by firing at them, something the Americans could ill afford to do.[35]

During the night, four more volunteers had been wounded, bringing the casualty total to eight dead and twenty wounded. In addition, some men had become ill from both dehydration and the bad water brought in by John Sherrard. William and his officers struggled to come up with a strategy for getting the army out of the trap, but their dwindling numbers further limited their options.[36]

In the enemy camp, Captain Elliott was more than happy to continue his present strategy. The heat and lack of water were taking their toll, wearing down William's small army. Moreover, their slow loss of men and ammunition was preferable to a massive assault. An attack was sure to result in numerous casualties, something Elliot needed to avoid to retain his Native American allies' cooperation. Native American war chiefs always tried to save their men's lives, and in the warrior culture of the woodland nations, no victory could ever justify heavy casualties.[37]

William spent the morning discussing their next moves with his officers. Once again, Colonel Williamson was adamant that aggressive offensive action was the only answer. He proposed a counterattack against the warriors positioned within fifty yards of the grove. His plan entailed an attack by fifty men on foot straight at the Indian position, while Major Rose attacked their flanks with 150 men on the best horses. William immediately dismissed the idea. Such an attack might further weaken the army at great cost in both men and horses, accomplishing little. Crawford argued that the Wyandot and Delaware were defending their homes, and such an attack would not cause them to abandon that defense. The discussion between William and his deputy quickly escalated into another ugly quarrel before William ended the council meeting. For now, the army would hold their ground and watch for any opportunity to turn the tide in their favor.[38]

As the morning grew hotter, the water supply again became an issue. Despite the fact that some men had become sick from the water he had brought, John Sherrard was urged by his comrades to fill the canteens once more. This time, he would have to do so in broad daylight. Sherrard crawled slowly out through the tall grass, trying hard to avoid detection by the enemy. When he reached the spot where the puddle had been the night before, Sherrard discovered it was bone dry. Luckily, he saw another puddle only a few feet away. He filled the first canteens and made his way back, repeating the process several times over the course of the morning. Finally, after filling one last batch of canteens, Sherrard was overcome by a lack of sleep and he dozed off leaning against the fallen tree between the two lines. After almost two hours, a warrior spotted him sleeping by the tree and fired a shot that missed Sherrard's head by inches. The ball slivered bark off the tree and fell on Sherrard's face, waking him from his perilous nap. He quickly crawled back to the grove, dragging the last of the filled canteens with him.[39]

As afternoon arrived, the June sun continued to bear down on the battlefield, making the heat even more unbearable. One soldier, John Walters, recalled that as the day grew warmer, "the stench of the dead and wounded became almost intolerable." If this were not bad enough, when Walters and his comrades looked to the north, what they saw almost certainly made their spirits sink.[40]

One of William's men had spotted an ominous cloud of dust moving along the road from the north. Soon, William could see a large group of mounted men wearing the conspicuous green Ranger uniform. Although the Rangers had yet to bring up their artillery, the addition of these skilled fighters to the Indian forces was a bad sign for the Americans.

Once the main body of Rangers arrived, the warriors and Rangers started shouting to William's army across the prairie grass. They called for the Americans to give up, telling them that anyone who surrendered would not be harmed. Some volunteers yelled back that they would never surrender to "slaves and Indians." Then, a lone rider appeared on a horse, moving towards the grove carrying a white flag. William saw the red bandana wrapped around the rider's head and realized immediately that it was Simon Girty.[41]

Elliott had sent Girty forward to see if he could convince William to surrender his forces. Girty advanced slowly across a space of about 150 yards until he was close enough to be heard by the Americans. He called out loudly, telling Crawford that Captain Elliott was willing to parley. Hearing no reply and not knowing exactly where William might be in the trees, he turned in different directions, shouting the same message each time. William watched Girty in silence. He pondered whether to ride out and meet with him, but in the end he decided not to reply to the request of his old comrade. After hearing nothing but silence, Girty finally wheeled his horse about and rode until he was out of sight. One volunteer later claimed that he had drawn a bead on Girty from a position high in the oak trees and began to squeeze the trigger just as Girty passed from his view.[42]

Not long after Girty's gesture requesting surrender, the reason for Elliott's confidence became clear. William's men, who were perched high in the trees spotted more enemy reinforcements in the distance. This time the reserves came from the south in the form of about 150 Shawnee warriors, led by a war chief carrying a large red banner. The Shawnee fell into line next to the Delaware, completing the encirclement of the American position. The only gaps in the Indian line were the road back to Dunquat's abandoned town and the deep cranberry marsh to the southwest. As they arrived, the Shawnee shot several volleys into the grove and then raised their muskets skyward. They fired their guns into the air in what Rose called a "Feu de joie," literally a "Fire of Joy." This was intended to send William's men the clear message that, with the Shawnee arrival on the field, the Americans had no hope.[43]

William called a final council meeting. He told his officers that they had no recourse except to attempt a getaway. Escape was now the only option.

A Desperate Breakout

William's officers unanimously agreed that "prudence dictated a retreat." The arrival of the British Rangers and the Shawnee, and the fact that enemy reinforcements "kept pouring in hourly" even convinced the combative, insolent Williamson that the Americans were in dire straits. Since only an escape during darkness afforded any chance of success, William directed that preparations begin for a breakout that night.[44]

The plan William devised was simple. Once darkness fell, the army would form in four divisions, with Major McClelland in the lead, Major Brinton in the rear, and the wounded placed at the center of the column. At the last moment, the sentinels would be called in to take their place in line. Then, when William gave the command, the army would gallop out of the grove heading south down the road toward the abandoned Wyandot town, fighting their way through if necessary.[45]

Men began throwing together horse-litters to carry the seven most severely wounded men, since Dr. Knight deemed the remaining thirteen as being able to ride. The dead whose bodies lay within the grove were collected for burial. Once interred, men lit fires over the burial sites to eliminate any sign of a grave for fear the Indians might dig them up and mutilate the corpses.[46]

Not long after sunset, the men mounted their horses and took their assigned positions among the four divisions. The only sounds besides the muffled rattle of gear and the urgent whispers of officers were the occasional musket shots and war cries from the enemy lines. As William mounted his own horse and prepared to call in the outlying sentinels, a group of soldiers led by Captain Hardin decided they stood a better chance on their own. They galloped out of the grove heading south, leaving the rest of the army behind. Exasperated, William ordered that everyone remain in position as he charged after Hardin and his men, but it was too late. Within minutes, Indian sentries had detected Hardin's men riding towards them in the darkness and had fired warning shots, alerting the entire encircling force.[47]

William turned around and dashed back into the grove. The enemy warning shots and war cries filled the night air, and panic ran rampant through the assembled volunteers. Groups of men galloped out of hiding and into the night, lashing their horses in a desperate race for survival. Many rode behind their panicked officers crashing down the road towards Dunquat's abandoned town. Major McClelland, who had given his horse to a wounded soldier, tried to restore order, but his men rode right over him. Though badly injured, McClelland survived the trampling only to be later captured and tortured to death. As the mob fled Battle Island, Colonel Williamson led the largest group of deserters, proving that he was both a scoundrel and a coward.

The fleeing volunteers abandoned not only their commanding

officer, but also left behind the badly wounded and the sentinels, some of whom were unaware of the army's sudden flight. William, Dr. Knight, and a few others who had not run away helped the wounded mount some horses. One of the severely wounded, Captain Ezekiel Rose, believed his wound was fatal and refused to mount up until he had recited the Lord's Prayer. In shock, he kept making mistakes and starting over despite the fact that his comrades were pleading with him to get on his horse. Finally, Major Daniel Leet grabbed his friend and unceremoniously shoved him up into the arms of another soldier who waited in the saddle to ride with him. Despite these heroic efforts, at least two of the wounded were accidently left behind in the dark. Soon they would be discovered and scalped.[48]

As for the sentinels, some heard the clatter resulting from the army's disorganized retreat, found their horses, and made their own way to safety. Others were not so lucky. In their exhausted state, some sentinels had fallen asleep, only to be found by warriors the next morning and killed on the spot. At least two managed to escape the battlefield on foot but were found weeks later by warriors, lying dead behind a log, having starved to death.[49]

Chaos gripped those left behind in the grove, and the rest of the army careened south down the road toward the small gap between the camps of the Delaware and Shawnee warriors. Having heard the warning shots, warriors ran into the road to block the Americans' escape route. As the first group of volunteers galloped down on them, the warriors opened fire. The Americans following immediately behind saw the flashes of rifle fire up ahead and veered off the road to the southwest towards the edge of the cranberry marsh. Struggling to find their way in the dark, a few managed to get around the bog. They dismounted and made their way on foot when the thickets of brush tangled their horses so badly they could not proceed. Others were not so fortunate. These men rode directly into the marsh, where both they and their horses became hopelessly mired. Before long, the shadowy figures of Shawnee warriors emerged out of the night to club them down with tomahawks and take their scalps.

The rear guard division under Major Brinton came under fire almost as soon as it rode out of the grove, but Brinton, now wounded, swayed in his saddle. Major Leet assumed command, ordering the riders to wheel to the west, away from the worst gunfire. The forty men rode straight through the enemy's lines unscathed and took an alternate trail homeward, eventually arriving safely. William's son, John, was among them. For the rest, the night soon became a dark whirlwind of individual nightmares.

John Slover was busy feeding several horses when the army began its mad retreat. He quickly mounted his own horse and tried in vain to catch up with the groups thundering down the road. Unfortunately, Slover chose to follow those who plunged into the cranberry marsh. Within minutes his horse was completely bogged down. He dismounted and made his way across the morass, where he came upon six other men who had also lost their horses in the mire. Slover led them on a path intended to double back on the Indians by heading north towards Lake Erie and the Shawnee towns.

Three days later, as Slover and the others turned and made their way towards the Muskingum, they encountered several groups of warriors. The warriors killed two of the Americans outright in the ensuing fight. Two escaped to safety, but Slover and two others were captured. Taken to a large Shawnee town, Slover's two companions were beaten to death, their bodies dumped with those of other recently executed volunteers, including William's son-in-law, William Harrison. The Shawnee held Slover in the town for several weeks until they decided to burn him at the stake. On the day appointed for his execution, a thunderstorm arrived as the Shawnee lit the wood, dousing the fire. Slover was untied and the Shawnee said they would burn him the next day. That night as his Shawnee guards slept, Slover slipped out of his lodge, stole a horse, and rode away, reaching safety a few days later.[50]

Mike Myers also ended up in the muck of the cranberry marsh. As he approached it on foot, a group of warriors surrounded him. They closed in, and he began swinging his rifle at them, clubbing several before one got close enough to smash his hand with a tomahawk blow, dislocating his thumb. An arrow struck him in the leg just as the attackers grabbed him, their combined weight forcing him to his knees. Still, Myers managed to fight off the warriors, jerk the arrow out of his leg, and outrace his pursuers to the marsh. He struggled through the slime and past floating logs, wading through swamp water up to his armpits and escaping to safety.[51]

As for the larger groups of volunteers, one party of approximately fifty men led by Major Rose galloped into the dark. In the confusion, Rose escorted these men west, instead of south, but when the moon rose they discovered that they were headed in the wrong direction. "Unmindful that the Shawnee path did take off at the same place," Rose later wrote in his journal, "we fell upon it and followed it for near 2 miles." Rose added that he was "deceived by the trails on each side" until the moon rose, allowing him to see his error. At that point, Rose and his fifty men found the correct trail, about three miles from Dunquat's abandoned town. Once they arrived at the Wyandot village, Colonel Williamson and his group of about 250 volunteers joined them.[52]

Williamson now took command and led the ragged survivors down the trail towards the spring where they had camped two days before. The men moved as fast as the condition of the wounded would allow, knowing a pursuit would surely overtake them at some point. Williamson and Rose hoped to reach the woods before any of the enemy could catch them; fighting in the open plain would make any effective defense difficult. Soon, sniper fire erupted from each small stand of trees as the column became more strung out, quickly cutting down those who straggled too far behind.

By noon, groups of mounted Rangers began attacking the head of the column. In one attack, Rose was able to outrace his pursuers. The warriors, however, tomahawked and scalped a volunteer, an "unfortunate boy" named John Hayes, and ripped half of the scalp from his head.[53]

About a mile from the protective cover of the woods, Williamson called for a halt to water the horses. Rose tried in vain to make him understand this was unwise, but Williamson insisted on stopping. Thirsty men and horses, desperate for relief, rushed towards the water. The volunteers began drinking, and a force of mounted Rangers and Indians immediately appeared on the horizon. Seeing their advantage, the pursuers pressed an attack on the Americans' rear. The advance American guard quickly mounted and galloped into the woods, trying to clear it of any potential foes. Meanwhile, the rear guard engaged the enemy, while confused volunteers in the middle milled about the spring, unsure of

This monument standing in the Ohio countryside commemorates the Battle of Olentangy, which occurred within few miles of the spot. (*Author photo*)

what to do. In what became known as the Battle of Olentangy, the rear guard battled with the Rangers and Indian warriors at close range for nearly an hour, eventually driving the enemy away.[54]

After the men under Williamson's command reached the woods, some rode off, deserting their comrades. Others became lost in the dense forest. The Indians hunted down and killed many of them, but a few would manage to straggle into Mingo Bottom or Fort McIntosh several days later. The army pressed on, and rain began to fall in torrents. At first, the rain brought great relief to men who had been suffering from extreme heat for several days, but when the army finally made camp around 6:00 p.m., many shivered in their cold, wet clothing and the wounded suffered badly. The rain stopped, and Williamson and Rose thought it was safe to light large fires, giving the wounded some comfort. Williamson planned only a short rest, hoping to march on around 1:00 a.m., but the night proved so dark that he and Rose realized they would never find their way. They decided to let the men rest until dawn the next morning.[55]

The following day, the army struggled eastward with little order, strung out for miles. Luckily, after the battle at the edge of the woods, their pursuers lost any desire to persist in their attacks. The Americans marched, and small groups of stragglers appeared, joining the main body. The largest of these consisted of the forty men under Daniel Leet, a group which included John Crawford. As the army crossed the Muskingum on June 10, Rose took count and roughly estimated that 380 men had come through alive. Finally, at noon on June 13, they arrived at Mingo Bottom after an expedition of seventeen harrowing days.[56]

The next day, Major Rose composed a letter to General Irvine in which he summarized the events of the campaign. His journal reflected an estimated loss of between forty and fifty killed and missing, with another twenty-eight wounded, but Rose officially reported the loss of no more than thirty killed and missing, none of which correlated with his count of 380 survivors on June 10. His account ended with a telling sentence: "Colonel Crawford has not been heard of since the night of the 5th instant, and I fear is among the killed."[57]

Where was William Crawford?

Chapter 11

TRIAL AND PUNISHMENT

The morning of June 6, 1782 dawned with another bright blue sky over the prairie surrounding the Sandusky River. This heralded what might otherwise might have been a tranquil late spring day in the Native American towns that dotted the river's shoreline. The brilliant blue sky was smudged by smoke that drifted lazily upward from the remains of the fires that ringed Battle Island. It was also filled with large flocks of crows and buzzards who circled ominously above the prairie. The scars from hundreds of musket balls marked the trees on the small island of green and the trees' dark shade covered the carcasses of dead horses, already swelling and bursting from the rising heat. Most telling, however, was the blood from horses and men that streaked the prairie grass.

The landscape in and around the trees was littered with cast off supplies and equipment. Wyandot villagers from the nearby towns, as well as the Delaware and Shawnee warriors, scavenged the area for whatever they might find useful. This included wandering horses and the refuse of the American volunteers, an abundance of blankets, bundles of rope, halters, cooking utensils, saddles, and knapsacks. As the Indians searched, the circling birds feasted on the bodies of the American sentinels who had been left behind and killed when their army retreated. Once the birds had had their fill, the Native Americans would drag the dismembered body parts back to their villages for public display. A sacrificial burning of the bodies intended to appease the angry spirits of their own dead warriors typically followed.

British officers reported their decisive victory to Major DePeyster at Fort Detroit. Lieutenant John Turney of Butler's Rangers praised the efforts of both his own men and the warriors of their Indian allies, noting, "No people could behave better." He officially reported the loss of one Ranger killed with two others wounded. He also documented the death of the French interpreter, Le Villier, along with four warriors dead and eight more wounded. As for the invaders, Turney stated there were one hundred Americans dead, a number he was certain was accurate.[1]

On that same morning, Simon Girty's colleague, Alexander McKee, conveyed similar numbers to DePeyster but added that warriors were still bringing in scalps. He also stated that the Indians continued to pursue the enemy and bring in American prisoners.[2]

One of those prisoners would be William Crawford.

Escape

As the army dashed off into the night in panic, William had mounted his horse and rode after his fleeing volunteers. He only rode about a quarter of a mile before he found part of the disorganized, panicked mob that had once been his command. The fighting up the road had brought the men to a complete halt, but the welfare of William's family members now became his primary concern. He rode up and down the line of men trying to escape the enemy, desperately calling for his son, John, his son-in-law, William Harrison, and his nephew, William. No reply came, and when Dr. Knight arrived William was in an anxious state. The surgeon shouted to William that he believed they had gone ahead with other groups.

"Is that Dr. Knight I hear?" William replied. Knight rode up beside him, and William turned to the doctor telling him that he feared his son and the others were not in front. Crawford begged Knight to stay with him. He believed his horse would not last long and "wished some of his best friends remain with him." William then cursed Williamson and the other volunteers for violating his orders by running off and abandoning the wounded. Finally, the frightened pack of volunteers began to move. As they passed, William saw no sign of his family and he realized it was time for him and the doctor to make their own exit. They turned to leave, and two more volunteers, an old man and a young lad, joined William and the doctor as they fled the battlefield.[3]

TRIAL AND PUNISHMENT

The four men headed north in the darkness, trying to avoid the fighting on the road to the southwest. Once they had gone about two miles, they turned east. William and the others rode single file, being careful to stay no more than fifteen to twenty yards apart in the darkness. To keep their course eastward, they tracked the North Star off their left shoulder. After a while, the old man began lagging behind and repeatedly called out for them to slow down and allow him to catch up. As they neared the Sandusky, he called out very loudly, causing both William and the doctor to scold him for making so much noise. Moments later, they heard the bone chilling sound of an Indian war cry about 150 yards behind them. They did not hear or see the old man again.[4]

About dawn on June 6, William's horse gave out, as did the one carrying the young volunteer. Leaving the horses behind, the two men marched east on foot, with only Dr. Knight still on horseback. Around 2:00 p.m., they saw a small party approaching and prepared for the worst. They crouched in the tall grass with their weapons cocked for a fight. The gang of men drew closer, and they could see that it was another group from the army, consisting of two enlisted volunteers with Ensign Ashby and Captain Biggs. Biggs held on to Ashby, who was badly wounded and pale from loss of blood. William conferred briefly with Biggs about their situation and the group continued moving eastward. Darkening clouds overtook them from the southwest and around 4:00 p.m., and it became apparent that heavy rains would soon be closing in. William ordered the men to camp in a nearby glade. They debarked four or five trees to use as fuel and started a small campfire, which they huddled around as they spent a cold, wet night before moving on at dawn on June 7.[5]

The next morning, the group had gone about three miles where they found the remains of a recently killed deer. The animal had been dressed, with the meat lying nearby wrapped up in its skin. The men gathered up the meat, and after walking another mile, they saw the smoke from a small fire in the distance. Leaving the wounded ensign behind with the young soldiers, William, Captain Biggs, and Dr. Knight advanced cautiously towards the smoke. When they reached the spot, they found the fire abandoned, but from belongings left behind they deduced that the fire must have belonged to other volunteers.

William called for Ashby and the young soldiers to join them. As they started roasting the venison, they saw another young volunteer moving slowly towards them from a small grove of trees. William waved to him and he came up quickly, greatly relieved to see they were not a party of pursuing warriors. The soldier told them that he had killed the deer but had left it to hide in a nearby thicket when he saw them in the distance. After eating, William and his party continued their march east.[6]

Around 2:00 p.m., they reached the road the army had followed during its westward advance and paused to discuss their options. Captain Biggs and Dr. Knight argued against following the same path for fear of an Indian pursuit and suggested they strike off in a different direction. William considered their views, but said he did not believe the Indians would follow them any further than the edge of the plains that they had now passed by several miles. With that, they walked down the road with Ensign Ashby mounted on Captain Biggs' horse, with Biggs astride the doctor's mount. William and Dr. Knight walked one hundred yards in front, with Biggs and Ashby in the center, and the two younger men bringing up the rear.

After traveling two miles farther, three warriors suddenly jumped up from the undergrowth. Dr. Knight recorded the moment later, writing, "…several Indians started up within fifteen or twenty steps of the Colonel and me. As we at first discovered only three, I immediately got behind a large black oak, made ready my piece and raised it up to take sight, when the Colonel called to me twice not to fire, upon that one of the Indians ran up to the Colonel and took him by the hand." Soon, more warriors appeared. Biggs fired at them but missed. The warriors, who were Delaware from Wingenund's town, quickly took William and Dr. Knight as prisoners, while the rest of the American party fled.[7]

The warriors marched their captives to a nearby campsite, where they held them into the next day. Soon eight other captured soldiers joined them. Delaware warriors delivered six of the new prisoners, and a small party of Chippewa brought Michael Walters and Christopher Coffman. The Chippewa did not allow either Walters or Coffman to speak to their commander Instead they rushed off with their prisoners, in fear that the Delaware would try to take their captives, thus denying the Chippewa the ransom they hoped to get for the two Americans from the British. That evening, five more Delaware warriors arrived, bringing Biggs' and Ashby's scalps. William asked about the fate of the two young soldiers and the warriors told him they had gotten away.[8]

Girty and the Trial

Early the next morning, the Delaware roughly kicked and shook their captives awake before beginning a forced march back to the Sandusky. Along the way, the warriors repeatedly beat them, especially William, who they identified as the "big captain" of the American army. When the warriors sent runners ahead with the momentous news of his capture, Crawford asked them to relay a request that he be allowed to speak with Simon Girty. William realized that his old comrade might be his and his mens' only hope for survival. As the day steadily wore on, they trudged back to the west, with the runners sprinting ahead. Soon, the word of the big captain's capture began to spread throughout the Sandusky towns.

When the news reached Dunquat's new village on the lower Sandusky, the chief told Simon Girty that the captured American officer wished to see him. Most of the prisoners were headed for Dunquat's abandoned town, but not William. The runners told Girty that Hopocan insisted Girty meet with the captive at the home of Alex McCormick, a British trader. Hopocan feared that, if he brought the American to Dunquat's village, the more powerful Wyandot would deliver him to the British for ransom. The Delaware chief also had the runners tell Girty that he intended to put the captive officer on trial and burn him. This led Girty to mistakenly believe that the Delaware had captured David Williamson.[9]

Girty immediately rode off to meet with the prisoner, relishing the thought of seeing the much-despised Williamson in captivity. He reached McCormick's house just after nightfall and was led to the room where the American waited. In the dim light Girty saw Elizabeth Turner, a twenty-year-old white, adopted captive of the Wyandot, and a young Christian Delaware named Tom Jelloway. Nodding to them, Girty turned to the captured officer nearby, whose head was drooping with exhaustion.

As Girty stood over him, the man raised his head. To his shock, Girty immediately recognized the bruised, dirty, and bloodied countenance of his old friend William Crawford.

William's face was drawn from the effects of fatigue, fear, and desperation. Girty took a deep breath and told William that his situation was grave. From what Girty could gather, Hopocan blamed William for the massacre at Gnadenhutten. Crawford was dumbstruck. This was utterly unexpected. He told Girty that he had nothing to do with Gnadenhutten, that Williamson bore the entire responsibility for the massacre, and that he would never have committed such an atrocity. Girty nodded in agreement. William begged him to intercede on his behalf and convince the Delaware chief of his innocence. William added that, if Girty could get him to Fort Detroit for ransom to the British, he would agree to divulge some military matters of intelligence value to DePeyster, but only if Girty could guarantee his freedom.[10]

Girty promised to do all he could to save him, but told him a ransom might be difficult under these circumstances. Hopocan saw this as a classic blood feud issue and emotions were running very high. Girty offered an alternative—one he said was William's best chance: escape.[11]

Girty told him that only one warrior would be guarding him that night and he was almost certain to fall asleep at some point. When that happened, William could slip out undetected and make his way to the corral. Girty's black slave, Sam Wells, would be waiting with his horse, saddled and ready to go. The road to Fort Detroit was only four miles away to the west of McCormick's house. Wells would guide William to the road and then follow him to make sure William escaped. Once William was safely on the road, Wells would return. Girty told William that he would be safe as soon as he arrived at the fort and surrendered himself to the British.[12]

William listened without replying, appearing "disheartened and with no pluck to make the effort." Looking him in the eye, Girty said, "This, my friend, is all I can do for you. You can easily get away if you will. If not, tomorrow must seal your fate." William finally shook his head and told Girty he did not have the strength to make such an escape. Apparently, the days of marching, the beatings, and a lack of food and water had worn down both William's body and spirit. With that, Girty promised to act as William's interpreter and argue his defense when Hopocan convened a council meeting to determine William's fate. As Girty left, the Delaware guard returned to watch William for the night.[13]

On the morning of June 10, Hopocan arrived at the abandoned Wyandot town where William's fellow prisoners were being held. He painted the faces of all the American prisoners black, the traditional symbol placed on all those facing the stake. An hour later, a group of Delaware warriors arrived, bringing William with them, after marching over from McCormick's house. As soon as Hopocan saw him, he painted William's face black as well. Now reunited with the colonel, Dr. Knight asked him if he had seen Girty, and Crawford replied that he had. He explained the reasons for the Delaware's anger and that Girty promised to do all he could to help them. The Delaware then marched the group out of the town, heading north toward Hopocan's village.[14]

Led by warriors escorting nine other prisoners, William and Dr. Knight followed at a distance with Hopocan just in front of them and William's old friend, Wingenund, following behind. William stole glances at Wingenund, but the Delaware chief gave no sign that he recognized him. Crawford secretly hoped that if all else failed the Delaware chief might find a way to save him. After they had marched a few miles, William and Knight saw the body of one of the other nine prisoners lying by the path, tomahawked and scalped. A half-mile further on, they passed another body, followed soon by two more. When they were a half-mile from Hopocan's town, they saw the remaining five prisoners sitting on the ground near the path. There, Knight was given to a Shawnee warrior and told he would be taken to one of their towns. Before being led onward, they witnessed the brutal execution of the other five prisoners, who were hacked to death and scalped by an angry mob of Delaware women and boys.[15]

As William and the doctor were led closer to Hopocan's town, they saw that a gauntlet had been assembled for them. This tradition was often used as a means for captives to demonstrate their bravery before being adopted into the tribe. In this instance, however, it was an opportunity for the villagers to vent their anger and grief. William and the doctor staggered between the two parallel lines of men, women, and children who lashed out at them, beating them about the head and shoulders with sticks, fists, and even lighted torches. Their guards met them at the end of the gauntlet and led them away, William to one lodge and Knight, with his Shawnee guard, to another.[16]

Meanwhile, Simon Girty arrived in the village. Before leaving McCormick's house, he had sent an urgent message to Matthew Elliott, requesting assistance in freeing William from the Delaware. Upon receiving the dispatch, Elliot relayed messages to Alexander McKee, as well as nearby British traders, hoping they could help in gathering trade goods and gold with which to ransom William.[17]

The day wore on, and increasing numbers of Delaware villagers arrived at Hopocan's town, all anxious to see what fate would befall the Americans' big captain. As darkness fell, the guards led William to the lodge where the council would hear his story and pass judgment. Jeers erupted from the crowd as they watched him walk past, with men and women shouting angry obscenities in the Lenape language. Once inside the council chamber, William saw Hopocan sitting at one end of the room, with his council of chiefs on either side, Wingenund among them. In the center of the room a fire burned brightly, casting long shadows on the walls, its smoke rising in wisps through a hole cut in the council house roof. Opposite the council, Girty waited in expectation. The guards led William to Girty's side and forced him to sit.

Led by Hopocan, the chiefs began the trial just as Girty had predicted, by accusing William of being responsible for the massacre at Gnadenhutten. One after another, they hurled accusations at him, lamenting the horrific cruelties inflicted on their Christian brothers and sisters. Then William's old friend, Wingenund, rose to speak and William hoped he might now hear some words spoken in his defense. Instead, Wingenund eloquently described the Delaware's deep anger:

> These Indians however believed all that their teachers told them, of what was written in the book, and believing it, strove to act accordingly! It was on account of the great book you have, that these Indians trusted so much to what you told them! We knew

you better than they did! We often warned them to beware of you, and your pretended friendship; but they would not believe us!—they believed nothing but good of you, and for this they paid with their lives![18]

They gave William an opportunity to respond, with Girty acting as his interpreter. Clearly stung by Wingenund's remarks, William told the council that he was not present at Gnadenhutten and that he would never have allowed those events to occur had he been there. William added that he had been appointed to command the recent expedition to make certain that no such atrocities were committed against the Delaware, and that he had acted with honor throughout the campaign.

Hopocan remained unconvinced. He angrily retorted that, if this were true, why did William allow David Williamson and those who had done the killing at Gnadenhutten to be part of his army? Furthermore, if William was determined to prevent another massacre, what about the threatening messages the scouts had discovered at Mingo Bottom that said no Indians would escape them—not man, woman, or child? As far as the Delaware chief was concerned, it quickly became obvious that William's protestations of innocence and good intentions rang hollow.

In response, William said that, as proof of his good intentions toward the Delaware, he had "very much favored the Indians at the Salk Licks of the Mahoning [during the Squaw Campaign]." Some on the council had listened intently to his defense, but with this reference to his conduct during the Squaw Campaign, William had committed a huge error.[19]

Hopocan motioned an elderly woman to step forward from the shadows, and William peered toward her as she walked across the council chamber. As she entered the light of the fire, he immediately recognized her—it was Michikapeche, Hopocan's sister-in-law. Holding up the hand that was missing a finger as a result of rifle fire from William's militiamen, she told the council in an angry, anguished voice that the accused had led the troops who killed her husband, Hopocan's brother, as well as Hopocan's mother.

William begged her to remember that he was the man who had saved her, who had stopped the other white soldiers from killing her, and who had made sure she returned to her people in safety. Michikapeche made no reply. She wanted her revenge for the murder of her family members, and she would have it. William turned to Girty, hoping his friend would confirm his story. Girty, of course, had been a witness to the events William described, but it was clear neither Girty nor Michikapeche had told the Delaware that Girty was there that day. If Girty revealed that fact now, he would likely join William at the stake. Girty said nothing.

Michikapeche finished her testimony, and Hopocan ordered that William be condemned to death by fire. With the council nodding their agreement, Girty leaped to William's defense, offering to pay any price required in ransom. He offered his horse, saddle, rifle, and a supply of liquor. Hopocan waved him away, and Girty fell to his knees promising gold in addition to the other valuables offered. Hopocan replied that William was the commander of the white soldiers and that he must suffer; someone, he added, must pay for what happened at Gnadenhutten. Had William been a common soldier, Hopocan continued, it would be different, and he would gladly accept Girty's offer of ransom. That was not the case, and William must suffer his fate.[20]

With the trial over and Girty's ransom offer rejected, the guards dragged William back to his lodge where he would spend a long, sleepless night awaiting his execution.

Execution

June 11, 1782 was another bright, late spring day. It was destined to be William Crawford's last. He spent the morning thinking those private thoughts that must come to every condemned man in the final hours of his life. Hoping to make one final appeal for his life, William asked his guards to summon Wingenund to the lodge. Shortly before noon, the Delaware chief arrived. He entered the darkened lodge and stood silently opposite William, exhibiting all the firmness and dignity of the renowned diplomat and warrior that he was. Years later, Wingenund described his conversation with William Crawford in detail to John Heckewelder, a United Brethren missionary. After a few moments, William said, "Do you

TRIAL AND PUNISHMENT

recollect me, Wingenund?" The chief replied that he did, and a moment of difficult silence followed. William spoke again, saying, "I am glad to see you." The chief's only response was, "Yes, indeed."[21]

William continued, trying to tap into their previous years of friendship. "Do you recollect the friendship that always existed between us," he asked, "and that we were always glad to see each other?" Wingenund replied, saying, "I recollect all this. I remember that we have drunk many a bowl of punch together. I remember also other acts of kindness that you have done me."[22]

William said he hoped that same friendship still existed between them, but Wingenund told him that could not be the case any longer. "It would, of course, be the same," he said, "were you in your proper place and not here." William asked him why things were different now and put forth the hope that his old friend would support him at this critical moment.[23]

At this, Wingenund looked sharply at William. "Colonel Crawford," he said, "you have placed yourself in a situation which puts it out of my power and that of others of your friends to do anything for you." Astonished by this statement, William asked why that was so. The old chief responded by pointing out that it was Crawford's association with David Williamson that made it impossible to help him. Wingenund forcefully described Williamson as a man "...who, but the other day, murdered such a number of the Moravian Indians, knowing them to be friends, knowing that he ran no risk in murdering a people who would not fight, and whose only business was praying!"[24]

William again professed his innocence saying, "Wingenund, I assure you, that had I been with him at the time, this would not have happened; not I alone but all your friends and all good men, wherever they are, reprobate acts of this kind." Wingenund acknowledged that, while that might be the truth, the Delaware seemed to see Crawford's expedition as one intended by Williamson and his friends to "kill the remainder of those inoffensive, yet foolish Moravian Indians." He continued saying that he considered them foolish because they chose to believe the Americans rather than their own kinsmen.[25]

Hearing this, William reminded Wingenund that he had been sent specifically for the purpose of preventing another atrocity. The chief responded, saying that his people would not believe this, even if it were he who told them so. William stared at his friend and then asked why they would not believe it. Wingenund replied that no one would believe William had the power to stop Williamson. At this, William reminded Wingenund that none of the Christian Delaware had been harmed during the campaign, which Wingenund acknowledged was true.[26]

But then the elderly chieftain added what was a damning fact as far as Hopocan and the other Delaware chiefs were concerned—the American army's path through Gnadenhutten on their way to the Sandusky. In their minds, the route William had taken meant that the Christian Delaware villages on the Tuscarawas were the real objective of the American army. They believed that once the Americans found the villages empty, only then did they continue to the Sandusky.[27]

This news stunned William. If the Delaware chiefs believed William's army intended to slaughter more of the Christian Delaware, he could see that no defense was going to convince them of his innocence. Pleadingly, he looked at Wingenund and asked, "What do they intend to do with me? Can you tell me?"[28]

William's old friend told him with sadness that, since "Williamson and his whole cowardly host ran off in the night," the Delaware were determined to take their revenge on William instead. William then pleaded with Wingenund, asking if there was any way the chief could save him. Wingenund shook his head sadly, saying "Had Williamson been taken with you, I and some friends, by making use of what you have told me, might perhaps, have succeeded to save you." He added that the "King of England himself, were he to come to this spot, with all his wealth and treasures," he could not change William's fate. William sank at this news, saying, "Then it seems my fate is decided, and I must prepare to meet death in its worst form."[29]

The two men tearfully embraced and the Delaware whispered, "Yes, Colonel, I am sorry for it; but cannot do anything for you. Had you attended to the Indian principle, that as good and evil cannot dwell together in the same heart, so a good man ought not to go into evil company; you would not be in this lamentable situation. You see now, when it is too late, after Williamson has deserted you, what a bad man he must be. Nothing now remains for you but to meet your fate like a brave man. Farewell, Colonel Crawford." Wingenund left the lodge and went to be alone in the woods, unable to watch the coming execution.[30]

As he left, William's guards entered the lodge, grabbed him by the arms, and began the long walk toward a grove of nearby oak trees where the Delaware held their rituals. Behind William walked Dr. Knight, under escort by his own Shawnee guard, apparently coming to serve as a witness.[31]

As he approached the grove next to Tymochtee Creek, William could see a large crowd gathered around a fifteen-foot-high post. The crowd included men, women, and children. Elizabeth Turner was there, along with several other white captives, all of whom had been ordered to attend. Finally, William spotted his friend and defender at the trial, Simon Girty. A pile of small hickory poles was stacked about seven feet away from the tall post. These poles were burnt almost through in the middle, with the remaining ends of each about six feet long. Lighting the fire at a distance from the post prolonged the condemned person's agony. This also allowed Delaware observers to come forward and add their own brutality to the process. In the Delaware belief system, this was the only way to appease the grief and anger of those who had lost relatives in the fighting against the whites.[32]

The guards ripped off William's clothes, leaving him naked, and forced him to sit by the edge of the fire pit. Knight sat nearby, but the two men were not allowed to speak. Next, individual Delaware walked up and struck each man with sticks and their fists. Finally, the guards pulled William to his feet and tied his hands behind him with rope. As they led him to the post, the guards added another length of rope that ran from his wrists to the base of the post. This final rope was long enough to allow William to walk around the post once or twice in either direction.[33]

William turned to Girty and called out, asking him if they truly intended to burn him. Girty replied with a simple but agonized, "Yes."

William nodded silently, and then said quietly, "I shall take it all patiently."

Then the torture began.

First, seventy warriors walked up to William, one after another and discharged a rifle loaded only with black powder onto William's body at

Artist Frank Halbedel's painting of William Crawford's execution.
(*Wyandot County Historical Society*)

close range, burning his skin, and leaving bloody blackened wounds. In agony, William began to pray in a low voice, and one warrior remembered this later saying, "...talked much God and all the time looking up."[34]

As a warrior lit the fire, Girty turned to Hopocan once more and bargained desperately for a ransom. This time, Girty offered "£300 in gold, 3 negroes, wampum," and all his other property, including his horse, saddle, and rifle. Again, Hopocan rejected the offer. The chief told Girty that, if he valued his friend's life so highly, then he could take his place at the stake. Only then, would he release William. Girty's response was a horrified silence.[35]

Hopocan stepped into the pit and approached William. Reaching into his belt, the chief pulled out a dull knife. William screamed, as Hopocan severed both his ears until they hung from the sides of his head. Hopocan turned and walked away as blood streamed down William's neck and onto his shoulders. William raised his head and looked at Girty; he begged his friend to shoot him. Girty replied that "he dared not" as it was custom that no one could interfere with a prisoner condemned to death, without being shot down on the spot for attempting to resist the nation's decision.[36]

Monument near the spot where William Crawford was executed by the Delaware. (*Author photo*)

As the fire grew in intensity, villagers began to approach William one after another. Some grabbed burning sticks and poked him with them, steadily adding more and more burns to his body. A few of the women advanced carrying broad boards which they used to scoop up burning coals and embers before throwing them on William's pain-wracked body. Soon, the post was surrounded by hot coals and ashes, leaving William no choice but to stand on them as they scorched his bare feet.[37]

About this time, the British traders summoned by Matthew Elliott and Alexander McKee arrived, but they saw it was too late to intervene on William's behalf. Elizabeth Turner, standing next to Girty, saw tears streaming down his cheeks. Girty could not stand to watch his friend's agony any longer. He turned, mounted his white horse, and rode away.[38]

William's torture lasted for two more long hours, during which he said nothing, only uttering low moans. Finally, he fell to his knees. Sensing the end was near, an apostate Christian Delaware named Joseph jumped into the pit and ripped William's scalp away with his knife. With William's face covered in blood and his body covered with ghastly burns, an old woman forced him to stand and made him walk around the post once more. William staggered around the stake like a man who no longer saw, heard, or felt anything. Coming to stop after one turn around the post, he stood erect for a moment and then pitched face down in the coals and ashes. William Crawford was dead.[39]

As the sun began to set, the crowd drifted away, and a small group Delaware warriors threw what was left of the mortal remains of William Crawford into the fire.

Chapter 12

LEGACIES

On June 16, 1782, General Irvine wrote a brief dispatch to Washington informing him about the failed expedition to the Sandusky, attaching a copy of both Colonel Williamson's and Major Rose's reports. Irvine made no mention of William's status in his letter, but in Major Rose's report the commander in chief read a line that said, "Col. Crawford has not been heard off since the night of the 5th instant; and I fear is among the killed." Deeply saddened by the news regarding his former friend and business partner, Washington replied on July 10: "I cannot but regret the misfortune & more especially for the loss of Colo. Crawford, for whom I had a very great regard."[1]

A few weeks later, on July 4, Dr. Knight was found alive. The surgeon had escaped from his Shawnee guard and then survived an arduous journey back across the Ohio Country on foot. He told Irvine and the rest of the Western Department staff about William's fate. Soon, the story was spread across the American frontier. Irvine wrote to Washington again to confirm William's excruciating torture, execution, and death. He said that the story "has struck the people of this country with a strange mixture of fear and resentment, their solicitations for making another excursion are increasing daily." Upon hearing the details of what had happened to William, Washington replied in his typically understated manner that he was "particularly affected with the disastrous fate of Colo. Crawford." Washington astutely added that he understood why William had met his death as he did, given the Indians' "present exasperation…for the treatment given their Moravian friends."[2]

As Irvine indicated, the public reaction was predictable: news of William's death spawned calls for a new expedition to revenge Williams' fate. On July 23, the *Pennsylvania Journal and Weekly Advertiser* boldly declared, "The militia are greatly enraged and determined on having ample satisfaction." The *Pennsylvania Packet*, referring to William's death as a "barbarous murder," printed dire warnings of massacres to come. They warned, "This and other similar acts of barbarity the Indians said they did in revenge for the murders and robberies committed by our frontier inhabitants on their relations, the Moravians, and that in future they would spare none of our people."[3]

News of William's death also reverberated throughout the British military in Canada. General Frederick Haldimand, the Royal Governor of Quebec and Major DePeyster's superior, reprimanded his officers at Fort Detroit, believing they could have done more to prevent the execution. The general also reported the affair to Sir Guy Carleton, Governor General of British North America, telling him, "This act of cruelty is to be more regretted, as it awakens in the Indians that barbarity to prisoners which the unwearied efforts of His Majesty's ministers had totally extinguished." DePeyster wrote Haldimand, telling the general that he met with the Delaware and made them understand His Majesty's government's "utter abhorrence of such proceedings." DePeyster also sent messages out to all the towns on the Sandusky insisting such acts stop and threatening to withdraw British support if they did not.[4]

There would be no more American expeditions against the villages on the Sandusky. Moreover, with the news of the signing of the Treaty of Paris in 1783, official British military support for the Native Americans ended. The tribes along the Sandusky did continue to struggle against American expansion into the Ohio Country, and the British quietly encouraged their raids, but they no longer provided any direct military assistance.

The new American government began negotiating a series of treaties with the woodland nations. The Indians first surrendered Kentucky in the vain hope that the Americans would allow them to continue to live in the Ohio Country. Sadly, the United States began a policy pattern that would continue into the late nineteenth century: they would promise much, but repudiate their promises, later insisting on negotiating a new treaty. As one broken treaty followed another, the Native Americans were always required to relinquish more of their land. All the while, their warriors maintained a steady pattern of small raids up and down the American frontier, burning farms and taking captives for adoption. Finally, the struggle ended with the American victory at the Battle of Fallen Timbers in 1794. Following their defeat, representatives of twelve woodland nations met with General Anthony Wayne to sign the Treaty of Greenville. As the nineteenth century began, each of the woodland nations were steadily forced to move further west; the Wyandot were the last to go in 1843.

As for William's execution, Simon Girty's daughter later said her father maintained that many Native Americans spoke openly of William's courage, and "regretted they had burned so brave a warrior."[5]

George Washington

Following the Treaty of Paris, Washington retired from public life, returning to the role of a planter at his beloved Mount Vernon. However, turmoil in the new nation over the Articles of Confederation forced him to end his retirement. In 1787, he served as the president of the Constitutional Convention in Philadelphia. His tireless efforts resulted in both the creation of the new Constitution as well as its eventual ratification by the states. Washington hoped to retire once more, but he was elected to serve as the nation's first president in 1789, and he remained in office for a second term until 1797. He would at last return to Mount Vernon, before dying on December 14, 1799.

In the years following the American Revolution, Washington had continued to manage the lands he and William marked along the Ohio in 1770, as well as those that William surveyed in Pennsylvania in the years before the war. This proved to be a daunting task. In 1775, a clerk in Williamsburg alleged that William did not swear to the required oaths of office as a surveyor, causing Lord Dunmore to disallow all William's surveys just before the Royal Governor fled the country. It was not until the middle of the war that the Virginia House of Delegates voted to validate William's original surveys, and the final American victory at Yorktown sealed their validation once and for all. In the years that followed, squatters, as well as some who continued to challenge William's commission and rights as a surveyor, plagued Washington with a series of lawsuits over ownership.

David Williamson

In his report to General Irvine filed after the Sandusky Expedition, Colonel David Williamson appeared humble and gave credit to Irvine's aide, Major Rose, as well as Irvine himself, for authorizing the expedition. "I hope when your honor takes into consideration the distress of the brave men in the present expedition, and the distress of our country in general, you will do us the favor to call the officers together, as our dependence is entirely upon you, and we are ready and willing to obey your commands when called upon." Williamson was not only lobbying for another campaign but was also putting himself forward to be its commander. General Irvine, however, had learned his lesson; he would never sanction a similar operation by militia volunteers. Not surprisingly, while trying to feather his nest with the general, Williamson's only mention of William came as an afterthought in the form of a brief postscript that read, "Colonel Crawford, our commandant, we can give no account of since the night of the retreat."[6]

Williamson was a butcher who massacred almost one hundred innocent Christian Delaware men, women, and children. He followed that heinous act by behaving as a corrosive force during the Sandusky Expedition, eating away at any command cohesion. In the end, he flagrantly disobeyed orders, fleeing like a coward from the battlefield, abandoning his commanding officer as well as badly wounded soldiers in the process. Despite this, Williamson remained very popular in Washington County by carefully grooming and managing his image.

He was first elected as county lieutenant, and later as sheriff in 1787. In spite of this, he was unsuccessful in his business efforts and was eventually reduced to poverty. He died a hopeless alcoholic in 1814, buried in an unmarked grave in the county's "potter's field" cemetery. Perhaps no man was more deserving of such a fate.[7]

LEGACIES

Simon Girty

When Dr. Knight returned to Fort Pitt and told his story, he unknowingly laid the final groundwork for Simon Girty's infamous reputation, one that would last for almost two hundred years. Knight related his story to an unscrupulous lawyer and Indian hater named Hugh H. Brackenridge. Brackenridge heavily edited the doctor's words and told an entirely different tale from what actually occurred at William's trial and execution. In the version Brackenridge published and sold, there was no trial. The published narrative also stated that Girty promised assistance but provided none, and worse, that Girty laughed at William's request for a merciful shooting, urging on the "savage" Delaware in their brutal tortures.

Breckenridge's pamphlet forever cemented Girty's place in American folklore. As a result, Simon Girty became one of the least understood figures in American history. Americans referred to him as the "White Savage" and his service to the British and Indian nations earned not only their hatred, but their fear as well. They saw him as the worst sort of Loyalist, a "renegade" who used his relationship with the Indians to wreak havoc on the frontier. One contemporary referred to him as "a savage in manner and principle, who spent his life in the perpetration of a demonic vengeance against his countrymen."[8]

Girty even inspired tall tales about the horrors he supposedly perpetrated on innocent settlers. These were so awful that parents used them to frighten their children into obedience. A generation of frontier girls and boys were told that, if they were not good, Simon Girty, the "Fiend of the Frontier," a "White Beast in human form," or, simply, "Dirty Girty" would come to snatch them away in the night. Stephen Vincent Benet gave Girty his most noteworthy place in American legend in Benet's famous 1937 short story, "The Devil and Daniel Webster." In that tale, the Devil summons the jury to determine Jabez Stone's fate, and Girty is among the cast of murderers and miscreants assembled to pass judgment. Benet describes Girty as "the renegade, who saw white men burned at the stake and whooped with the Indians to see them burn. His eyes were green, like a catamount's, and the stains on his hunting shirt did not come from the blood of the deer."[9]

237

The real Girty continued his support for the Native Americans he loved and admired, even after the end of the war between Great Britain and the United States. He could no longer render military assistance, but he provided advice and counsel, helping to prepare the tribal chiefs for their treaty conferences with American commissioners. He was also instrumental in negotiating the ransom and release of hundreds of American captives who were then able to return home to their families.[10]

Throughout his remaining years, Girty spoke of William "in the tenderest terms as a particular friend" and maintained that he had done all he could to save him. Former captives, such as Elizabeth Turner, along with members of Girty's family, fought to resurrect his reputation, but no one in the United States would listen. Following the British transfer of Fort Detroit to American authorities, Girty returned to his farm across the river in Canada. He continued to work for the British government as an interpreter, but, in 1811, his sight started to fade and by 1813 he was completely blind. He died in his home on February 18, 1818.[11]

Hopocan

Following the Revolutionary War, Hopocan chose to seek and maintain peace with the new American government. In June 1783, the first official American emissary arrived on the Sandusky and reported that Hopocan greeted him "with every demonstration of joy" and welcomed him "in the most friendly manner," treating him "with greater civility than is usual with them in the time of profound peace." Hopocan then facilitated the emissary's visits with the Wyandot and Shawnee, a role he would continue to play in coming years.[12]

Hopocan joined Wingenund and Dunquat in working with American officials, and he signed three major treaties, the Treaty of Fort McIntosh in 1785, Treaty of Fort Finney in 1786, and the Treaty of Fort Harmer in 1789. But as Americans continued to lie and break every treaty, Hopocan once again took up the hatchet, leading his warriors to victory over the Americans in the battle at Fort Recovery in November 1791.[13]

In the end, the old warrior again urged peace and participated in negotiations with American commissioners in 1793 that would have made the Ohio River the permanent boundary between the whites and Native Americans. Unfortunately, the Shawnee rejected Hopocan's support for the proposal, resulting in war with the Americans in 1794. In July, a month before the final battle at Fallen Timbers, Hopocan died at age seventy in his village near Tymochtee Creek.[14]

Wingenund

In the years that followed the expedition on the Sandusky, Wingenund, like Hopocan, urged his fellow Native Americans to seek peace with the Americans. As for William's death, John Heckewelder said that the chief never spoke of those events "without strong emotions of grief." The missionary was at Fort Detroit when Wingenund met with British authorities for the first time following the execution of his friend. When Wingenund heard several of the British staff conversing nearby and criticizing him for not doing more to save William, he listened calmly, turned to Heckewelder, and said in Lenape, "These men talk like fools." Wingenund then turned to the British and said in English, "If King George himself, if your king had been on the spot with all his ships laden with goods and treasures, he could not have ransomed my friend, nor saved his life from the rage of a justly exasperated multitude."[15]

Although Wingenund, along with Hopocan and Dunquat, signed the major treaties of the 1780s and 1790s with the United States, he joined Hopocan in fighting the Americans at Fort Recovery. Eventually, he seems to have faded into history, with no record of the place and time of his death.

Hannah Crawford

Within a few days of the army's return to Mingo Bottom, John Crawford arrived at Spring Garden. Without doubt, Hannah was joyous that her son was alive, but the news that John carried regarding his father was ominous. At that moment, all he could tell his mother was that William had not rejoined the army during its retreat across the Ohio Country. There was still hope, for William was an experienced frontiersman and could survive a journey home on his own.

Shortly after Dr. Knight arrived at Fort Pitt, General Irvine sent word to Hannah on William's fate. Within a few weeks, she would learn that her daughter, Sarah, had also lost her husband, William Harrison. Sarah would marry a second time, to Uriah Springer, while Hannah remained alone at Spring Garden for the next thirty-five years, in company with her slaves.

In this photo taken in the early twentieth century you can see the remains of the spring house William Crawford built at Spring Garden. (*Library of Congress*)

During those decades, Hannah struggled to keep her beloved farm. During William's retirement from military service, he had only been able to collect a few of the surveyor's fees due to him. As a result, he had only paid off a tiny portion of the debts he had accrued. Facing massive debt and numerous claims against the remaining estate, Hannah wrote Washington in June 1784. She told Washington that, after examining William's accounts, she discovered that the State of Virginia owed

William's estate a sum of £1,100 in Virginia currency. She appealed to Washington to help ensure that this money was paid, pleading, "I am very much harassed by the creditors for debts due by the estate."[16]

Washington helped her secure the funds from Virginia, but the money was not nearly enough to solve Hannah's financial problems. In May 1786, word reached Washington that Hannah would soon to be forced to sell her slaves in order to pay the debt owed to a Mr. James Cleveland. Once the slaves were gone, there would be no way for Hannah to maintain Spring Garden by herself. To avoid this, Washington wrote to his business agent, who also worked for Mr. Cleveland, instructing the agent to pay the debt for Hannah, with some "security" from her to repay him.[17]

Less than year later, Hannah again wrote to Washington. This time, she wanted his support to obtain a pension in William's name from the Commonwealth of Virginia. Hannah promised to use any pension funds "to make you satisfaction for your great kindness" in paying off her debt to James Cleveland. She stipulated that she would have "the bond paid up as soon as I draw the first year's allowance." With Washington's help, Hannah began drawing William's Virginia pension in April 1790 at a rate of £135 per year for five years.[18]

Not long after Hannah received the first pension payment, her son John left Pennsylvania for the new wilderness of Kentucky. This left her on the farm with one old slave named Daniel who would look after her until he passed away. Luckily, her daughter Sarah was still nearby, and Hannah must have taken some delight in helping to raise her grandchildren. Unfortunately, debt continued to plague her.

The Virginia pension funds dried up, but Hannah was able to apply for a new pension from Pennsylvania. The Commonwealth approved her application, and in 1794 she received the first of 25 annual payments of $120. In an effort to gain a little more financial support, Hannah petitioned Congress in November 1804 for permanent relief in the form of a federal pension.[19]

The petition recounted William's history of military service as well as his ultimate fate. It asked that "in view of the fact that the petitioner was aged, infirm, and indigent, that your honorable body will grant such relief and support as in your wisdom, justice, and discretion for the services

and loss of her said husband your petitioner may be justly entitled to."
In December 1804, the petition was referred to the House Committee
of Claims, who rejected Hannah's request in February 1806, apparently
feeling that her Virginia pension was enough to sustain her. Luckily, this
pension provided just enough money to keep Spring Garden, and Hannah
would remain in the small cabin William had built for them until the end
of her life.[20]

Regarding her husband, Hannah had been deprived of a funeral, a
grave, and the final certainty those things provide in the grieving process.
As a result, she mourned for William far longer than anyone should have
to. Eventually, she sought some relief that would provide the closure she
needed so desperately. In 1806, almost twenty-five years after William
failed to come home, Hannah asked her grandson, Billy, to accompany
her on a journey to the Sandusky Plains. Billy agreed, and at the age
of eighty-two Hannah made a difficult journey for someone her age,
traveling over 250 miles from Spring Garden to the site of the Delaware
ceremonial grove along the banks of Tymochtee Creek. Once they reached
the Sandusky, she and Billy met a small group of Wyandot who agreed to
guide them the final miles to the site where the Delaware had executed
her husband. Riding along on her favorite horse, a mare named Jenny, she
finally arrived at the spot next to the creek where William had died. She
dismounted and quietly walked about the site. Even then, the place where
the coals and embers had burned was clearly visible; no grass would grow
there. She knelt down, placed her hand on the ground, and silently prayed
as tears streamed down her cheeks. After a while, she stood, mounted
Jenny, and with Billy following behind her turned towards home.[21]

Hannah Crawford was a woman of great resilience and strength of
inner spirit, like many frontier women of the time. One of her neighbors
recalled the elderly widow coming for a visit in 1807, a year after her
journey to the Sandusky. Hannah rode over on Jenny and when she started
to mount her horse for the return trip to Spring Garden, a neighbor's son
called out for her to wait until he could locate a horse-block. "I don't
want a horse-block, my boy, to mount upon Jenny's back," she replied,
"I'm better than fifty horse-blocks." With that, Hannah walked up to
Jenny's side, placed one hand on the saddle horn with the other on the

mare's back, and slipped firmly into the saddle. "There," Hannah shouted to everyone's laughter, "what do you suppose I want of horse-blocks?" In 1818, Hannah became ill and went to stay at Sarah's home in nearby New Haven. There, one month before she would turn ninety-four years old, Hannah Crawford passed away.[22]

William Crawford

Within months of his death, William Crawford became a figure of legend in the public memory. For the majority of Americans who knew his story, he was a selfless, heroic martyr to the cause of American independence and western expansion. At some point around 1791, a ballad about William titled "A Song, Called Crawford's Defeat by the Indians, On the Fourth Day of June, 1782," was written by an unknown author and published in a broadside by the American Antiquarian Society in Worcester, Massachusetts. Sung to many different tunes, it had no less than twenty-four stanzas that were often adapted and even deleted as people made changes over the years.

> *Come all ye good people wherever you be,*
> *Pray draw near awhile, and listen to me,*
> *A story I'll tell you that happen'd of late,*
> *Concerning brave Crawford's most cruel defeat.*
>
> *A bold-hearted company, as we do hear,*
> *Equip'd themselves, being all volunteers;*
> *Their number was four hundred eighty and nine,*
> *To take the Sandusky towns was their design.*
>
> *In seventeen hundred eighty and two,*
> *The twenty-sixth of May, as I tell unto you,*
> *They cross'd the Ohio, as we understand,*
> *Where brave Colonel Crawford he gave the command.*

DISASTER ON THE SANDUSKY

With courage undaunted away they did steer,
Through the Indian's country without dread or fear;
Where Nicholson Slover and Jonathan Zeans
Conducted them over the Sandusky plains.

There was brave Colonel Crawford, an officer bold,
The fourth day of June did the Indians behold;
On the plains of Sandusky, at three the same day,
Both armies did meet there in battle array.

The Indians on horseback, Girtee gave them command,
On the side of the plains they boldly did stand;
Our men like brave heroes upon them did fire,
Until backwards the Indians were forced to retire.

Our Rifles did rattle and bullets did fly,
Until some of our men on the ground they did lie,
Some being wounded, to the others they said
"Fight on brother-soldiers and be not dismay'd."

There was brave Colonel Williamson, as I understand,
He wanted two hundred men at his command;
If the same had been granted, I make no great doubt,
He soon would have put the proud Indians to rout.

This brave commander like a hero so bold
Behaved himself like David of old;
When with the Philistines as he did war,
He returned home without ever a scar.

Like a hero of old there was brave Major Light,
Who encouraged his men for to stand and to fight,
With courage and conduct his men did command,
Like a Grecian that hero in battle did stand.

LEGACIES

There was brave Major Brinton, the fourth in command;
In the front of the battle he boldly did stand,
With courage and conduct his part did maintain,
Though the bullets like hail in great showers they came.

Oh! as this brave hero was giving command,
The Rifles did rattle on every hand;
He received a ball, but his life did not yield,
He returned with the wounded men out of the field.

There was brave Bigs and Ogle received each a ball,
On the Plains of Sandusky was their lot to fall;
Oh! not them alone, but several men
Had the honour of dying on the Sandusky plain.

There was brave Captain Mun like a hero of old,
Likewise Captain Rase, another as bold,
Receiv'd each a ball, but did not expire,
But into the camps they were forc'd to retire.

There was brave Captain Hogland I will not go past,
He fought it out bravely while the battle did last;
But on his return till a fire did go,
What came of him after we never could know.

Our officers all so bravely did fight,
And likewise our men two days until night;
Until a reinforcement of Indians there came,
Which made us to leave the Sandusky plain.

"Now," says our commander, "Since we have lost ground,
With superior number they do us surround;
We'll gather the wounded men, and let us save
All that's able to go, the rest we must leave."

DISASTER ON THE SANDUSKY

There was brave Ensign Majaster another as brave,
He fought many battles his country to save;
On the plains of Sandusky received a wound,
Not being able to go he was left on the ground.
There was brave Colonel Crawford upon his retreat,
Likewise Major Harrison, and brave Doctor Knight,
With Slover their pilot and several men
Was unfortunately taken on the Sandusky plain.

Now they have taken these men of renown,
And has drag'd them away to the Sandusky town,
Where in their council condemned for to be,
Burn'd at a stake by most cruel Girtee.

Like young Diabolians they this act did pursue,
And Girtee the head of this infernal crew,
This insinuator was a stander by,
While they in the fire their bodies did fry.

Their Scalps off their heads while alive they did tear,
Their bodies with irons red hot they did sear;
They bravely expir'd without ever a groan,
That might melt a heart that was harder than stone.

After our brave heroes were burnt at the stake,
Brave Knight and brave Slover they made their escape;
With kind Heaven's assistance they brought us the news,
So none need the truth of these tidings refuse.

So from East unto West let it be understood,
Let ever one rise to revenge Crawford's blood;
And likewise the blood of those men of renown,
That were taken and burnt at the Sandusky towns.[23]

The ballad, filled with historical inaccuracies, was obviously influenced by the racial and cultural prejudices of the time. However, it serves as an example of the foundation set for William's legacy, both in history and folklore. In the decades immediately following his death, the sentiments expressed in the final stanza, those calling for Americans to "rise to revenge Crawford's blood," dominated American public opinion, and even official government policy towards Native Americans reflected this same opinion.

This view of both William and the Sandusky Expedition would persist for a very long time. In an 1896 speech given at the monument placed near the site of William's execution, he was described as "Great Crawford," a man who was "Unselfish, magnanimous, heroic." This speech, given by Judge James H. Anderson, a prominent member and trustee of the Ohio State Archaeological and Historical Society, was later printed in the society's historical journal. Anderson also said:

> If Socrates died like a philosopher, and Jesus Christ like a God, then verily this manly, courageous soul, whose sufferings were a thousand fold greater, died like a hero, and patriot, and martyr. His name should live in the great American heart, and in the pantheon of history, while true patriotism is cherished, and the memory of the father of our country revered...This spot of ground is now immortal, consecrated by the blood and martyrdom of the illustrious hero.[1]

This portrayal of William was also maintained in the histories about the expedition written in the nineteenth century, particularly those of Consul W. Butterfield, who wrote what was long considered the definitive history of the Sandusky Expedition. In these accounts the Indians were "savages," Simon Girty was an evil fiend, David Williamson was a hero, the volunteers were courageous and righteous, and William was a bold, heroic figure. Although the martyrdom aspect of his legacy would fade over time, the simplistic view of William as "pioneer and patriot" persisted until recent decades.

Of course, as with all of us, the reality of who we are and what influences our decisions and choices is far more complex than that indicated by simple phrases. As a young man, William clearly had his own ambitions for wealth. He embraced land speculation and supported expansion into the lands where the woodland nations sought refuge. When viewed over two hundred years later, his ambition, along with that of his friend and business partner, George Washington, seems self-serving and greedy. Like many on the frontier, he was swept up in the fervor for independence from Great Britain, and his business goals were likely the greatest influence for his particular brand of patriotism.

He also appears to have been an adulterer. His relationship with Ann Connell casts doubts on his moral character. To have an illicit relationship with someone related by marriage, make a place for her to live only a short distance from his home, and then share her with other men in the family is reprehensible.

Regarding his abilities as a military leader, there is little doubt William possessed the physical courage required of a leader in those times. As it was with every other officer, dealing with militia volunteers was a challenge for him. His experiences in the French and Indian War, Lord Dunmore's War, and the Revolutionary War taught him much about the reliability of militia and their elected officers. Sadly, this did not stop him from accepting command of the Sandusky Expedition which ultimately proved to be his own undoing.

Why he chose to answer General Irvine's call will always be viewed as somewhat perplexing. With his retirement from military duties and his return to Spring Garden, it appeared that his ambitions for greater command responsibilities and success on the battlefield had finally faded. Instead, he chose to serve, and did so in a campaign that faced so many potential obstacles that it was almost doomed to failure before it even began. William's hesitance to agree to Irvine's offer indicates he knew the challenges ahead, and likely feared for the worst.

The historical evidence indicates that his decision to command was probably influenced by General Irvine's deep concern that, if left to their own devices, David Williamson and the volunteers would perpetrate another massacre, a fear William seems to have shared. William also likely felt that the expedition only had chance of overcoming the countless

Statue of William Crawford in Connellsville, Pennsylvania. (*Author photo*)

hardships it would face if someone with his experience were in command. In the end, he paid dearly for his decision.

It is also clear that William Crawford was no military genius, nor a charismatic leader. He knew the expedition's success rested on total surprise. As soon as the Native American scouts spotted the army near the Muskingum, William should have ordered an immediate withdrawal. Instead, he allowed democracy to hold sway, permitting the views of amateurs to overrule his own judgment and authority.

The use of "councils of war" played a key role in the eventual disaster along the Sandusky. Allowing votes on command decisions by Williamson and the other volunteer officers was a critical mistake, even though this was an accepted practice in commanding the militia volunteers of the time. Many of these officers were men whose only qualification for leadership was their personal popularity with their hometown volunteers. Although this democratic review process might have been common, acting on these volunteers' views was a grievous error, especially in light of the fact that William knew better. Ironically, those like Williamson, men who pressed for aggressive offensive action, were the first to run when things got worse.

It might be easy to dismiss William Crawford as an unprincipled adulterer, a greedy land speculator, an ambitious expansionist who was motivated entirely by personal gain, and a man ill-suited to a military leadership position. The evidence, however, reveals a man that commands respect. Despite the popularity of cruel, barbaric tactics such as those advocated by men like David Williamson, William seems to have come to resist such views. In the end, his desire to ensure there was not a repeat of Gnadenhutten in the villages along the Sandusky cost him his life. It is tragically ironic that he died in an act of revenge for the very thing he was determined to thwart, and even more so, that his death prompted calls for more acts of bloodthirsty barbarism. This is not the legacy William Crawford would have wanted, nor is it the one he deserves.

ENDNOTES

Introduction (pages xiv-xvi)

1. Franklin Ellis, ed. History of Fayette County, Pennsylvania, With Biographical Sketches of Many of Its Pioneers and Prominent Men (Philadelphia: L.H. Everts & Co., 1882), 525.

Chapter 1: Frontier Farmer and Surveyor (pages 1-13)

1. Allen W. Scholl, *The Brothers Crawford: Colonel William, 1722-1782 and Valentine Jr., 1724-1777, Volume I* (Westminster, Maryland: Heritage Books, Inc., 2007), 1, 44. Dr. Scholl's study is a definitive genealogical history of William Crawford's family and resolves many historical errors, the first being Crawford's actual date of birth. For many years, authors and historians accepted his year of birth as 1732 because it was the same as George Washington. The only evidence that supported this date is contained in one of the early biographies of Washington, *History of the Life and Death, Virtues and Exploits of General George Washington*, written by the former rector of the Mount Vernon Parish, Mason L. Weems. In this wildly inaccurate book that also created the famous cherry tree myth, Weems alludes to a teenage Washington participating in athletic games with the Crawford brothers during Washington's first visit to the Shenandoah Valley in 1749. Therefore, Weems and a host of historians that followed merely assumed these two men were the same age when, in fact, Crawford was ten years Washington's senior and a married man with several children when they first met; Scholl, The Brothers Crawford, xii.
2. Ibid.
3. Ibid.
4. J.E. Norris, ed., *The History of the Lower Shenandoah Valley Counties of Frederick, Berkeley, Jefferson and Clarke* (Chicago: A. Warner & Co., Publishers, 1890), 50.
5. James M. Volo and Dorothy Denneen Volo, *Daily Life on the Old Colonial Frontier* (Westport, Connecticut: Greenwood Press, 2002), 128.
6. John M. Boback, "Indian Warfare, Household Competency, and the Settlement of the Western Virginia Frontier, 1749 to 1794" (PhD dissertation,

West Virginia University, 2007), 26; Ronald W. Moxley, "The Orchard Site: A Proto-Historic Fort Ancient Site in Mason County, West Virginia," *West Virginia Archeologist 40* (Spring 1988): 32.
7. Grace U. Emahiser, *From River Clyde to Tymochtee and Col. William Crawford* (Fostoria, Ohio: Lithographed by the Commercial Press, 1969), 13.
8. Scholl, *The Brothers Crawford*, 275.
9. Emahiser, From River Clyde to Tymochtee, 39; Scholl, *The Brothers Crawford*, 275. Note: Many genealogical web sites and family trees state that the Crawfords had four children, but these are all incorrect. Allen Scholl's definitive geology of the Crawfords shows that all legal documents, affidavits, letters, and even rulings of the United States Congress show that William and Hannah Crawford had only three children.
10. Scholl, *The Brothers Crawford*, 275.
11. Lyman Copeland Draper Collection (Wisconsin State Historical Society, Madison, Wisconsin), MSS 3S, 150.
12. Scholl, *The Brothers Crawford*, 275; Emahiser, *From River Clyde to Tymochtee*, 40-41; Deed Book B, page 135, Frederick County, Virginia.
13. John E. Ferling, *The First of Men: A Life of George Washington* (Knoxville, Tennessee: University of Tennessee Press, 1988), 37.
14. Ferling, *The First of Men*, 11.
15. Ibid.
16. Silvio A. Bedini, "George Washington (1732-1799) Surveyor and Cartographer, Part 1" *Professional Surveyor Magazine*, September 2000, http://archives.profsurv.com/magazine/article.aspx?i=639#sthash.i9ipoa2l.dpuf, accessed 24 March 2015.
17. Ferling, *The First of Men,* 13. In this era, surveyors used a plane surveying compass to determine the bearing of a survey line, and they measured distances using a chain. These were carried by chainmen who measured the distances along the survey lines. A full surveyor's chain consisted of one hundred equal links and was 66 feet long. Each link represented a decimal of the chain, and 25 links was an English statutory pole. The standard chain equaled four poles and 80 chains equaled one mile. Although the full chain was the standard in England, surveyors like Washington and Crawford knew that dragging a 66-foot chain through the brush of colonial Virginia's forests was impractical, to say the least. A long chain would hang on brush or logs and the dense vegetation often made it difficult for the chain carriers to see each other. Therefore, they typically used a half- or two-pole-chain that had 50 links and was only 33 feet long.

To measure distances once Washington had sighted the correct bearing, William, as the lead chainman, would walk toward the mark that Washington determined with his compass. The rear chainman, who was another local man hired by Washington, played out the chain, keeping the tail end of the chain over the beginning point. At the end of the chain, William would stop and stick a 12-inch iron or wooden pin in the ground.

As soon as William set the pin, the rear chainman moved forward to that spot, and the process began again. As he advanced along the survey line, the rear chainman picked up the pin that William had left. Chainmen carried 10 pins. When all 10 were collected, the chainmen knew that they had measured five full chains, if they were using a half chain, or 10 full chains with a full chain. Source: Ron Bailey, "A Surveyor for the King," Colonial Williamsburg Journal, Summer 2001 (Williamsburg, Virginia: Colonial Williamsburg Foundation, 2001), online edition, http://www.history.org/foundation/journal/Summer01/Surveyor.cfm, accessed March 20, 2015.

18. *The Papers of George Washington*, W. W. Abbot, ed. (Charlottesville: University Press of Virginia, 1983-2006), Colonial Series, vol. 1, 8–37; Norris, *History of the Lower Shenandoah Valley*, 64.
19. George Mercer, Lois Mulkearn, ed., *George Mercer Papers Relating to the Ohio Company of Virginia* (Pittsburgh: University of Pittsburgh Press, 1954), 2-3; Ferling, *The First of Men*, 17.
20. Ferling, *The First of Men*, 18.
21. Dinwiddie to Hamilton, May 21, 1753, *Minutes of the Provincial Council Pennsylvania, From the Organization to the Termination of the Proprietary Government, Volume V, Containing The Proceedings of Council from December 17th 1745, to 20th March, 1754, Both Days Included* (Harrisburg, Pennsylvania: Theodore Penn & Co., 1851), 630.
22. Dinwiddie to the Board of Trade, 16 June 1753 (Public Record Office, Kew, Surrey, England), C.O. 5/1327, 292–94; K H Ledward, ed., *Journal, August 1753: Volume 61*, in *Journals of the Board of Trade and Plantations, Volume 9, January 1750 - December 1753* (London: H. M. Stationary Office, 1932), 451-452; Earl of Holderness to Dinwiddie, 28 August 1753 (Public Record Office, Kew, Surrey, England), C.O. 5/211, 21–40.

Chapter 2: The Surveyor Becomes a Soldier (pages 14-28)

1. *The Papers of George Washington*, Diaries, Donald Jackson, ed., et al. (Charlottesville: University of Virginia Press, 1976 – 1979), Vol. 1, 127-128; *Executive Journals of the Council of Colonial Virginia, Vol. V, November 1, 1739- May 7, 1754* (Richmond, Virginia: Commonwealth of Virginia Division of Purchase and Printing, 1945), 443-444; Robert Dinwiddie to French Commandant, October 30, 1753 (Public Record Office, Kew, Surrey,

England), C.O.5/1328, 45--46. Note: The Six Nations was a confederation of Native American nations, the Cayuga, Mohawk, Oneida, Onondaga, Seneca, and Tuscarora, which included the Delaware and Mingo.
2. Ferling, *The First of Men*, 22.
3. Ibid., 23-25.
4. Dinwiddie to Washington, January 1754, *The Papers of George Washington*, Colonial Series, Vol. 1, 63-67.
5. Ferling, *The First of Men*, 24.
6. *Executive Journals of the Council of Colonial Virginia, Vol. V, November 1, 1739-May 7, 1754*, 499-500; Washington to Dinwiddie, March 9, 1754, *The Papers of George Washington*, Colonial Series, Vol. 1, 75-77.
7. Ferling, *The First of Men*, 25; Washington to Dinwiddie, March 20, 1754, *The Papers of George Washington*, Colonial Series, vol. 1, 78-80.
8. Scholl, *The Brothers Crawford*, 275. The precise timing and nature of the first months of William Crawford's military experience is somewhat difficult to track. The militia records in the Old Court House in Winchester cited by Scholl indicate William and Valentine Crawford enlisted in 1754, shortly after Dinwiddie's proclamation. After that, the next clear mention of William Crawford is his promotion to ensign in December 1755. Washington, however, mentions a "Crawford" in a dispatch from June 3, 1754. Curiously, no one named Crawford is on the official rolls of the Virginia Regiment for those men present at the battle at Fort Necessity on July 2, 1754. Despite this, most historians do place Crawford with the regiment at that time. Historians also place Crawford with Braddock's expedition in the summer of 1755 despite the fact that he stated in a deposition to the state of Pennsylvania that he first became "familiar" with the Ohio Country during the Forbes Expedition of 1758. Given the scarcity of men willing to enlist in 1754, the timing of Adam Stephen mustering his small unit in Winchester, and the June 3, 1754 reference, it seems very likely that William Crawford served with Stephen, and was with the regiment during their movement across the Alleghenies in April-July 1754. Finally, as will be discussed later, when Virginia proceeded to grant lands only to those men who served in the original Virginia Regiment during Washington's expedition of 1754, William Crawford was among those former soldiers authorized a grant.
9. April 23, 1754, *The Papers of George Washington, Diaries*, Vol. 1, 177-180.
10. The National Archives (UK), Colonial Office Papers, CO 5/15, 194-195, cited in David L. Preston, *Braddock's Defeat: The Battle of the Monongahela and the Road to Revolution* (New York: Oxford University Press, 2015), 373.
11. April 23, 1754, *The Papers of George Washington, Diaries*, Vol. 1, 177-180.
12. May 11, 1754, *The Papers of George Washington*, Ibid., Vol. 1., 185-186; William

M. Darlington, *Christopher Gist's Journals with Historical, Geographical and Ethnological Notes and Biographies of his Contemporaries* (Pittsburgh: J.R. Weldin & Co., 1893), 90.

13. Adam Stephen, "The Ohio Expedition of 1754," *The Pennsylvania Magazine of Biography and History, Volume 18* (Philadelphia: The Historical Society of Pennsylvania, 1894), 44.
14. May 24, 1754, *The Papers of George Washington, Diaries*, Vol. 1, 187-188.
15. Ferling, *The First of Men*, 25; The National Archives (UK), CO 5/15, 194-195, cited in Preston, *Braddock's Defeat*, 373; May 27, 1754, *The Papers of George Washington, Diaries*, Vol. 1, 190-191.
16. May 27, 1754, *The Papers of George Washington, Diaries*, Vol. 1, 190-191.
17. Ibid., 194-199; Stephen, "The Ohio Expedition of 1754," 46.
18. Washington to Dinwiddie, May 29, 1754, *The Papers of George Washington*, Colonial Series, Vol. 1, 107-115; Ferling, 25-26; William R. Nester, *The Great Frontier War: Britain, France, and the Imperial Struggle for North America, 1607-1755* (Westport, Connecticut: Praeger, 2000), 186-187; Jacob Nicolas Moreau, *A Memorial Containing a Summary View of Facts, with Their Authorities. In Answer to the Observations Sent by the English Ministry to the Courts of Europe, Translated from the French* (New York: H. Gaine, 1757), 69-70; Stephen, "The Ohio Expedition of 1754, 46.
19. National Archives (UK), CO 5/15, 194-195, cited in Preston, *Braddock's Defeat*, 373.
20. Washington to William Fairfax, August 11, 1754, *The Papers of George Washington*, Colonial Series, Vol. 1, 180-188.
21. Ibid.
22. Ibid. Moreover, in a letter sent on August 3, 1754 by Governor Dinwiddie to Washington (*The Papers of George Washington*, Colonial Series, Vol. 1, 182-183), he mentions "Ringleaders" and the "want of proper command."
23. Note: Whitehall refers to the buildings along Whitehall street in London considered to be the center of His Majesty's Government; Ferling, *The First of Men*, 30; George Washington, John C. Fitzpatrick, ed., *The Writings of George Washington from the Original Manuscript Sources, 1745-1799*, Vol. 1, 104-105, 106n; *The Papers of George Washington*, Colonial Series, Vol. 1, 80n. The exact date of Washington's resignation is unknown, as his letter tendering his resignation to Governor Dinwiddie did not survive; however, on November 15, 1754, he responded to a letter from Colonel William Fitzhugh clearly declining any offers to return to active service; he said, "the disparity between the present offer of a Company, and my former Rank, too great to expect any real satisfaction or enjoyment in a Corps, where I once did, or thought I had a right to, command."

ENDNOTES

Chapter 3: Disaster on the Monongahela (pages 29-46)

1. Nester, *The Great Frontier War*, 2.
2. Ibid.
3. Richard Eburne, Louis B. Wright, ed., *A Plain Pathway to Plantations (1624)* (Ithaca, New York: Cornell University Press, 1962), 41.
4. Nester, *The Great Frontier War*, 217-219.
5. Ibid., 219.
6. Willard Sterne Randall, *George Washington: A Life* (New York: Henry Holt & Co. 1997), 143.
7. William Allen, Lewis Burd Walker, ed., *The Burd Papers: Extract from Chief Justice William Allen's Letter Book, Together with an Appendix Containing Pamphlets in the Controversy with Franklin* (Pottsville, Pennsylvania.: Standard Publishing Company, 1897), 23; Washington to William Fairfax, June 7, 1755, Washington, *The Writings of George Washington from the Original Manuscript Sources*, 1745-1799, vol. 1, 133.
8. Nester, *The Great Frontier War*, 222.
9. Stanley V. Pargellis, ed., *Military Affairs in North America, 1748-1765: Selected Documents from the Cumberland Papers in Windsor Castle* (New York: D. Appleton-Century Company, 1936), 84.
10. Colonel Henry Bouquet quoted in Fort Ligonier Association et al., *War for Empire in Western Pennsylvania* (Ligonier, Pennsylvania: Fort Ligonier Association, 1993), 7.
11. Nester, *The Great Frontier War*, 230.
12. Transcription of Adam Stephen's unpublished account, Paul E. Kopperman, *Braddock at the Monongahela* (Pittsburgh: University of Pittsburgh Press, 1977), 227.
13. Stephen's unpublished account, Kopperman, *Braddock at the Monongahela*, 227.
14. Kopperman, *Braddock at the Monongahela*, 14.
15. Nester, *The Great Frontier War*, 231.
16. Pargellis, ed., *Military Affairs in North America*, 129-132, 88-89; Nester, *The Great Frontier War: Britain, France, and the Imperial Struggle for North America, 1607-1755*, 230-231.
17. Nester, *The Great Frontier War: Britain, France, and the Imperial Struggle for North America, 1607-1755*, 230.
18. "Journal of the Operations of the Army from 22 July 30th September 1755," E. B. O'Callaghan, ed., *Documents Relative to the Colonial History, State of New York, Volume X* (Albany, New York: Weed, Parsons, and Company, 1858), 337.
19. Preston, *Braddock's Defeat*, 235.

ENDNOTES

20. Kopperman, *Braddock at the Monongahela*, 57, 60. Note: An after action report by British officers stated the fears of British Regulars was one of three major causes for a rapidly unfolding disaster. This report to Governor Shirley read, "The frequent conversations of the provincial troops and country people was, that if they engaged the Indians in their European manner of fighting, they would be beat, and this some of their officers declared as their opinion." Further, the report added that the "novelty of an invisible enemy and the nature of the country, which was entirely a forest" contributed to the poor performance of Braddock's Regulars (Charles Henry Lincoln, ed., Correspondence of William Shirley, Governor of Massachusetts and Military Commander in America, 1731-1760, Volume II (New York: The Macmillan Company, 1912), 313).
21. Washington to Dinwiddie, July 18, 1755, *The Papers of George Washington*, Colonial Series, Vol. 1, 339-342.
22. Pargellis, ed., *Military Affairs in North America*, 117.
23. Washington to Dinwiddie, July 18, 1755, *The Papers of George Washington*, Colonial Series, Vol. 1, 339-342.
24. Randall, *George Washington: A Life*, 173.
25. Pargellis, ed., *Military Affairs in North America*, 117.
26. Ibid., 98-99; Nester, *The Great Frontier War*, 233; Washington to Dinwiddie, July 18, 1755, *The Papers of George Washington*, Colonial Series, Vol. 1, 339-342.
27. Nathan G. Goodman, *A Franklin Reader* (New York: Thomas Y. Crowell Company, 1945), 175.

Chapter 4: An Officer of the King (pages 47-63)

1. Pargellis, *Military Affairs in North America*, 124.
2. Robert Dinwiddie, R.A. Brock, ed., *The Official Records of Robert Dinwiddie, Lieutenant-Governor of The Colony of Virginia, 1751-1758, Volume II* (Richmond, Virginia: The Virginia Historical Society, 1883), 170; Goodman, ed., *Benjamin Franklin Reader*, 175.
3. *Documents Relative to the Colonial History, State of New York, Volume X*, 423.
4. Charles Cecil Wall, *George Washington, Citizen-Soldier* (Charlottesville, Virginia: University of Virginia Press, 1980), 20-21; Commission, 14 August 1755, *The Papers of George Washington*, Colonial Series, Vol. 2, 3-4; Stephen to Washington, October 4, 1755, Ibid., 72-75.
5. Volo and Volo, *Daily Life on the Colonial Frontier*, 126.
6. Susannah Willard Johnson, *A Narrative of the Captivity of Mrs. Johnson* (Windsor, Vermont: Thomas Pomrot, 1814), 22–23.

ENDNOTES

7. Washington to Christopher Gist, 10 October 1755, *The Papers of George Washington*, Colonial Series, Vol. 2, 98-99; George Washington, John C. Fitzpatrick, ed., *The Writings of George Washington from the Original Manuscript Sources, 1745-1799, vol. 1*, 261; Memorandum, December 27, 1755, The Papers of George Washington, Colonial Series, Vol. 2, 235; Memorandum, January 7, 1756, *The Papers of George Washington*, Ibid., 254.
8. *The Papers of George Washington*, Colonial Series, Vol. 2, 242-243n.
9. Washington to Stephen, April 7, 1756, Ibid., 339-340; *The Papers of George Washington*, Ibid., 36-37n.
10. Washington to David Bell, April 25, 1756, Ibid.. 2, 52-53.
11. William R. Nester, *The First Global War: Britain, France, and the Fate of North America, 1756-1775* (Westport, Connecticut: Praeger Publishers, 2000), 26; George Washington, John C. Fitzpatrick, ed., *The Writings of George Washington from the Original Manuscript Sources, 1745-1799, vol. 1*, 505.
12. Washington to Dinwiddie, June 10, 1757, *The Papers of George Washington*, Colonial Series, Vol. 2, 192-198.
13. Washington to Crawford, July 20, 1757, Ibid., 320-321; General Court-Martial, July 25–26, 1757, Ibid., 329-335; Memoranda, July 29-August 3, 1757, Ibid., 339-340; George Washington to John Stanwix, 30 July 1757, Ibid., 353-355; Instructions to Company Captains, July 29, 1757, Ibid., 341-346.
14. Nester, *The First Global War*, 104-106.
15. Ibid., 105.
16. John Forbes, Alfred Procter James ed., *Writings of General John Forbes Relating to His Service in North America* (Menasha, Wisconsin: The Collegiate Press, 1938), 205.
17. Washington to John Stanwix, April 10, 1758, *The Papers of George Washington*, Colonial Series, Vol. 2, 117-120.
18. Nester, *The First Global War*, 107; Washington to Bouquet, August 2, 1758, *The Papers of George Washington*, Colonial Series, Vol. 2, 353-360; Ferling, *The First of Men*, 54-55.
19. Armstrong to Peters, October 3, 1758, *Pennsylvania Archives, Series I, Volume III* (Philadelphia: Joseph Severns &, Co., 1853), 552.
20. Nester, *The First Global War*, 109.
21. Forbes, *Writings of General John Forbes*, 232.
22. Niles Anderson, "The General Chooses a Road: The Forbes Campaign of 1758 to Capture Fort Duquesne," *Western Pennsylvania Historical Magazine, Volume 42, Number 4* (Pittsburgh: The Historical Society of Western Pennsylvania, 1959), 390.
23. Anderson, "The General Chooses a Road," 392.

24. *Niles' Weekly Register*, Baltimore, 1st ser., 14, (9 May 1818), 179-180; Nester, *The First Global War*, 111.
25. Anderson, "The General Chooses a Road," 393-395.
26. Forbes, *Writings of General John Forbes*, 267.
27. Scholl, *The Brothers Crawford*, 276.
28. James Hall, *Romance of Western History or Sketches of History, Life, and Manners in the West* (Cincinnati: Applegate & Company, 1857), 121-125. Note: This story was told to the James Hall by General Daniel Morgan's grandson, Morgan Neville.

Chapter 5: Over the Mountains (pages 64-88)

1. Diary Entry for May 6, 1760, *The Papers of George Washington*, Colonial Series, Vol. 2, 265, with endnote.
2. J. C. McClenathan, M. D., Reverend William A. Edie, Reverend Ellis B. Burgess, J. Aloysius Coll, Eugene T. Norton, *Centennial History of the Borough of Connellsville Pennsylvania, 1806-1906* (Columbus, Ohio: The Champlin Press, 1906), 30-31; Joseph Doddridge, *Notes on the Settlement and Indian Wars* (Akron, Ohio: New Werner Company, 1912), 94.
3. Bruce G. Trigger, *The Huron: Farmers of the North*, 2d ed. (Belmont, California: Wadsworth Group, 2002), 31; J.F.D. Smyth, Esq., *A Tour in the United States of America* (London: G. Robinson, J. Robson, J. Sewell, 1784), 94.
4. McClenathan, Edie, Burgess, Coll, and Norton, *Centennial History*, 31.
5. Trigger, *The Huron*, 33.
6. William Henry Engle, *Some Women of Pennsylvania During the War of the Revolution* (Harrisburg, Pennsylvania: Harrisburg Publishing Company, 1898), 59.
7. Ferling, *The First of Men*, 69-70.
8. Washington to Crawford, September 21, 1767, Consul W. Butterfield, ed., *The Washington-Crawford Letters, Being the Correspondence Between George Washington and William Crawford, From 1767 to 1781, Concerning Western Lands* (Cincinnati: Robert Clarke & Co., 1877), 1-3. Note: Although the numerous letters between Washington and Crawford are available through the National Archives and Library of Congress, I have chosen to cite Butterfield as a source because his versions of the letters between Washington and Crawford were edited from the originals for readability.
9. Ibid.
10. Ibid., 3.
11. Washington to Crawford, September 21, 1767 (Correct date is September 17), Butterfield, *Washington-Crawford Letters*, 3-4.

12. Crawford to Washington, September 29, 1767, Ibid., 5-10.
13. Crawford to Washington, January 7, 1769, Butterfield, *Washington-Crawford Letters*, 10-12; Washington to James Tilghman, May 25, 1769, *The Papers of George Washington*, Colonial Series, Vol. 8, 206-207; Crawford to Washington, October 13, 1769, Butterfield, *Washington-Crawford Letters*, 13.
14. Washington to Baron de Botetourt, December 8, 1769, *The Papers of George Washington*, Colonial Series, Vol. 8, 272-277; Petition to Baron de Botetourt, Ibid., 277-279 with endnote 1; Ferling, The First of Men, 72.
15. Advertisement, December 16, 1769, *The Papers of George Washington*, Colonial Series, Vol. 8, 280.
16. Johnson to Washington, December 20, 1769, Ibid., 281; Horrocks to Washington, December 21, 1769, Ibid., 282.
17. Diary Entry, March 4, 1770, *The Papers of George Washington*, Diaries, Vol. 2, 218-219; Diary Entry, March 23, 1770, Ibid., 222.
18. Butterfield, *Washington-Crawford Letters*, viii.
19. Diary Entry, August 2, 1770, *The Papers of George Washington*, Diaries, Vol. 2, 260-261 with endnote.
20. Diary Entry, October 5, 1770, Ibid., 277-280, Diary Entry, October 15, 1770, Ibid., 290.
21. Diary Entry, October 19, 1770, Ibid., 293-294.
22. Diary Entry, October 17, Ibid., 280-281.
23. Diary Entry, October 19, 1770, Ibid., 292-293.
24. Ibid.
25. William Cronon, *Changes in the Land: Indians, Colonists, and the Ecology of New England* (New York: Hill and Wang, 1983), 94-95; R. Douglas Hurt, *Indian Agriculture in America: Prehistory to Present* (Lawrence: University Press of Kansas, 1987), 65-66.
26. Black Hawk, Antoine Leclair, U.S. Interpreter and J.B. Patterson, ed., *Life of MA-KA-TAI-ME-SHE-KIA-KIAK* (Rock Island, Illinois: J.B. Patterson, 1882), 88.
27. Hurt, *Indian Agriculture in America*, 65-66.
28. Russell Thornton, *American Indian Holocaust and Survival: A Population History Since 1492* (Norman, Oklahoma: The University of Oklahoma Press, 1990), 26-32, 43.
29. Diary Entry, October 19, 1770, *The Papers of George Washington*, Diaries, Vol. 2, 293-294.
30. Diary Entry, October 22, 1770, Ibid., 296.
31. "Acct. of the Weather in October," 1770, Ibid., 285.
32. Diary Entry, October 28, 1770, Ibid., 304.
33. Phillip W. Hoffman, *Simon Girty: Turncoat Hero* (Franklin, Tennessee: Flying Camp Press, 2008), 25-27.

ENDNOTES

34. Diary Entry, October 28, 1770, *The Papers of George Washington*, Diaries, Vol. 2, 304.
35. Diary Entry, November 2, 1770, Ibid., 308.
36. Diary Entry, November 5, 1770, Ibid., 309-310.
37. "November, Where & how my time is Spent," 1770, Ibid., 325-326.
38. Butterfield, *Washington-Crawford Letters*, 16.
39. Minutes of the Meeting of the Officers of the Virginia Regiment of 1754, March 5, 1771, *The Papers of George Washington*, Colonial Series, Vol. 8, 439-441; Crawford to Washington, April 20, 1771, Butterfield, *Washington-Crawford Letters*, 19.
40. George Washington to Charles Washington, January 31, 1770, *The Papers of George Washington*, Colonial Series, Vol. 8, 300-304.
41. George Washington to Robert Adam, November 22, 1771, Ibid., 550-554 with endnote 1.
42. Washington to Charles Thruston, March 12, 1773, Ibid., 194-198.
43. Crawford to Washington, August 2, 1771, Butterfield, *Washington-Crawford Letters*, 21.
44. David McClure, Franklin B. Dexter, ed., *The Diary of David McClure, Doctor of Divinity, 1748-1820* (New York: The Knickerbocker Press, 1899), 108-109.
45. Nicholas Cresswell, Lincoln MacVeagh, ed., *The Journal of Nicholas Cresswell, 1774-1777* (New York: The Dial Press, 1924), 100.
46. Scholl, *The Brothers Crawford*, 42, 47, 201.

Chapter 6: Lord Dunmore's War (pages 89-108)

1. Washington to Lord Dunmore, April 13, 1773, Butterfield, *Washington-Crawford Letters*, 27-28; Crawford to Washington, November 12, 1773, Ibid., 34-36.
2. Percy B. Caley, "Lord Dunmore and the Pennsylvania Virginia Boundary Dispute," *Western Pennsylvania Historical Magazine, Volume 22, Number 2* (Pittsburgh: The Historical Society of Western Pennsylvania, 1939), 87.
3. Arthur St. Clair, *The St. Clair Papers: The Life and Services of Arthur St. Clair, Vol. I* (Cincinnati: Robert Clarke & Co., 1882), 260-261; Samuel Hazard, Pennsylvania Archives, Series 1, Vol. IV (Philadelphia: Joseph Severns & Co., 1853), 457-458, 466-467.
4. Connolly to Washington, August 29, 1773, *The Papers of George Washington*, Colonial Series, Vol. 8, 314-315.
5. Crawford to Washington, January 10, 1774, Butterfield, *Washington-Crawford Letters*, 40-41.

ENDNOTES

6. Crawford to John Penn, Ibid., 42-46.
7. David Jones, *A Journal of Two Visits Made to Some Nations of Indians on the West Side of the River Ohio, in the Years 1772 and 1773* (Burlington, New Jersey: Isaac Collins, 1774), 49-50.
8. John M. Boback, "Indian Warfare, Household Competency, and the Settlement of the Western Virginia Frontier, 1749 to 1794" (PhD dissertation, West Virginia University, 2007), 152.
9. Ibid., 153-54; Michael N. McConnell, *A Country Between: The Upper Ohio Valley and Its Peoples, 1724-1774* (Lincoln, Nebraska: University of Nebraska Press, 1992), 274-275.
10. Starkey, *European and Native American Warfare*, 28.
11. Crawford to Washington, May 8, 1774, Ibid., 48.
12. McClenathan, Edie, Burgess, Coll, and Norton, *Centennial History*, 35-36.
13. National Archives, Revolutionary War Pension 1800-1900, "Michael Swope," cited in Boback, "Indian Warfare," 166.
14. Doddridge, *Notes on the Settlement*, 95.
15. Crawford to Washington, May 8, 1774, Ibid., 49; Scholl, *The Brothers Crawford*, 280.
16. Virgil A. Lewis, *History of the Battle of Point Pleasant* (Charleston, West Virginia: The Tribune Printing Company, 1909), 19-20.
17. Ibid., 22; Crawford to Washington, September 20, 1774, Butterfield, *Washington-Crawford Letters*, 53.
18. Edward Butts, *Simon Girty: Wilderness Warrior* (Toronto: Dundurn, 2011), 17-19.
19. Russel B. Nye, *A Baker's Dozen: Thirteen Unusual Americans* (East Lansing, Michigan: Michigan State University Press, 1956), 99; Butts, *Simon Girty*, 20-22.
20. Nye, *A Baker's Dozen*, 99; Butts, *Simon Girty*, 24-27.
21. Ibid., 28-32.
22. Ibid., 34-37.
23. Phillip W. Hoffman, *Simon Girty: Turncoat Hero* (Franklin, Tennessee: Flying Camp Press, 2008), 32.
24. Ibid., 34; Butts, *Simon Girty*, 43.
25. Hoffman, *Simon Girty*, 38-39; Butts, *Simon Girty*, 44-45.
26. Hoffman, Simon Girty, 39.
27. Ibid., 42.
28. Ibid., 49.
29. Anthony F.C. Wallace, *Jefferson and the Indians: The Tragic Fate of the First Americans* (Cambridge, MA: Harvard University Press, 2001), xvi.
30. Caley, "Lord Dunmore and the Pennsylvania Virginia Boundary Dispute," 56.

31. Crawford to Washington, November 14, 1774, Butterfield, *Washington-Crawford Letters*, 55; Alfred E. Lee, *History of the City of Columbus, Capital of Ohio* (New York & Chicago: Munsell & Company, 1892), 98.
32. Crawford to Washington, November 14, 1774, Butterfield, *Washington-Crawford Letters*, 55-56.
33. Ibid.

Chapter 7: Revolution (pages 109-137)

1. Crawford to Washington, February 7, 1775, Butterfield, *Washington-Crawford Letters*, 57-59.
2. Nathaniel Philbrick, *Bunker Hill: A City, A Siege, A Revolution* (New York: Penguin Random House LLC, 2013), 125.
3. *American Archives, Series 4, Vol. 2,* 612-615.
4. *Journals of the Continental Congress, Edited from the Original Records in the Library of Congress, Volume 2* (Washington D.C.: U.S. Government Printing Office, 1904-1937), 89-90, 91, 95, 97.
5. Robert K. Wright, Jr., *The Continental Army* (Washington D.C.: Center for Military History, U.S. Army, 1983), 67-68.
6. *The Virginia Gazette, Number 52,* January 26, 1777, Williamsburg, Virginia, 3; *The Virginia Gazette, Number 1277,* January 27, 1776, Williamsburg, Virginia, 1.
7. Engle, *Some Women of Pennsylvania During the War of the Revolution,* 59.
8. F. B. Heitman, *Historical Register of Officers of the Continental Army During the War of the Revolution, April, 1775, to December, 1783* (Washington D.C.: W. H. Lowdermilk & Co., 1893), 51.
9. Ibid., 52; Wright, *The Continental Army,* 284-286.
10. Crawford to Washington, September 23, 1776, Butterfield, *Washington-Crawford Letters,* 58-59.
11. Wright, *The Continental Army,* 291.
12. *The Virginia Gazette, Number 95,* Williamsburg, Virginia, 3.
13. Crawford to Washington, February 12, 1777, Butterfield, *Washington-Crawford Letters,* 63.
14. Ibid.
15. H.J. Eckenrode, Archivist, *List of the Revolutionary Soldiers of Virginia* (Richmond, Virginia: Superintendent of Public Printing, 1913), 709; Crawford to Washington, February 12, 1777, Butterfield, *Washington-Crawford Letters,* 63-64, 65. Note: Some source documents only show Colonel William Russell as the commander of the 13th Virginia Regiment. On the other hand, the original War Department documents cited by Eckenrode clearly show

William Crawford as the regiment's original commanding officer. Moreover, in May 1778, Washington wrote Timothy Pickering and referenced a dispute between Russell and Crawford as to who was the regiment's commander, and Washington made it clear he supported Crawford: Washington to Pickering, May 23, 1778, *The Papers of George Washington*, W. W. Abbot, et. al. (Charlottesville: University of Virginia Press, 1987-2006), Revolutionary War Series, Vol. 15, 204–205.

16. Wright, *The Continental Army*, 291.
17. Edward w. Hocker, *The Fighting Parson of the American Revolution: A Biography of General Peter Muhlenberg, Lutheran Clergyman, Military Chieftain and Political Leader* (Philadelphia: Edward W. Hocker, 1936), 12, 19-20, 31, 55, 59-60, 68-73.
18. Gerald M. Carbone, *Nathanael Greene, A Biography of the American Revolution* (New York: Palgrave Macmillan, 2008), Kindle Editon, Kindle Location 176, 472, 613-614, 1092; Terry Golway, *Washington's General: Nathanael Greene and the Triumph of the American Revolution* (New York: Henry Holt and Company, 2005), Kindle Edition, Kindle Location 3701.
19. Thomas J. McGuire, *The Philadelphia Campaign: Volume One: Brandywine and the Fall of Philadelphia* (Mechanicsburg, Pennsylvania: Stackpole Books, 2006), Kindle Edition, Kindle Locations 144-145; Washington to Hancock, January 31, 1777, *The Papers of George Washington*, Revolutionary War Series, Vol. 8, 201–202.
20. McGuire, *Philadelphia Campaign, Volume One*, Kindle Locations 332-333.
21. John Ferling, *Almost a Miracle: The American Victory in the War of Independence* (Oxford: Oxford University Press, 2007), 242; Washington to Hancock, July 2, 1777, *The Papers of George Washington*, Revolutionary War Series, Vol. 10, 168-170.
22. Ferling, *Almost a Miracle*, 242; Washington to Hancock, July 25, 1777, *The Papers of George Washington*, Revolutionary War Series, Vol. 10, 410-412.
23. Washington to Hancock, July 31, 1777, *The Papers of George Washington*, Revolutionary War Series, Vol. 10, 471-472.
24. Persifor Frazer, *General Percifor Frazer: A Memoir Compiled Principally from His Own Papers by His Great-Grandson, Persifor Frazer* (Philadelphia: Unknown Publisher, 1907), 151.
25. General Orders, August 23, 1777, *The Papers of George Washington*, Revolutionary War Series, Vol. 11, 49–51.
26. John Adams to Abigail Adams, August 24, 1777, John Adams, L. H. Butterfield, ed., *The Adams Papers, Adams Family Correspondence, vol. 2, June 1776–March 1778* (Cambridge, Massachusetts: Harvard University Press, 1963), 327–328.
27. General Orders, August 24, 1777, *The Papers of George Washington*,

Revolutionary War Series, Vol. 10, 55-56.
28. McGuire, *Philadelphia Campaign, Volume One,* Kindle Locations 1816-1818.
29. Ibid., Kindle Locations 1935-1936.
30. Consul W. Butterfield, An *Historical Account of the Expedition against Sandusky Under Col. William Crawford in 1782* (Cincinnati, Ohio: Robert Clarke & Co., 1873), 104; Michael Harris, *Brandywine: A Military History of the Battle that Lost Philadelphia but Saved America, September 11, 1777* (El Dorado Hills, California: Savas Beatie, 2014), Kindle Edition, Kindle Location 2706-2707.
31. Jaeger were Hessian elite light infantry units made of the experienced hunters in the ranks.
32. Harris, *Brandywine*, Kindle Location 2865-2900; Butterfield, *Expedition against Sandusky*, 104.
33. William P. McMichael, "Diary of Lieutenant James McMichael, of the Pennsylvania Line, 1776-1778," *Pennsylvania Magazine of History and Biography, Vol XVI, No. 2* (Philadelphia: Pennsylvania Historical Society, 1892), 149.
34. McGuire, *Philadelphia Campaign, Volume One*. Kindle Location 2126-2196.
35. McMichael, "Diary of Lieutenant James McMichael," 149.
36. McGuire, *Philadelphia Campaign, Volume One*. Kindle Location 2292-2302.
37. Ibid., Kindle Location 2330, 2443.
38. Sullivan to Washington, 11 September 1777, *The Papers of George Washington*, Revolutionary War Series, Vol. 11, 198.
39. Harris, *Brandywine*, Kindle Locations 4921-4922.
40. Daniel Agnew, "A Biographical Sketch of Governor Richard Howell of New Jersey," *Pennsylvania Magazine of History and Biography, Vol XXI* (Philadelphia: Pennsylvania Historical Society, 1898), 224.
41. Richard K. Showman, Robert M. McCarthy, and Margaret Cobb, eds., *The Papers of General Nathanael Greene, vol. 2, 1 January 1777 - 16 October 1778* (Chapel Hill, North Carolina: University of North Carolina Press, 1980), 471.
42. Harris, *Brandywine*, Kindle Locations 6282-6310.
43. McMichael, "Diary of Lieutenant James McMichael," 150.
44. Joseph Foulke, *Memoirs of Jacob Ritter, A Faithful Minister in the Society of Friends* (Philadelphia: T. E. Chapman, 1844), 15.
45. McMichael, "Diary of Lieutenant James McMichael," 151.
46. Jared Sparks and Henry Reed, *The Lives of Charles Lee and Joseph Reed* (Boston: Charles C. Little and James Brown, 1846), 384; Reed to Washington, September 23, 1777, *The Papers of George Washington*, Revolutionary War Series, Vol. 11, 306-308.
47. Ferling, *Almost a Miracle*, 253.
48. Comments of Col. Elias Dayton, George Washington, *The Papers of George Washington*, Revolutionary War Series, Vol. 11, 393-401n.

49. Ferling, *Almost a Miracle*, 254; Comments of Col. Elias Dayton, George Washington, *The Papers of George Washington*, Revolutionary War Series, Vol. 11, 393-401n.
50. McMichael, "Diary of Lieutenant James McMichael," 153.
51. Quoted in Ferling, *Almost a Miracle*, 256.
52. Peter Gabriel Muhlenberg, "Orderly Book of Gen. John Peter Gabriel Muhlenberg, March 26-December 20, 1777," *The Pennsylvania Magazine of History and Biography, Vol. 35, No. 1* (Philadelphia: Pennsylvania Historical Society, 1911), 70; General Orders, October 11, 1777, Ibid., 480-482; General Orders, October 13, 1777, Ibid., 11, 496-497; General Orders, October 14, 1777, Ibid., 502-503.

Chapter 8: War on the Frontier (pages 138-164)

1. *Journals of the Continental Congress, Volume 9*, 942.
2. Ibid., 943-944.
3. Washington to Laurens, November 26-27, 1777, *The Papers of George Washington*, Revolutionary War Series, Vol. 12, 420–422.
4. Allan W. Eckert, *Sorrow in Our Heart: The Life of Tecumseh* (New York: Bantam Books, 1992), ix.
5. William I. Barnholth, *Hopocan (Capt. Pipe) The Delaware Chief* (Akron, Ohio: The Summit County Historical Society, 1966), 2.
6. Ibid., 2-3.
7. Parker B. Brown, "The Historical Accuracy of the Captivity Narrative of Doctor John Knight," *The Western Pennsylvania Historical Magazine, Vol. 70, No. 1* (Pittsburgh: The Western Pennsylvania Historical Society, 1987), 58.
8. Butts, *Simon Girty*, 62-63.
9. Ibid.
10. Ibid., 63; Consul W. Butterfield, *History of the Girtys* (Cincinnati: Robert Clarke & Co., 1890), 41.
11. Butts, Simon Girty, 64-66; Butterfield, *History of the Girtys*, 45.
12. Allan W. Eckert, *That Dark and Bloody River* (New York: Bantam Books, 1995), 217.
13. Hand to Crawford, February 5, 1778, Butterfield, *Washington-Crawford Letters*, 66-67.
14. Butts, *Simon Girty*, 68-69.
15. Eckert, *That Dark and Bloody River*, 218.
16. Butts, *Simon Girty*, 68-71; Butterfield, *History of the Girtys*, 47-48; Hoffman, 93-97; Eckert, *That Dark and Bloody River*, 219.

ENDNOTES

17. Butts, *Simon Girty*, 68-71; Butterfield, *History of the Girtys*, 47-48; Hoffman, *Simon Girty*, 93-97.
18. Ibid.
19. Ibid.
20. John Heckewelder, *A Narrative of the Mission of the United Brethren Among the Delaware and Mohegan Indians, From Its Commencement, in the Year 1740, to the Close of the Year 1808* (Philadelphia: McCarty & Davis, 1820), 143; Barnholth, 1, 4.
21. Butts, *Simon Girty*, 68-71; Butterfield, *History of the Girtys*, 47-48; Hoffman, *Simon Girty*, 93-97.
22. Ibid.
23. Nye, *A Baker's Dozen*, 101-104; Butts, 72-73; Butterfield, *History of the Girtys*, 50-52; "General Edward Hand to General Horatio Gates," Reuben Gold Thwaites and Louise Phelps Kellogg, eds., *Frontier Defense on the Upper Ohio, 1777-1778* (Oshkosh, Wisconsin: Castle-Pierce Printing Company, 1912), 250.
24. Heckewelder, *A Narrative of the Mission of the United Brethren, 174-175*.
25. General Edward Hand to Colonel William Crawford, March 30, 1778, Thwaites and Kellogg, 252-253.
26. Nye, *A Baker's Dozen*, 109.
27. Butts, *Simon Girty*, 78.
28. Nelson, *A Man of Distinction among Them*, 117.
29. Nye, *A Baker's Dozen*, 103-104.
30. Nye, *A Baker's Dozen*, 105; Butts, *Simon Girty*, 97; "Colonel Arthur Campbell to Colonel William Davies, October 3, 1782," William P. Palmer, ed., *Calendar of Virginia State Papers and Other Manuscripts, Vol. III* (Richmond, Virginia: James E. Goode, 1883), 337-338.
31. Washington to Laurens, May 12, 1778, *The Papers of George Washington*, Revolutionary War Series, Vol. 15, 108–110; McIntosh to Washington, February 161776, *The Papers of George Washington*, Revolutionary War Series, Vol. 3, 325–328n.
32. Washington to Pickering, May 23, 1778, *The Papers of George Washington*, Revolutionary War Series, Vol. 15, 204-205; Washington to Laurens, May 28, 1778, Ibid., 247; Washington to Colonel William Russell, Sr., May 28, 1778, Ibid., 249.
33. Scholl, *The Brothers Crawford*, 283-284.
34. *Journals of the Continental Congress, Volume XI*, 589; Thomas I. Pieper and James B. Gidney, *Fort Laurens, 1778-1779: The Revolutionary War in Ohio* (Kent, Ohio: Kent State University Press, 1976), 21-22.
35. Edward G. Williams, "A Revolutionary Journal and Orderly Book of

General Lachlan Mcintosh's Expedition, 1778 (Second Installment)," *The Western Pennsylvania Historical Magazine, Volume 43, No. 2* (Pittsburgh: The Historical Society of Western Pennsylvania, 1960), 165; Pieper and Gidney, 25.

36. Note: The Orderly Books maintained by Robert McReady, an Orderly Sergeant in (William Crawford's half-brother) Colonel John Stephenson's regiment, indicate a total of ten separate courts martial ordered by General McIntosh from October 17, 1778 through December 8, 1778. Source: Williams, Second Installment, 165-169; Edward G. Williams, "A Revolutionary Journal and Orderly Book of General Lachlan Mcintosh's Expedition, 1778 (Third Installment)," *The Western Pennsylvania Historical Magazine, Volume 43, No. 3* (Pittsburgh: The Historical Society of Western Pennsylvania, 1960), 267-282.
37. Williams, Second Installment, 166.
38. Ibid., 168.
39. Ibid.
40. Pieper and Gidney, *Fort Laurens*, 28.
41. Williams, Third Installment, 274. 276.
42. Pieper and Gidney, *Fort Laurens*, 36.
43. Williams, Third Installment, 276.
44. Ibid., 277.
45. Louise Phelps Kellogg, ed., "Recollections of John Cuppy," *Frontier Advance on the Upper Ohio, 1778-1779* (Madison, Wisconsin: Wisconsin Historical Society, 1916), 159-160.
46. Williams, Third Installment, 279; Williams, Second Installment, 161.
47. Williams, Third Installment, 279-280.
48. Ibid.
49. Ibid., 282; Pieper and Gidney, *Fort Laurens*, 41.
50. Louise Phelps Kellogg, ed., "Recollections of Capt. Jacob White," *Frontier Advance on the Upper Ohio*, 163.
51. "Recollections of Henry Jolly," Ibid., 184-185.
52. "Recollections of Capt. Jacob White," Ibid., 163.
53. Crawford to Washington, July 12, 1779, Butterfield, *Washington-Crawford Letters*, 70-71
54. Ibid., 72.
55. Butterfield, *Washington-Crawford Letters*, 72; Daniel Brodhead to George Washington, September 16, 1779, *The Papers of George Washington*, Revolutionary War Series, Vol. 22, 433-438.
56. Ibid., 75.

ENDNOTES

Chapter 9: An Expedition to the Sandusky (pages 165-189)

1. *The Parliamentary History of England from the Earliest Period to the Year 1803, Volume XXII* (London: T.C. Hanspard, 1814), 1089.
2. Consul W. Butterfield, *Washington-Irvine Correspondence: The Official Letters Which Passed Between Washington and Brig.-Gen. William Irvine and Between Irvine and Others Concerning Military Affairs in the West from 1781 To 1783* (Madison, Wisconsin: David Atwood, 1882) 65-67; Irvine to Washington, March 22, 1782, 103.
3. David Zeisberger, *The Diary of David Zeisberger, A Moravian Missionary* (Cincinnati: Historical and Philosophical Society of Ohio, 1885), 4.
4. Eckhert, *Dark and Bloody River*, 380-381.
5. Heckewelder, *A Narrative of the Mission of the United Brethren*, 68.
6. Ibid., 316.
7. Nelson, *A Man of Distinction*, 124.
8. Heckewelder, *A Narrative of the Mission of the United Brethren*, 320; Zeisberger, *The Diary of David Zeisberger*, 79-81.
9. John Heckewelder, *History, Manners, and Customs of the Indian Nations Who Once Inhabited Pennsylvania and the Neighbouring States* (Philadelphia: Publication Fund of the Historical Society of Pennsylvania, 1881), 81.
10. Butterfield, *Expedition Against Sandusky*, 49, 61.
11. John Knight and John Slover, *Narratives of the Perils and Sufferings of Dr. Knight and John Slover* (Cincinnati: U.P. James, 1867), 2;
12. Butterfield, *Expedition Against Sandusky*, 52.
13. Ibid., 53.
14. Ibid., 56-57.
15. Ibid., 115-116.
16. William Crawford, *Last Will and Testament of William Crawford*, Westmoreland County, Pennsylvania, Probate Court, Will Book No. 1, 6.
17. Butterfield, *Expedition Against Sandusky*, 118.
18. Ibid., 118-119; Parker B. Brown, "The Battle of Sandusky: June 4-6, 1782," *The Western Pennsylvania Historical Magazine, Volume 65, No. 2* (Pittsburgh: The Historical Society of Western Pennsylvania, 1982), 121.
19. Brown, "The Battle of Sandusky," 122-123.
20. Irvine to Washington, May 21, 1782, Butterfield, *Washington-Irvine Letters*, 114-115; Irvine Orders to Expedition Commander, Fort Pitt, May 14, 1782, Ibid., 119-120, note 1.
21. Irvine Orders to Expedition Commander, Fort Pitt, May 14, 1782, Ibid., 119-120, note 1.

22. Ibid.
23. Butterfield, *Expedition Against Sandusky*, 62-63; Crawford to Irvine, May 24, 1782, Butterfield, *Washington-Irvine Letters*, 364.
24. Butterfield, *Expedition Against Sandusky*, 76-77; Rose to Irvine, May 24, 1782, Butterfield, *Washington-Irvine Letters*, 364.
25. George Pilar Von Pilchau, Baron de Rosenthal and William L. Stone, "Journal of a Volunteer Expedition to Sandusky, from May 24 to June 13, 1782," *The Pennsylvania Magazine of History and Biography, Vol. 18, No. 3* (Philadelphia: Historical Society of Pennsylvania, 1894), 293.
26. Ibid., 293
27. Ibid.
28. Butterfield, *Expedition Against Sandusky*, 125; Butterfield, *Washington-Irvine Letters*, 117, note 2.
29. George Pilar Von Pilchau, Baron de Rosenthal and William L. Stone, "Journal of a Volunteer Expedition to Sandusky, from May 24 to June 13, 1782," *The Pennsylvania Magazine of History and Biography, Vol. 18, No. 2* (Philadelphia: Historical Society of Pennsylvania, 1894), 137-139.
30. Ibid., 295.
31. Butterfield, *Expedition Against Sandusky*, 65-66.
32. Crawford to Irvine, May 24, 1782, Butterfield, *Washington-Irvine Letters*, 363-364.
33. Von Pilchau, Rosenthal, and Stone, "Journal of a Volunteer Expedition to Sandusky," Vol. 18, No. 2, 139; Knight and Slover, *Narratives*, 11.
34. Butterfield, *Expedition Against Sandusky*, 126-128.
35. Ibid., 126-129.
36. Von Pilchau, Rosenthal, and Stone, "Journal of a Volunteer Expedition to Sandusky," Vol. 18, No. 3, 300.
37. Ibid.
38. Ibid., 299.
39. Ibid., 295-297.
40. Von Pilchau, Rosenthal, and Stone, "Journal of a Volunteer Expedition to Sandusky," Vol. 18, No.2, 140.
41. Von Pilchau, Rosenthal, and Stone, "Journal of a Volunteer Expedition to Sandusky," Vol. 18, No. 3, 300-301.
42. Von Pilchau, Rosenthal, and Stone, "Journal of a Volunteer Expedition to Sandusky," Vol. 18, No.2, 142-143.
43. Ibid., 145-146.
44. Butterfield, *Expedition Against Sandusky*, 149.
45. Von Pilchau, Rosenthal, and Stone, "Journal of a Volunteer Expedition to Sandusky," Vol. 18, No.2, 148.

ENDNOTES

Chapter 10: Battle Island (pages 190-216)

1. Girty to DePeyster, May 12, 1782, Consul W. Butterfield, *History of the Girtys*, 164.
2. Heckewelder, *Narrative of the Mission of the United Brethren*, 341-342.
3. DePeyster to Powell, May 16, 1782, *Historical Collections: Collections and Researches Made by the Michigan Pioneer and Historical Society, Vol. XX* (Lansing, Michigan: Wynkoop Uallenreck Crawford Co., 1912), 18-19; Butterfield, *Expedition Against Sandusky*, 173-174.
4. Georges E. Sioui, *Huron Wendat: The Heritage of the Circle* (East Lansing, Michigan: Michigan State University Press, 1999), 3, 207.
5. Ibid., 6, 22.
6. Ibid., 84-86.
7. Larry K. Hanks, *The Emigrant Tribes, Wyandot, Delaware, and Shawnee: A Chronology* (Kansas City, Kansas: Unpublished, 1998), 7.
8. John R. Swanton, *The Indian Tribes of North America* (Washington, DC: U.S. Government Printing Office, 1952) 235–36.
9. Ibid., 6–7.
10. Butterfield, *Expedition Against Sandusky*, 194; Butterfield, *History of the Girtys*, 162.
11. Butterfield, *Expedition Against Sandusky*, 167.69, 172, Butterfield, *History of the Girtys*, 162.
12. Heckewelder, *History, Manners, and Customs of the Indian Nations*, 285.
13. John Heckewelder, *History, Manners, and Customs of the Indian Nations Who Once Inhabited Pennsylvania and the Neighbouring States* (Philadelphia: Publication Fund of the Historical Society of Pennsylvania, 1881), 284-285.
14. John Leith, *Leith's Narrative: A Short Biography of John Leith with a Brief Account of his Life Among the Indians* (Cincinnati: Robert Clarke & Co., 1883), 45-48.
15. Hoffman, *Simon Girty*, 167.
16. Butts, *Simon Girty*, 135.
17. Note: The story of hearing cannon fire in the hours after dawn on June 4 was reported by both Major Rose (Von Pilchau, Rosenthal, and Stone, "Journal of a Volunteer Expedition to Sandusky," Vol. 18, No. 2, 148) and John Leith (Leith, Leith's Narrative, 48). At the time, the Ranger's artillery was still downriver and had not arrived at the battleground. Therefore, it seems most probable that this incident involved some test firing of the guns after their journey across Lake Erie.
18. Von Pilchau, Rosenthal, and Stone, "Journal of a Volunteer Expedition to Sandusky," Vol. 18, No. 2, 148; Brown, *Battle of Sandusky*, 137.

19. Brown, *Battle of Sandusky*, 137.
20. Butterfield, *Expedition Against Sandusky*, 203; Knight and Slover, *Narratives*, 12; Brown, *Battle of Sandusky*, 137.
21. Butterfield, *Expedition Against Sandusky*, 204-205.
22. Ibid., 206; Brown, *Battle of Sandusky*, 137-138, note 62.
23. Von Pilchau, Rosenthal, and Stone, "Journal of a Volunteer Expedition to Sandusky," Vol. 18, No. 2, 150; Pension application, "Williams, James. Md., Penn., Va. S.3590," October 5, 1832, National Archives.
24. Tuney to DePeyster, June 7, 1782, Butterfield, *Washington-Irvine*, 368. Note: Given Caldwell's experience and Elliot's lack thereof, this proved to be something of a turning point in the battle's eventual outcome. Caldwell would later write, "If I had not been so unlucky I am induced to think, from the influence I have with the Indians, the enemy would not have left the place we surrounded them in." (Caldwell to DePeyster, June 11, 1782, Butterfield, Washington-Irvine, 371).
25. Draper MSS 4 S 135-36.
26. Butterfield, *Expedition Against Sandusky*, 210.
27. Ibid.
28. Draper MSS 4 S 135-36.
29. Butterfield, *Expedition Against Sandusky*, 211.
30. John Leith, *Leith's Narrative*, 48; Caldwell to DePeyster, June 11, 1782, Butterfield, *Washington-Irvine*, 371.
31. Von Pilchau, Rosenthal, and Stone, "Journal of a Volunteer Expedition to Sandusky," Vol. 18, No. 2, 151; Butterfield, *Expedition Against Sandusky*, 212-213.
32. Robert Andrew Sherrard, Thomas Johnson Sherrard, ed., *The Sherrard Family of Steubenville* (Philadelphia: The Jas. B. Rodgers Printing Company, 1890), 11.
33. Williams, Pension Application, 9; Draper MSS 4 S 137; Hoffman, *Simon Girty*, 168.
34. Von Pilchau, Rosenthal, and Stone, "Journal of a Volunteer Expedition to Sandusky," Vol. 18, No. 3, 297.
35. Von Pilchau, Rosenthal, and Stone, "Journal of a Volunteer Expedition to Sandusky," Vol. 18, No. 2, 151.
36. Knight and Slover, *Narratives*, 14.
37. Starkey, European and Native American Warfare, 18.
38. Brown, *Battle of Sandusky*, 139-140; Butts, *Simon Girty*, 138.
39. Robert Andrew Sherrard, Thomas Johnson Sherrard, ed., *Sherrard Family*, 12.
40. Pension application, "Walters, John. Penn., S.17753," June 3, 1833, National Archives.

41. Michael Walters, J.P. Maclean, ed., *Journal of Michael Walters, A Member of the Expedition Against Sandusky in the Year 1782* (Cleveland: Western Reserve Historical Society, 1899), 18.
42. Hoffman, *Simon Girty*, 169; Butts, *Simon Girty*, 138; Draper MSS 4 S 137-38.
43. Von Pilchau, Rosenthal, and Stone, "Journal of a Volunteer Expedition to Sandusky," Vol. 18, No. 2, 151; Brown, *Battle of Sandusky*, 140-141.
44. Rose to Irvine, June 14, 1782, Butterfield, *Washington-Irvine*, 371.
45. Brown, *Battle of Sandusky*, 141.
46. Knight and Slover, *Narratives*, 14; Brown, *Battle of Sandusky*, 141; Butterfield, *Expedition Against Sandusky*, 218.
47. Von Pilchau, Rosenthal, and Stone, "Journal of a Volunteer Expedition to Sandusky," Vol. 18, No. 2, 152.
48. Brown, *Battle of Sandusky*, 143.
49. Heckewelder, *Narrative of the Mission of the United Brethren*, 338; Parker B. Brown, "The Fate of Crawford Volunteers Captured by Indians Following the Battle Of Sandusky in 1782," *The Western Pennsylvania Historical Magazine, Volume 65, Number 4* (Pittsburgh: Western Pennsylvania Historical Society, 1982), 325.
50. Knight and Slover, *Narratives*, 37-59.
51. Draper MSS 4 S 138-42.
52. Von Pilchau, Rosenthal, and Stone, "Journal of a Volunteer Expedition to Sandusky," Vol. 18, No. 2, 152.
53. Ibid., 152, 154; Draper MSS 10 E 79.
54. Von Pilchau, Rosenthal, and Stone, "Journal of a Volunteer Expedition to Sandusky," Vol. 18, No. 2, 153-154; Von Pilchau, Rosenthal, and Stone, "Journal of a Volunteer Expedition to Sandusky," Vol. 18, No. 3, 309.
55. Von Pilchau, Rosenthal, and Stone, "Journal of a Volunteer Expedition to Sandusky," Vol. 18, No. 2, 154.
56. Ibid.
57. Ibid., 156; Rose to Irvine, June 14, 1782, Butterfield, *Washington-Irvine Letters*, 373.

Chapter 11: Trial and Punishment (pages 217-232)

1. This number, although much higher than either the 40-50 casualties Major Rose recorded in his journal, or the 30 killed and wounded that he officially reported to General Irvine, more closely correlates with the data derived by modern historians. Parker B. Brown calculates 41 killed, 16 wounded, and 7 captured, with more unaccounted (Parker B. Brown, "The Fate of Crawford Volunteers Captured by Indians Following the Battle of

Sandusky in 1782," *The Western Pennsylvania Historical Magazine, Volume 65, No. 4* [Pittsburgh: The Historical Society of Western Pennsylvania, 1982], 339-340). Additionally, Allen W. Eckert's unofficial calculation from a variety of letters, journals, diaries and incidental reports, indicates that approximately 138 volunteers were killed in the battle or in the retreat that followed, later died of wounds received, or were executed after being captured (Eckert, *Dark and Bloody River*, Note 595, 786).

2. Turney to DePeyster, June 7, 1782, Butterfield, *Washington-Irvine*, 368-369; McKee to DePeyster, June 7, 1782, Butterfield, *Washington-Irvine*, 370.
3. Knight and Slover, *Narratives*, 15.
4. Ibid., 15-16.
5. Ibid., 16-17; Parker B. Brown, "The Historical Accuracy of the Captivity Narrative of Doctor John Knight," 60.
6. Knight and Slover, *Narratives*, 17-18.
7. Ibid., 18.
8. Ibid., 18-19; Brown, "Historical Accuracy of the Captivity Narrative," 60; Walters, J.P. Maclean, ed. *Journal of Michael Walters*, 183.
9. Hoffman, *Simon Girty*, 169-170.
10. Brown, "Historical Accuracy of the Captivity Narrative," 60.
11. Knight and Slover, *Narratives*, 20.
12. Draper MSS 17 S 204-205; Hoffman, *Simon Girty*, note 2, 316.
13. Draper MSS 17 S 204-205.
14. Knight and Slover, *Narratives*, 20.
15. Heckewelder, *History, Manners, and Customs of the Indian Nations*, 284-285; Brown, "Historical Accuracy of the Captivity Narrative," 61; Knight and Slover, *Narratives*, 21.
16. Brown, "Historical Accuracy of the Captivity Narrative," 61; Boback, "Indian Warfare," 58-59.
17. Hoffman, *Simon Girty*, 172.
18. Heckewelder, *A Narrative of the Mission of the United Brethren*, 341.
19. Draper MSS 4 S 185.
20. Draper MSS 11 C 62.33
21. Heckewelder, *History, Manners, and Customs of the Indian Nations*, 285.
22. Ibid., 285-286
23. Ibid., 286.
24. Ibid.
25. Ibid.
26. Ibid., 287

27. Ibid.
28. Ibid.
29. Ibid., 287-288.
30. Ibid., 288.
31. Brown, "Historical Accuracy of the Captivity Narrative," 61.
32. Knight and Slover, *Narratives*, 22-23; Parker B. Brown, "The Fate of Crawford Volunteers", 326-327. Note: Despite the stereotype presented in nineteenth century American literature and even Hollywood films of the twentieth century, burnings at the stake and other ritualistic executions were the exception and one must look at the customs of Native Americans in order to understand why these did happen on occasion. They were not merely savage expressions of frenzied cruelty. Native American custom dictated their own laws of war and these were closely regulated. For example, warriors departing for battle underwent purification rituals and painted themselves in order to be handsome should they be killed and presented to the Great Spirit. In the same way, scalps and even captives were taken as trophies of combat and were significant as symbols of either mourning, to appease ghosts, or even as offerings to supernatural spirits.

    The tortures and executions that followed Crawford's defeat seem all the more barbaric because, as in his case, the Delaware tried to keep him alive and in as much pain as possible. This was not done strictly to be ghoulish or cruel, but because long standing customs and rules demanded it. Furthermore, the torture must be seen through Native American eyes as a deeply felt expression of religious belief and conviction. In addition, the protracted torture was also a reflection of an outpouring of grief by wives and children whose warrior husbands and fathers had died in combat with whites.
33. Parker B. Brown, "The Fate of Crawford Volunteers," 326.
34. Knight and Slover, *Narratives*, 23; Shellhouse letter, C. W. Butterfield Scrapbooks, Series 3, Number 8:70, Western Reserve Historical Society, Cleveland, Ohio.
35. Draper MSS 10 E 146-147, MSS 17 S 191, MSS 20 S 200-201.
36. Draper MSS 10 E 147, MSS 20 S 201.
37. Knight and Slover, *Narratives*, 23.
38. Draper MSS 17 S 205.
39. Zeisberger, *The Diary of David Zeisberger*, 431; Shellhouse letter, Butterfield Scrapbooks, Series 3, Number 8:71.

ENDNOTES

Chapter 12: Legacies (pages 233-250)

1. Irvine to Washington, June 16, 1782, Butterfield, *Washington-Irvine*, 121; Rose to Irvine, June 14, 1782, Ibid., 378; Washington to Irvine, July 10, 1782, Ibid., 125.
2. Irvine to Washington, July 11, 1782, Ibid., 128; Washington to Irvine, August 6, 1782, August 6, 1782, 131-132.
3. Butterfield, Ibid., Notes IV, V, and VI, 376-377.
4. Haldimand to Carlton, July 28, 1782, Ibid., Note VIII, 373; DePeyster to Haldimand, August 18, 1782, Ibid., Note IX, 373.
5. Draper MSS 20 S 201.
6. Butterfield, *Washington-Irvine*, 366-367.
7. Ibid.
8. Nye, *A Baker's Dozen*, 114.
9. Butts, *Simon Girty*, 13; Stephen Vincent Benet, *The Devil and Daniel Webster* (Los Angeles: Library of Alexandria, 2011), 10; Nook ebook version.
10. One of these captives was my fifth great grandmother, Phebe Tucker Cunningham. Captured on August 31, 1785 by a Wyandot raiding party near what is now Peoria, West Virginia, she watched the warriors kill her four young children, and then marched with them on foot almost 250 miles to their village in the Ohio Country. She was adopted into the tribe and lived with them for three years until Girty ransomed her in October 1788. She returned to her husband and lived to the age of eight-four.
11. Draper MSS 17 S 205; MSS 17 S 191.
12. Report of Ephraim Douglass to the Secretary of War, August 18, 1783, cited in Barnholth, 9.
13. Barnholth, 10-12.
14. Ibid., 12.
15. Ibid., 288.
16. Hannah Crawford to Washington, June 4, 1784, *The Papers of George Washington*, (Charlottesville, Virginia: University Press of Virginia, 1992), Confederation Series, Vol. 1, 423.
17. Washington to Thomas Freeman, May 8, 1786, *The Papers of George Washington*, Confederation Series, Vol. 4, 36.
18. Hannah Crawford to Washington, March 16, 1787, *The Papers of George Washington*, Confederation Series, Vol. 4, 89-90; Scholl, *The Brothers Crawford*, 33-34.
19. Scholl, *The Brothers Crawford*, 37.
20. Franklin Ellis, ed., *History of Fayette County, Pennsylvania, With Biographical Sketches of Many of Its Pioneers and Prominent Men* (Philadelphia: L.H. Everts

& Co., 1882), 526; *Journal of the House of Representatives of the United States, Volume V* (Washington, D.C: Gales & Seaton, 1826), 56, 194, 96.
21. Parker B. Brown, "The Search for the Colonel William Crawford Burn Site: An Investigative Report," *The Western Pennsylvania Historical Magazine Volume 68, No. 1* (Pittsburgh: The Western Pennsylvania Historical Society, 1985), 66.
22. Franklin Ellis, ed., *History of Fayette County, Pennsylvania, With Biographical Sketches of Many of Its Pioneers and Prominent Men* (Philadelphia: L.H. Everts & Co., 1882), 526; Scholl, The Brothers Crawford, 37.
23. Parker B. Brown "Crawford's Defeat: A Ballad," *The Western Pennsylvania Historical Magazine, Volume 65, No. 4* (Pittsburgh: The Historical Society of Western Pennsylvania, 1982), 312-315.
24. Anderson, "Colonel William Crawford," 34.

BIBLIOGRAPHY

Adams, John, L. H. Butterfield, ed. *The Adams Papers, Adams Family Correspondence, Vol. 2, June 1776–March 1778.* Cambridge, Massachusetts: Harvard University Press, 1963.

Agnew, Daniel. "A Biographical Sketch of Governor Richard Howell of New Jersey," *Pennsylvania Magazine of History and Biography, Vol XXI.* Philadelphia: Pennsylvania Historical Society, 1898.

Allen, William. Lewis Burd Walker, ed. *The Burd Papers: Extract from Chief Justice William Allen's Letter Book, Together with an Appendix Containing Pamphlets in the Controversy with Franklin.* Pottsville, Pennsylvania: Standard Publishing Company, 1897.

American Archives: Consisting of a Collection of Authentick Records, State Papers, Debates, and Letters and other Notices of Publick Affairs. Washington, D.C.: M. St. Clair Clarke and Peter Force, 1833.

Anderson, James H. Speech presented to the Wyandot Pioneer Association, June 11, 1896, "Colonel William Crawford," *Ohio Archaeological and Historical Publications, Volume VI.* Columbus, Ohio: Fred J. Herr, 1896.

Anderson, Niles. "The General Chooses a Road: The Forbes Campaign of 1758 to Capture Fort Duquesne," *Western Pennsylvania Historical Magazine, Volume 42, Number 4.* Pittsburgh: The Historical Society of Western Pennsylvania, 1959.

Asbury, Francis. *The Letters of Francis Asbury, Vol. I.* The Wesley Center (online), accessed October 4, 2012; http://wesley.nnu.edu/other-theologians/francis-asbury/the-journal-and-letters-of-francis-asbury-volume-i/francis-asbury-the-journal-vol-1.

Axtell, James, ed. *The Indian Peoples of Eastern America: A Documentary History of the Sexes.* New York: Oxford University Press, 1981.

Bailey, Ron. "A Surveyor for the King," *Colonial Williamsburg Journal,* Summer 2001. Williamsburg, Virginia: Colonial Williamsburg Foundation, 2001.

Barbeau, C.M. *Huron and Wyandot Mythology.* Ottawa: Government Printing Bureau, 1915.

Barnholth, William I. *Hopocan (Capt. Pipe) The Delaware Chief.* Akron, Ohio: The Summit County Historical Society, 1966.

Barnes, Celia. *Native American Power in the United States, 1783–1795.* Madison, New Jersey: Farleigh Dickinson University Press, 2003.

BIBLIOGRAPHY

Bedini, Silvio A. "George Washington (1732-1799) Surveyor and Cartographer, Part 1" *Professional Surveyor Magazine,* September 2000.

Benet, Stephen Vincent. *The Devil and Daniel Webster.* Los Angeles: Library of Alexandria, 2011, Nook ebook version.

Boback, John M. "Indian Warfare, Household Competency, and the Settlement of the Western Virginia Frontier, 1749 to 1794." PhD dissertation, West Virginia University, 2007.

Bockstruck, Lloyd DeWitt. *Virginia's Colonial Soldiers.* Baltimore: Genealogical Publishing Company, Inc., 1988.

Boulware, Tyler. "At the Crossroads: Indians and Empires on a Mid-Atlantic Frontier, 1700–1763/Breaking the Backcountry: The Seven Years' War in Virginia and Pennsylvania, 1754–1765." *South Carolina Historical Magazine 106, no. 1* (2005)

Brown, Parker B. "The Battle of Sandusky: June 4-6, 1782," *The Western Pennsylvania Historical Magazine, Volume 65, No. 2.* Pittsburgh: The Historical Society of Western Pennsylvania, 1982.

———. "Crawford's Defeat: A Ballad," *The Western Pennsylvania Historical Magazine, Volume 65, No. 4.* Pittsburgh: The Historical Society of Western Pennsylvania, 1982.

———. "The Fate of Crawford Volunteers Captured by Indians Following the Battle Of Sandusky in 1782," *The Western Pennsylvania Historical Magazine, Volume 65, Number 4.* Pittsburgh: Western Pennsylvania Historical Society, 1982.

———. "The Search for the Colonel William Crawford Burn Site: An Investigative Report," *The Western Pennsylvania Historical Magazine Volume 68, No. 1.* Pittsburgh: The Western Pennsylvania Historical Society, 1985.

———. "The Historical Accuracy of the Captivity Narrative of Doctor John Knight," *The Western Pennsylvania Historical Magazine, Vol. 70, No. 1.* Pittsburgh: The Western Pennsylvania Historical Society, 1987.

Butterfield, Consul W., ed. *The Washington-Crawford Letters, Being the Correspondence Between George Washington and William Crawford, From 1767 to 1781,* Concerning Western Lands. Cincinnati: Robert Clarke & Co., 1877.

———. *History of the Girtys.* Cincinnati: Robert Clarke & Co., 1890.

———. *Washington-Irvine Correspondence: The Official Letters Which Passed Between Washington and Brig.-Gen. William Irvine and Between Irvine and Others Concerning Military Affairs in the West from 1781 To 1783,* Madison, Wisconsin: David Atwood, 1882.

———. *An Historical Account of the Expedition against Sandusky Under Col. William Crawford in 1782.* Cincinnati, Ohio: Robert Clarke & Co., 1873.

Butts, Edward. *Simon Girty: Wilderness Warrior.* Toronto: Dundurn Press, 2011.

Caley, Percy B. "Lord Dunmore and the Pennsylvania Virginia Boundary Dispute," *Western Pennsylvania Historical Magazine, Volume 22, Number 2.* Pittsburgh: The Historical Society of Western Pennsylvania, 1939.

Calloway, Colin G. *The American Revolution in Indian Country: Crisis and Diversity in Native American Communities.* New York: Cambridge University Press, 1995.

Carbone, Gerald M. *Nathanael Greene: A Biography of the American Revolution.* New York: Palgrave MacMillan, 2008.

Crawford, William. *Last Will and Testament of William Crawford.* Westmoreland County, Pennsylvania, Probate Court, Will Book No. 1, 6

Cresswell, Nicholas, Lincoln MacVeagh, ed. *The Journal of Nicholas Cresswell, 1774-1777.* New York: The Dial Press, 1924.

Cronon, William. *Changes in the Land: Indians, Colonists, and the Ecology of New England.* New York: Hill and Wang, 1983.

Darlington, William M. *Christopher Gist's Journals with Historical, Geographical and Ethnological Notes and Biographies of his Contemporaries.* Pittsburgh: J.R. Weldin & Co., 1893.

de Crevecoeur, J. Hector St. John. *Letters from an American Farmer.* New York: Fox, Duffield, 1904.

Dinwiddie, Robert, R.A. Brock, ed., *The Official Records of Robert Dinwiddie, Lieutenant-Governor of The Colony of Virginia, 1751-1758, Volume II.* Richmond, Virginia: The Virginia Historical Society, 1883.

Doddridge, Joseph. *Notes on the Settlement and Indian Wars.* Akron, Ohio: New Werner Company, 1912.

Draper, Lyman Copeland. *Lyman Copeland Draper Collection.* Wisconsin State Historical Society, Madison, Wisconsin, 1830-1880.

Eburne, Richard. Louis B. Wright, ed. *A Plain Pathway to Plantations (1624.* Ithaca, New York: Cornell University Press, 1962.

Eckenrode, H. J. Archivist. *List of the Revolutionary Soldiers of Virginia.* Richmond, Virginia: Superintendent of Public Printing, 1913.

Eckert, Allan W. *That Dark and Bloody River.* New York: Bantam Books, 1995.

———. *Sorrow in Our Heart: The Life of Tecumseh.* New York: Bantam Books, 1992.

Ellis, Franklin, ed. *History of Fayette County, Pennsylvania, With Biographical Sketches of Many of Its Pioneers and Prominent Men.* Philadelphia: L.H. Everts & Co., 1882.

Emahiser, Grace U. *From River Clyde to Tymochtee and Col. William Crawford.* Fostoria, Ohio: Lithographed by the Commercial Press, 1969.

Engle, William Henry. *Some Women of Pennsylvania During the War of the Revolution.* Harrisburg, Pennsylvania: Harrisburg Publishing Company, 1898.

Executive Journals of the Council of Colonial Virginia, Vol. V, November 1, 1739-

May 7, 1754. Richmond, Virginia: Commonwealth of Virginia Division of Purchase and Printing, 1945.

Ferling, John E. *Almost a Miracle: The American Victory in the War of Independence.* Oxford: Oxford University Press, 2007.

———. *The First of Men: A Life of George Washington.* Knoxville, Tennessee: University of Tennessee Press, 1988.

Fitzpatrick, John C., ed. *The Diaries of George Washington, 1748-1799.* Boston: Houghton Mifflin, 1925.

Forbes, John, Alfred Procter James, ed. *Writings of General John Forbes Relating to His Service in North America.* Menasha, Wisconsin: The Collegiate Press, 1938.

Fort Ligonier Association et al. *War for Empire in Western Pennsylvania.* Ligonier, Pennsylvania: Fort Ligonier Association, 1993.

Foulke, Joseph. *Memoirs of Jacob Ritter, A Faithful Minister in the Society of Friends.* Philadelphia: T. E. Chapman, 1844.

Frazer, Persifor. *General Persifor Frazer: A Memoir Compiled Principally from His Own Papers by His Great-Grandson, Persifor Frazer.* Philadelphia: Unknown Publisher, 1907.

Gipson, Lawrence Henry. *The Great War for Empire: The Years of Defeat, 1754–1757.* New York: Alfred A. Knopf, 1959.

Goodman, Nathan G. *A Franklin Reader.* New York: Thomas Y. Crowell Company, 1945.

Hanks, Larry K. *The Emigrant Tribes, Wyandot, Delaware, and Shawnee: A Chronology.* Kansas City, Kansas: Unpublished, 1998.

Harris, Michael. *Brandywine: A Military History of the Battle that Lost Philadelphia but Saved America, September 11, 1777.* El Dorado Hills, California: Savas Beatie, 2014.

Hawk, Black. *Life of MA-KA-TAI-ME-SHE-KIA-KIAK or Black Hawk.* Iowa City: State Historical Society of Iowa, 1932.

Hazard, Samuel, ed. *Pennsylvania Archive.* Philadelphia: Joseph Severns, 1853.

Heckewelder, John. *A Narrative of the Mission of the United Brethren Among the Delaware and Mohegan Indians, From Its Commencement, in the Year 1740, to the Close of the Year 1808.* Philadelphia: McCarty & Davis, 1820.

———. *History, Manners, and Customs of the Indian Nations Who Once Inhabited Pennsylvania and the Neighbouring States.* Philadelphia: Publication Fund of the Historical Society of Pennsylvania, 1881.

Heitman, F. B. *Historical Register of Officers of the Continental Army During The War of the Revolution, April, 1775, to December, 1783.* Washington D.C.: W. H. Lowdermilk & Co., 1893.

Historical Collections: Report of the Pioneer Society of the State of Michigan, Vol. IX. Lansing, Michigan: Wynkoop, Hallenbeck, Crawford Company, 1908.

Historical Collections: Collections and Researches Made by the Michigan Pioneer and Historical Society, Vol. XX. Lansing, Michigan: Wynkoop Hallenreck Crawford Co., 1912.

Hocker, Edward W. *The Fighting Parson of the American Revolution: A Biography of General Peter Muhlenberg, Lutheran Clergyman, Military Chieftain and Political Leader.* Philadelphia: Edward W. Hocker, 1936.

Hoffman, Phillip W. *Simon Girty: Turncoat Hero.* Franklin, Tennessee: Flying Camp Press, 2008.

Hurt, Douglas. *Indian Agriculture in America: Prehistory to Present.* Lawrence, Kansas: University Press of Kansas, 1987.

Johansen, Bruce E., ed. *Enduring Legacies: Native American Treaties and Contemporary Controversies.* Westport, Connecticut: Praeger, 2004.

Johnson, Susannah Willard. *A Narrative of the Captivity of Mrs. Johnson.* Windsor, Vermont: Thomas Pomrot, 1814.

Jones, David. *A Journal of Two Visits Made to Some Nations of Indians on the West Side of the River Ohio, in the Years 1772 and 1773.* Burlington, New Jersey: Isaac Collins, 1774.

Journals of the Continental Congress, Edited from the Original Records in the Library of Congress. Washington D.C.: U.S. Government Printing Office, 1904-1937.

Kellogg, Louise Phelps ed., *Frontier Advance on the Upper Ohio, 1778-1779.* Madison, Wisconsin: Wisconsin Historical Society, 1916.

Knepper, George W. *Ohio and Its People.* Kent, Ohio: Kent State University Press, 2003.

Knight, John, and John Slover. *Narratives of the Perils and Sufferings of Dr. Knight and John Slover.* Cincinnati: U.P. James, 1867.

Kopperman, Paul E. *Braddock at the Monongahela.* Pittsburgh: University of Pittsburgh Press, 1977.

Ledward, K.H. ed., *Journal, August 1753: Volume 61, in Journals of the Board of Trade and Plantations, Volume 9, January 1750 - December 1753.* London: H. M. Stationary Office, 1932.

Lee, Alfred E. *History of the City of Columbus, Capital of Ohio.* New York & Chicago: Munsell & Company, 1892.

Leith, John. *Leith's Narrative: A Short Biography of John Leith with a Brief Account of his Life Among the Indians.* Cincinnati: Robert Clarke & Co., 1883.

Letters and Correspondence, Public Record Office, Kew, Surrey, England.

Lewis, Virgil A. *History of the Battle of Point Pleasant.* Charleston, West Virginia: The Tribune Printing Company, 1909.

Lincoln, Charles Henry, ed., *Correspondence of William Shirley, Governor of Massachusetts and Military Commander in America, 1731-1760, Volume II.* New York: The Macmillan Company, 1912.

BIBLIOGRAPHY

Mann, Barbara Alice. *George Washington's War on Native America.* Westport, Connecticut: Praeger, 2005.

Mercer, George. Lois Mulkearn, ed., *George Mercer Papers Relating to the Ohio Company of Virginia.* Pittsburgh: University of Pittsburgh Press, 1954.

McClenathan, J. C. M. D., Reverend William A. Edie, Reverend Ellis B. Burgess, J. Aloysius Coll, Eugene T. Norton. *Centennial History of the Borough of Connellsville Pennsylvania, 1806 -1906.* Columbus, Ohio: The Champlin Press, 1906.

McClure, David, Franklin B. Dexter, ed. *The Diary of David McClure, Doctor of Divinity, 1748-1820.* New York: The Knickerbocker Press, 1899.

McConnell, Michael N. *A Country Between: The Upper Ohio Valley and Its Peoples, 1724–1774.* Lincoln, Nebraska: University of Nebraska Press, 1992.

McGuire. Thomas J. *The Philadelphia Campaign: Volume One: Brandywine and the Fall of Philadelphia.* Mechanicsburg, Pennsylvania: Stackpole Books, 2006.

———. *The Philadelphia Campaign: Volume Two: Germantown and the Roads to Valley Forge.* Mechanicsburg, Pennsylvania: Stackpole Books, 2007.

McMichael, William P. "Diary of Lieutenant James McMichael, of the Pennsylvania Line, 1776-1778," *Pennsylvania Magazine of History and Biography, Vol XVI, No. 2.* Philadelphia: Pennsylvania Historical Society, 1892.

McWhorter, Lucullus Virgil. *The Border Settlers of Northwest Virginia, From 1768 to 1795.* Hamilton, Ohio: Republican Publishing Co., 1915.

Minutes of the Provincial Council Pennsylvania, From the Organization to the Termination of the Proprietary Government, Volume V, Containing The Proceedings of Council From December 17th 1745, to 20th March, 1754, Both Days Included. Harrisburg, Pennsylvania: Theodore Penn & Co., 1851.

Moreau, Jacob Nicolas. *A Memorial Containing a Summary View of Facts, with Their Authorities. In Answer to the Observations Sent by the English Ministry to the Courts of Europe, Translated from the French.* New York: H. Gaine, 1757.

Muhlenberg, Peter Gabriel. "Orderly Book of Gen. John Peter Gabriel Muhlenberg, March 26-December 20, 1777," *The Pennsylvania Magazine of History and Biography, Vol. 35, No. 1.* Philadelphia: Pennsylvania Historical Society, 1911.

Nelson, Larry L. *A Man of Distinction among Them: Alexander McKee and British-Indian Affairs along the Ohio Country Frontier, 1754–1799.* Kent, Ohio: Kent State University Press, 1999.

Nester, William R. *The Great Frontier War: Britain, France, and the Imperial Struggle for North America, 1607–1755.* Westport, Connecticut: Praeger, 2000.

———. *The First Global War: Britain, France, and the Fate of North America, 1756-1775.* Westport, Connecticut: Praeger Publishers, 2000.

Norris J.E., ed. *The History of the Lower Shenandoah Valley Counties of Frederick, Berkeley, Jefferson and Clarke*. Chicago: A. Warner & Co., 1890.

Nye, Russel B. *A Baker's Dozen: Thirteen Unusual Americans*. East Lansing, Michigan: Michigan State University Press, 1956.

O'Callaghan, E. B., ed., *Documents Relative to the Colonial History, State of New York, Volume X*. Albany, New York: Weed, Parsons, and Company, 1858.

Olmstead, Earl P., and David Zeisberger. *David Zeisberger: A Life among the Indians*. Kent, Ohio: Kent State University Press, 1997.

Palmer, William P., ed. *Calendar of Virginia State Papers and Other Manuscripts, Vol. III*. Richmond, Virginia: James E. Goode, 1883.

The Papers of George Washington, W.W. Abbot, ed., et al. Charlottesville: University Press of Virginia, 1983-2006.

The Papers of George Washington, Diaries, Donald Jackson, ed., et al. Charlottesville: University of Virginia Press, 1976-1979.

Pargellis, Stanley V., ed. *Military Affairs in North America, 1748- 1765: Selected Documents from the Cumberland Papers in Windsor Castle*. New York: D. Appleton-Century Company, 1936.

The Parliamentary History of England from the Earliest Period to the Year 1803, Volume XXII. London: T.C. Hanspard, 1814.

Perkins, Elizabeth A. *Border Life: Experience and Memory in the Revolutionary Ohio Valley*. Chapel Hill, North Carolina: University of North Carolina Press, 1998.

Philbreck, Nathaniel. *Bunker Hill: A City, A Siege, A Revolution*. New York: Penguin Random House LLC, 2013.

Post, Christian Frederick. *The Second Journal of Christian Frederick Post, On a Message from the Governor of Pennsylvania to the Indians on the Ohio*. London: J. Wilkie, 1769.

Pieper Thomas I., and James B. Gidney. *Fort Laurens, 1778-1779: The Revolutionary War in Ohio*. Kent, Ohio: Kent State University Press, 1976.

Preston, David L. *Braddock's Defeat: The Battle of the Monongahela and the Road to Revolution*. New York: Oxford University Press, 2015.

Randall, Willard Sterne. *George Washington: A Life*. New York: Henry Holt & Co. 1997.

"Revolutionary War Pension and Bounty Land Warrant Application Files." National Archives, Washington, D.C.

Richter, Daniel K. *Facing East from Indian Country: A Native History of Early America*. Cambridge, Massachusetts: Harvard University Press, 2001.

Scholl, Allen W. *The Brothers Crawford: Colonel William, 1722-1782 and Valentine Jr., 1724-1777, Volume I*. Westminster, Maryland: Heritage Books, Inc., 2007.

Seed, Patricia. *Ceremonies of Possession in Europe's Conquest of the New World*. New

York: Cambridge University Press, 1995.

Seeman, Eric R. *The Huron-Wendat Feast of the Dead*. Baltimore: Johns Hopkins University Press, 2011.

Shellhouse letter, C. W. Butterfield Scrapbooks, Series 3, Number 8, Western Reserve Historical Society, Cleveland, Ohio.

Sherrard, Robert Andrew, Thomas Johnson Sherrard, ed. *The Sherrard Family of Steubenville*. Philadelphia: The Jas. B. Rodgers Printing Company, 1890.

Showman, Richard K., Robert M. McCarthy, and Margaret Cobb, eds. *The Papers of General Nathaniel Greene, vol. 2, 1 January 1777 - 16 October 1778*. Chapel Hill, North Carolina: University of North Carolina Press, 1980.

Sipe, C. Hale. *The Indian Wars of Pennsylvania: An Account of the Indian Events, in Pennsylvania, of The French and Indian War, Pontiac s War, Lord Dunmore's War, The Revolutionary War and the Indian Uprising from 1789 to 1795*. Harrisburg, Pennsylvania: The Telegraph Press, 1929.

Smyth, J.F.D., Esq. *A Tour in the United States of America*. London: G. Robinson, J. Robson, J. Sewell, 1784.

Sioui, Georges E. *Huron Wendat: The Heritage of the Circle*. East Lansing, Michigan: Michigan State University Press, 1999.

Sparks, Jared and Henry Reed. *The Lives of Charles Lee and Joseph Reed*. Boston: Charles C. Little and James Brown, 1846.

St. Clair, Arthur. *The St. Clair Papers: The Life and Services of Arthur St. Clair, Vol. I*. Cincinnati: Robert Clarke & Co., 1882.

Starkey, Armstrong. *European and Native American Warfare, 1675–1815*. London: UCL Press, 1998.

Stephen, Adam. "The Ohio Expedition of 1754," *The Pennsylvania Magazine of Biography and History, Volume 18*. Philadelphia: The Historical Society of Pennsylvania, 1894.

Stevens, S.K, and D.H. Kent, eds. *The Papers of Henry Bouquet, Series 21634, Northwestern Pennsylvania Series*. Harrisburg, Pennsylvania: Pennsylvania Historical Commission, 1940.

Swanton, John R. *The Indian Tribes of North America*. Washington, DC: U.S. Government Printing Office, 1952.

Thornton, Russell. *American Indian Holocaust and Survival: A Population History Since 1492*. Norman, Oklahoma: The University of Oklahoma Press, 1990.

Thwaites, Reuben G., and Louise Phelps Kellogg, eds. *Frontier Defense on the Upper Ohio, 1777–1778*. Oshkosh, Wisconsin: Castle-Pierce Printing Company, 1912.

The Virginia Gazette, Number 1277, January 27, 1776, Williamsburg, Virginia.

Trigger, Bruce G. *The Huron: Farmers of the North*, 2d ed. Belmont, CA: Wadsworth Group, 2002.

Volo James M., and Dorothy Denneen Volo, *Daily Life on the Old Colonial Frontier*. Westport, Connecticut: Greenwood Press, 2002.

Von Pilchau, George Pilar, Baron de Rosenthal and William L. Stone. "Journal of a Volunteer Expedition to Sandusky, from May 24 to June 13, 1782," *The Pennsylvania Magazine of History and Biography, Vol. 18, No. 2*. Philadelphia: Historical Society of Pennsylvania, 1894.

———. "Journal of a Volunteer Expedition to Sandusky, from May 24 to June 13, 1782," *The Pennsylvania Magazine of History and Biography, Vol. 18, No. 3*. Philadelphia: Historical Society of Pennsylvania, 1894.

Wall, Charles Cecil. *George Washington, Citizen-Soldier*. Charlottesville, Virginia: University of Virginia Press, 1980.

Wallace, Anthony F.C. *Jefferson and the Indians: The Tragic Fate of the First Americans*. Cambridge, Massachusetts: Harvard University Press, 2001.

Walters, Michael, J.P. Maclean, ed. *Journal of Michael Walters, A Member of the Expedition Against Sandusky in the Year 1782*. Cleveland: Western Reserve Historical Society, 1899.

Washington, George. John C. Fitzpatrick, ed., *The Writings of George Washington from the Original Manuscript Sources, 1745-1799, Vol. 1* (Washington, DC: U. S. Government Printing Office, 1931.

Williams, Edward G. "A Revolutionary Journal and Orderly Book of General Lachlan Mcintosh's Expedition, 1778 (Second Installment)," *The Western Pennsylvania Historical Magazine, Volume 43, No. 2*. Pittsburgh: The Historical Society of Western Pennsylvania, 1960.

———. "A Revolutionary Journal and Orderly Book of General Lachlan Mcintosh's Expedition, 1778 (Third Installment)," *The Western Pennsylvania Historical Magazine, Volume 43, No. 3*. Pittsburgh: The Historical Society of Western Pennsylvania, 1960.

White, Richard. *The Middle Ground: Indians, Empires, and Republics in the Great Lakes Region, 1650–1815*. Cambridge: Cambridge University Press, 1991.

Williams, Roger, John Russell Bartlett, ed. *Letters of Roger Williams, 1632–1682*. Providence, Rhode Island: Narragansett Club, 1874.

Withers, Alexander Scott. *Chronicles of Border Warfare*. Cleveland: Arthur H. Clark Company, 1895.

Zeisberger, David. *The Diary of David Zeisberger, A Moravian Missionary*. Cincinnati: Historical and Philosophical Society of Ohio, 1885.

INDEX
(i) = illustration

2nd Grenadiers Battalion (British), 129-130
2nd Regiment (British), 134
40th Regiment of Foot (British), 134-135
4th Brigade (British), 129-130
A Song, Called Crawford's Defeat by the Indians, On the Fourth Day of June, 1782, 243
Abercrombie, James, General, 58
Adams, Abigail (Smith), 122
Adams, John, 122
Allegheny Campaign, 162
Allegheny Mountains, 10, 27, 32, 35, 54, 56-57, 65-66, 69-70, 72, 87, 92, 112, 140, 151
Allegheny Plateau, 4, 9, 11, 14-16, 20, 31, 48, 65, 72, 92, 95
Allegheny River, 77, 101, 142
Allen, William, 34
American Antiquarian Society, 243
American Revolution, 63, 110, 112, 140, 163, 235, 238, 248
Appalachian Mountains, 30
Armstrong, John, 73
Articles of Confederation, 235
Ashby, Hankerson, Ensign, 219, 220, 221
Battle Island, 198(i), 200(i), 202(i), 211-213, 217
Baynton, Wharton, and Morgan, 103
Beaver River, 145, 154
Bell, Robert, 76, 79
Berkeley Regiment, 97-98
Berkeley, Norborne, 4th Baron de Botetourt, 73-74
Big Captain Johnny, 204
Biggs, John, Captain, 184, 219-221
Bland, Theodorick Jr., Colonel, 127
Blue Ridge Mountains, 3, 8
Boone, Daniel, 93
Boone, James, 93

Boston Harbor, 112
Bouquet, Henry, Colonel, 35, 55-57, 61, 65
Brackenridge, Hugh H., 237
Braddock Road, 55-57, 59, 66, 68-69, 72, 84-85
Braddock, Edward, General, 31-40, 42-48, 53, 55, 66, 77, 84, 148
  death of, 46
Brady, William, 145-146, 203
Brandywine Creek, 122, 124-126, 128
Brandywine, battle of, 126-128, 130, 181
Breed's Hill, 112
Brinton, James, Major, 210, 212
Brinton's Ford, 125
Bristol Ford, 127
British Indian Department, 103, 105, 150
British Rangers, 176, 188, 191, 195, 203, 210
Brodhead, Daniel, Colonel, 154, 161-163, 165-166(i), 185
Buffalo Creek, 174
Bull, 146, 147
Bullskin Creek, 51
Bullskin Run, 2, 64
Bunker Hill, battle of, 112-113, 119
Burgoyne, John, General, 120
Butler's Rangers, 217
Butterfield, Consul W., 247
Byrne, George, 7
Caldwell, William, Captain, 195, 203
  death of, 203
Camp Charlotte, 99, 105-107, 149
Camp Point Pleasant, 98-99
Canon, Daniel, 203
Captina Creek, 93
Carleton, Sir Guy, Governor General, 234
Cattail Run, 5-6

INDEX

Chadd's Ford, 124-127
Charles River, 110
Chartier's Creek, 71-72
Chequamigon Bay, 193
Cherokee Expedition, 85
Cherokee Tribe, 72, 93
Chew, Benjamin, 134
Chiksika, Chief, 140
Chippewa Tribe, 220
Christian Delaware Tribe, 157, 167-173, 180, 186, 196, 221, 228, 232-233, 236
Christiana Creek, 123
Clark, George Rogers, Colonel, 163
Cleveland, James, 241
Cliveden (Benjamin Chew House), 134(i)-135
Clove, encampment, 120
Coffman, Christopher, 220
Connell, Ann Matthews, 87-88, 115, 176, 248
Connell, James, 87, 177
Connell, Nancy, 177
Connell, Polly, 177
Connell, William, 177
Connewago (Seneca village), 142
Connolly, John M.D., 91-92, 97
Constitutional Convention (United States), 235
Continental Army, 113, 118-119, 122, 124, 179
Contrecoeur, Claude-Pierre Pécaudy de, Colonel, 39, 48
Cooch's Mill, 123
Corbley, Rev. John, 174
Cornstalk, Chief, 99, 140
Cornwallis, Lord Charles, 1st Marquess and 2nd Earl Cornwallis, 119, 128
  surrender at Yorktown, 163
Coryell's Ferry, 120
Coulon de Villiers de Jumonville, Joseph, Ensign, 21, 23-26, 44
Cowpens, battle of, 63
Craik, James, 76-77, 79
Crawford, Hannah (Vance), 5(i), 13, 49, 52, 64, 68-69, 76, 87, 115, 163, 176-177, 194, 239-243
  death of, 243
Crawford, John, 5, 49, 76, 87, 176-177, 213, 216, 218, 239, 241
Crawford, Moses, 176
Crawford, Ophelia "Effie", 5, 49
Crawford, Richard, 176
Crawford, Valentine, 1-2, 4, 18, 64, 70, 87, 95, 117
  death of, 117
Crawford, William III (father of WC IV), 1
  death of, 1
Crawford, William IV, 13, 73, 125, 230-231(i), 249
  accepts Command of Sandusky Expedition, 176
  accused of being a Tory sympathizer, 114
  aids wounded at Battle Island, 212
  aligns himself with the patriot cause, 112
  apprenticeship of, 4
  argues with Col. Williamson, 208
  argues with Col. Williamson over dividing forces, 197
  as Brigade Commander, 137
  as chainman, 8-9
  as Commander of Sandusky Expedition, 182(i), 185, 188, 196, 201
  as Commander of militia troops of Ohio counties, 153
  as Ensign, 50
  as executor of brothers estate, 117
  as homesteader, 68
  as infantry officer, 55
  as Justice of the Peace, 75
  as Justice of the Peace for Youghiogheny County, 163
  as land agent, 71-73, 89, 108
  as President Judge, 75, 91
  as prisoner, 218
  as Ranger, 35-38, 42, 43-45, 47, 49
  as scout, 123
  as servant to Lord Dunmore, 96
  as soldier, 19-23, 27, 51-52, 59, 61, 96, 98, 107, 123-124, 127-128, 133, 136
  as soldier in Lord Dunmore's War, 107
  as surveyor, 72-74, 76, 79, 81-82, 84-85, 90, 109

INDEX

asked to lead expedition, 175
asks Simon Girty to have him sent to Fort Detroit for ransom to the British, 222
assigned to Fort Pitt, 139
at Squaw Campaign, 147
at the Battle of Germantown, 135
begins expedition to Sandusky, 183
birth of, 1
birth of children, 5
calls for war council meeting to discuss options, 188-189
capture of, 220
condemned to death by Chief Hopocan, 226
considers his army's field disadvantage at Battle Island, 207
creates his final Will & Testament, 176
death of, 232
disavows being a Tory sympathizer in letter to Editor, 114
dismisses men for insubordination, 160
early years, 1-2
education of, 4
escorted to his execution by Delaware guard, 229
family moves to Sheandoah Valley, 2
friendship with Chief Wingenund, 194
informs war council of decision to retreat from Battle Island, 210
joins Virginia militia, 18
leads expedition into deserted Indian village, 197
leads party East after Battle Island retreat, 218-220
leads Sandusky Expedition, 190
letter from Gen E. Hand (2/5/1778), 144
listens undercover while Simon Girty asks for his surrender, 209
looses command of Thirteenth Virginia Regiment, 153
made Commander of Brigade, 136
marriage of, 5
meets Moravian Indians, 157
meets Simon Girty, 99
moves family to Pennsylvania, 66, 68

opens fire on 2nd Grenadier Battalion, 130
orders army to hold ground on Battle Island, 208
orders army to march through Gnadenhutten, 187
orders remaining army to advance to Battle Island, 201
organizes brigade construction of Fort Laurens, 158
pleads with Chief Wingenund for freedom, 228
pledges allegiance to VA, 96
promoted to Colonel & Commander of Seventh Virginia Regiment, 116
promotion to Captain, 62
promotion to Colonel, 97
promotion to Lieutenant, 52
promotion to Lt. Colonel and 2nd in Command of regiment, 115
proposes to GW an expedition against Shawnee towns, 162
purchase of property in VA, 5
recovering from scabies/psoriasis, 143
releases his brigade and sends them home, 161
requests audience with Chief Wingenund, 226
resigns from militia, 64
retires from the Army, 163
takes Command of Fort Crawford, 153
takes stand at Battle Island, 202
torture of, 224, 229-232
transferred to Thirteenth Virginia Regiment, 116
trial of, 221, 224
wins election to lead expedition, 180
with scouting unit, 123
writes "final" letter to GW in May 1781, 163
Cresap, Michael, Colonel, 91, 93-94, 106
Creswell, Nicholas, 87
Croghan, George, 38, 40, 77, 79, 91
Crooked Billet, battle of, 124
Cumberland River, 103
Cuppy, John, 158

Cuyahoga River, 143, 145
Darcy, Lord Robert, 4th Earl of Holderness, 12
Dawes, William, 110
de Beaujeu, Daniel Hyacinthe Mary Lienard, Captain, 39-41
de Charlevoix, Pierre Francois Xavier, 193
de Corbiere, Lieutenant, 59-60
Delaware
    New Castle, 123
    Newport, 123
    Wilmington, 122-124
Delaware Capes, 120
Delaware River, 90, 120
Delaware Tribe, 14, 24, 65, 87, 93, 99-102, 138, 140, 146-148, 155, 157, 174, 184, 193-195, 200, 203, 207-208, 210, 212, 217, 220-221, 223, 225-226, 229, 232, 237, 242
DePeyster, Arent, Major, 150, 167-168, 190-191, 217-218, 222, 234
The Devil and Daniel Webster (Benet), 237
Dinwiddie, Robert, Governor, 10-12, 14-19, 22-24, 26-28, 43, 46, 48, 51-52, 55, 73-74
du Motier, Gilbert, Marquis de Lafayette, 122
Dumas, Jean-Daniel, Captain, 48
Dunbar, Thomas, Colonel, 32, 37, 47, 48
Dunleavy, Francis, 204
Dunquat, Chief, 167-168, 189-191, 193-195, 201, 210-211, 221, 238-239
Duquesne de Menneville, Michel-Ange, Marquis Duquesne, 11
Eburne, Richard, 30
Eighth Pennsylvania Regiment, 153-154, 161
Eighth Virginia Regiment, 118
Elk River, 122
Elliott, Matthew, Captain, 99, 149-150, 195, 203, 208-210, 224, 231
Erie Tribe, 193
Fairfax, George William, 7-8, 26-27
Fairfax, Thomas, 6th Lord Fairfax, Baron of Cameron, 6, 8
Fairfax, Thomas, Colonel, 7-8

Faith (British ship), 191
Fallen Timbers, battle of, 235, 239
Fifth Virginia Regiment, 115
First Connecticut Brigade, 135-136
First Virginia Regiment, 55, 57-59, 61-62, 64, 69, 75, 113, 118, 121, 129, 135-136
Forbes Expedition, 57-62, 73
Forbes, John, General, 53-62, 65-66, 85
Fort Bedford, 55-57, 59
Fort Crawford, 153
Fort Cumberland, 26, 34-36, 47-48, 51, 55, 62-63
Fort Detroit, 138, 141, 143, 149-153, 155, 157, 165, 167, 190-191, 194, 217, 222, 234, 238-239
Fort Dunmore, 97
Fort Duquesne, 18, 20-22, 26, 32-33, 35-40, 47-48, 53-59, 61-63, 65, 100-101
Fort Fincastle, 96-97
Fort Gower, 98-99, 107-108
Fort Granville, 100-101
Fort Laurens, 102(i), 152, 157-161
    description of, 159
Fort Laurens Expedition, 185
Fort Laurens Historic Site, 160
Fort Laurens Museum, 156
Fort LeBoeuf, 11, 15
Fort Ligonier, 56(i)-59, 61
Fort Loudon, 52
Fort McIntosh, 154(i)-155, 159-161, 179, 215
Fort Necessity, 25(i)-26, 44, 46(i), 84
Fort Necessity National Battlefield, 25(i)
Fort Niagara, 32, 141, 143
Fort Nonsense, 158(1)-159
Fort Pitt, 62, 65-66, 71-72, 76-77, 79, 81-82, 89-92, 96-97, 102-104, 111-112, 116, 137-141, 143-148, 151-154, 159, 161, 163, 165-166, 169-170, 172, 174, 177-178, 181, 183-184, 194, 237, 240
Fort Presque Isle, 11
Fort Randolph, 140
Fort Recovery, battle of, 238-239
Fort Ticonderoga, 120, 178
Fort Venango, 15

INDEX

Fourth Virginia Regiment, 116
Fox Nation, 29
Franklin, Benjamin, 48
Frederick Regiment, 97-98
French and Indian War, 40, 48, 81, 90, 100, 103, 140, 148, 248
Fry, Joshua, Colonel, 18, 26
Gaddis, Thomas, Colonel, 202
Gage, Thomas, Colonel, 38, 40, 91, 110
Genn, James, 7
George II, King of England, 9-10, 31-32
George III, King of England, 66, 70, 109, 111, 119, 149, 239
Georgian Bay, 191
Germantown, battle of, 134-136, 181
Gibson, John, Colonel, 153, 166, 174
Girty, George, 100-101, 149, 195
Girty, James, 100-102, 149
Girty, Simon, 99-106, 141-143, 145-152, 190-191, 193-195, 201, 204-205(i), 209-210, 218, 221-224, 226, 229-232, 235, 237-238, 247
  as interpreter for WC IV's trial, 225
  death of, 238
Girty, Thomas, 100-102, 149
Gist, Christopher, Captain, 10-11, 15-16, 20, 22, 50-52
Gnadenhutten Massacre, 166-167, 170-171(i), 173-175, 177-78, 190, 222, 224, 226, 250
Grant, James, General, 81
Grape Vine Town, 79
Great Kanawha River, 73-74, 78, 80, 82-85, 98
Great Meadows, 21-22, 25, 84
Greathouse, Daniel, 93-94
Green Bay, 193
Greene, Nathanael, General, 118-119, 123-124, 127, 129-136
Guyasuta, Chief, 81-82, 101-102, 105, 142-143
Haldimand, Frederick, General, 234
Halkett, Sir Peter, 32
Hamilton, Henry, Colonel, 138, 143, 150
Hamilton, James, Governor, 12
Hampshire County Militia, 158
Hancock, John, 119-120
Hand, Edward, General, 138-139(i), 141-146, 148-150, 152(i), 163, 193
Hardin, John, Captain, 211
Harrison, Lawrence, 69
Harrison, William, 69, 76, 79, 176-177, 218, 240
  death of, 213
Hayes, John, 214
Heckewelder, John, 194, 226, 239
Hessians, in American Revolution, 122-123, 126-128, 134
Higgins, John, 149
Hite, Jacob, 84
Hite, Jost, 51
Hocking River, 81, 97-98
Hollingshead, Joseph, 104
Hopocan, Chief, 146-148, 193-195, 200, 203, 221-226, 228, 230, 238-239
  death of, 239
Horrocks, James, 75
House Committee of Claims, 242
House of Commons of Great Britian, 165
House of Lords (UK Parliament), 98
Howe, Sir William, General, 118-128(i), 131-132, 135-136
Hudson River, 120
Hume, George, 7
Illinois
  Kaskaskia, 104
Innes, James, Colonel, 24
Iron Hill, 123
Iroquois Confederacy, 14, 19, 65, 192
Iroquois Nation, 29, 72
Irvine, William, General, 151, 165-166(i), 174-181, 183, 190, 216, 233, 236, 240, 248
James I, King of England, 30
Jamestown Settlement, 30
Jeffrey's Ford, 126-127
Jelloway, Tom, 221
Johnson, Josiah, 75
Johnson, Sir William, 65, 72, 102
Joncaire, Philippe Thomas, Captain, 15
Jones Ford, 126
Jones, David, 93

INDEX

Kanaghragait, Chief, 77, 79, 81-82
Kenton, Simon, 105
Killbuck Creek, 188
King George's War (War of the Austrian Succession, 1745-1748), 29
King William's War (League of Augsburg War, 1689-1697), 29
Kispoko Town, 94
Kittanning (village of), 101
Knight, John M.D., 181, 206, 211-212, 218-220, 223, 229, 237, 240
  capture of, 220
  escape of, 233
  torture of, 224
Knox, Henry, General, 135
Knyphausen, Wilhelm, Baron von, General, 123, 126-128
Lake Erie, 11, 143, 176, 213
Lake Huron, 193
Lake Simcoe, 191
Lake Superior, 193
Laurens, Henry, 139, 152, 158
Lawson, John, Major, 137
Le Gardeur, Louis, de St. Pierre de Repentigny, 15-16
Le Marchand de Lignery, Francois-Marie, 57-58, 61-62
Le Villier, Francis, 205, 218
Lee, Charles, General, 118
Leet, Daniel, Major, 213, 216
Leith, John, 194-195
Lenni-Lenape Tribe, 140
Leveson-Gower, John, 1st Earl of Gower, 98
Lewis, Andrew, General, 98-99
Lexington and Concord, battles of, 109-110
Lichtenau Moravian Mission, 157
Little Kanawha River, 85, 89, 109
Logan's Lament, 105-106
Lord Dunmore's War, 89, 94, 98(i), 104, 107, 112, 148, 185, 248
Louis XV, King of France and Navarre, 11
Lower Sandusky River, 191
Luken's Mill, 135
Mahoning River, 147, 225
Maidstone-on-the-Potomac, 50-52
Makataimeshekiakiak "Black Hawk",

Chief, 78
Manitoulin Island, 193
Mannucothe (Miami Tribe name for John Slover), 184
Marin, Pierre-Paul, de la Malgue, 11
Marshal, James, 174-175
Maryland
  Elk Ferry, 122
  Elkton, 122
  Fredericktown, 117
  Williamsport, 50
  Wills Creek (Cumberland), 15, 24, 26
Maryland Militia, 132-133
Massachusetts
  Boston, 108-109, 111, 113
  Cambridge, 119
  Concord, 110
  Lexington, 110-111
  Worcester, 243
Matthews, Elizabeth (Vance), 87
Maxwell, William "Scotch Willie", General, 123, 126
McClelland, John, Major, 210-211
McClure, Rev. David, 87
McCormick, Alex, 221-224
McCormick, Anne, 176
McCoy, Angus, 203
McDonald, Angus, Major, 96
McIntosh, Lachlan, General, 152(i)-157, 159-163
McKee, Alexander, 102-105, 141, 148-150, 152, 167, 195, 218, 224, 231
Mercer, George, Captain, 69
Mercer, Hugh, Colonel, 59-60
Miami Tribe, 184
Michikapeche, 146-147, 225-226
Michilimackinac, 193
Mingo Bottom, 177-179, 181, 183, 186, 189-190, 215-216, 225, 239
Mingo Island, 179
Mingo Nations, 92
Mingo Town, 79, 81-82
Mingo Tribe, 14, 34, 65, 79, 93, 96, 98-99, 104-107, 111, 150-151, 174, 194
Mississippi River, 103
Mohawk Tribe, 141
Monmouth, battle of, 165

292

INDEX

Monongahela River, 18, 20, 38-41(i), 43-45, 59, 72-73, 75, 84, 94
Monongahela Valley, 95
Montagu-Dunk, George, 2nd Earl of Halifax, 32
Montgomery, Archibald, Lt. Colonel, 61
Moravian Indians (Christian Delaware Tribe members), 157, 227
Morgan, Daniel, 62-63, 141-142, 174
Morgan, George, 103-104
Mount Vernon, 14, 16, 28, 63-64, 70, 72-76, 82, 85, 235
Muhlenberg, Peter, General, 118, 121, 129
Munn, James, Captain, 203
Murray, Lord John, Governor, 4th Earl of Dunmore, 89-92, 94, 96-99, 105-107, 113-114(i), 235
Muskingum River, 81, 87, 141, 157, 179, 183, 190, 193, 213, 216, 249
Myers, Mike, 204, 213
Natchez Nation, 29
Neutral Confederacy, 193
New France, 11, 16, 29-31, 39
New Jersey
   Morristown, 119
   Trenton, 117, 119
New Jersey Militia, 132-133
New River, 72-73
New York
   Manhattan, 120
   Onondaga, 141
New York Independent Company, 38
Nicholson, Joseph, 79, 105
Ninth Virginia Regiment, 136
Nutimus, Chief, 147
Ohio
   Bolivar, 157
   Chillicothe, 151
   Circleville, 99
   Columbus, 107
   Crestline, 194
   Gnadenhutten, 167-174, 177, 186-188, 190, 196, 222, 225, 228
   Mingo Junction, 79
   Salt Lick Town, 107, 177
   Upper Sandusky, 193

Wheeling, 184
Ohio Company, 10-11, 15-16, 19, 69
Ohio Country, 11, 13-14, 57, 77-78, 81-82, 92, 96, 99, 103, 112, 139, 141-142, 149-150, 167, 174, 181-182(i), 188, 195, 233-234, 240
Ohio River, 10, 14-15, 17, 19, 21, 70, 72, 76-77, 82, 85, 92-93, 96-100, 103, 105-106, 109, 154(i), 175-176, 185, 239
Ohio Valley, 72-73, 76, 81, 85
Old Point Comfort, 11
Old Will, 93
Olentangy, battle of, 215(i)
Oneida Tribe, 79
Opequon Creek, 51
Ottawa Tribe, 99
Pachgantschihilas, Chief, 172
Parker, John, 111
Parker, John, Captain, 110
Paxton Boys, 169, 171, 191
Peachy, William, Colonel, 115
Penn, Thomas, Governor, 75, 91-92, 96
Penn, William, 140
Pennsylvania
   Bedford County, 75
   Carlisle, 166
   Chester, 131
   Chester County, 124
   Connellsville, 66-67(i), 249(i)
   Cumberland County, 75
   Derby, 131
   Dilworth, 127, 129
   Erie, 11
   Germantown, 131-134
   Kennett Township, 124
   Lancaster, 55, 124, 131, 150
   Lancaster County, 100, 146
   Logstown, 14-15
   Paoli, 131
   Philadelphia, 47-48, 65, 75, 103-104, 113, 118-122, 124, 131-132, 137, 178, 235
   Pittsburgh, 14, 18, 76, 91, 106, 142, 149, 166
   Raystown, 55
   Reading, 131
   Sconneltown, 127
   Towamensing, 136

INDEX

Tyrone Township, 69
Washington County, 169, 174, 207, 236
Waterford, 11
Westmoreland County, 91
York, 131, 137, 139, 148, 152
Pennsylvania Journal and Weekly Advertiser, 234
Pennsylvania Militia, 132, 169
The Pennsylvania Packet, 234
Pennsylvania State Regiment, 136
Pennsylvania University, 118
Pennybecker's Mill, 131
Pépin, Michel, Ensign, 20-23, 25
Pheasant, 79
Philadelphia Campaign of 1777, 121(i)
Pickaway Plains, 99
Pitt, William, 53-54, 62
Pontiac's War (1763), 169
Post, Christopher, 54
Potawatomi Tribe, 40
Potomac River, 50
Prince William Augustus, Duke of Cumberland, 32-33
Princeton, battle of, 119
Puckerty Creek, 153
Purdie and Dixon's Virginia Gazette, 74, 114
Queen Anne's War (War of the Spanish Succession, 1702-1713), 29
Ranger Unit (French & Indian War), 35-38, 42-45, 47-48, 50
Reardon, Daniel, 76, 79
Redbud Run, 3(i)
Redstone Creek, 20-21
Reed, Joseph, Colonel, 131
USS *Revenge*, 178
Revere, Paul, 110
Rhode Island General Assembly, 119
Rhode Island's Army of Observation, 119
Rind's Virginia Gazette, 74
Ritchie, Craig, Captain, 204
Robinson, John, 51
Roche de Bout, 176
HMS *Roebuck*, 122
Rose, Ezekiel, Captain, 203, 212
Rose, John, Major, 177-183, 185-187, 189, 199-201, 207-208, 210, 214, 216, 233, 236,
his opinions of WC IV's personal and professional character, 180-181
Rosenthal, Baron Gustav Heinrich de. *See* Rose, John, Major
Royal Proclamation of 1763, 66, 70-71
Russell, William, Colonel, 153
Sandusky Expedition, 233, 236, 239, 247-249
Sandusky Plains, 184, 189-191, 193-194, 196, 234, 242
Sandusky River, 148, 156-157, 167-168, 170, 174-176, 181, 183-184(i), 188-190, 193-195, 197, 199-200, 217, 219, 221, 228, 242
Sandy Creek, 73
Sauk Tribe, 78
Scarouady (Monacatuatha or Monakaduto), 25, 34, 38
Schuylkill River, 131
Scioto River, 107, 162, 184
Second Continental Congress, 113, 116, 131, 137-138, 140-141, 145, 148, 151-153
Second Pennsylvania Brigade, 165
Second Virginia Regiment, 55, 58, 113, 124, 129, 135
Seneca Tribe, 14-15, 23-24, 81, 101-102, 105, 142, 162
Seventh Virginia Regiment, 116
Sharpe, Horatio, Governor, 28
Shawnee Tribe, 3-4, 24, 65, 92-94, 96-99, 101-105, 111, 138, 140, 148, 150-151, 162, 174, 184, 194, 204, 210, 212-213, 217, 223-224, 229, 233, 238-239
Sherrard, John, 206, 208-209
Six Nations, 14, 19, 25, 77, 141, 162
Sixth Pennsylvania Regiment, 165, 178
Sixth Virginia Regiment, 116
Skunks Ford, 126
Slover, John (*also see* Mannucothe), 184, 187-188, 193-194, 197, 213
Smith, Phillip, Private, 204
Smith, William, 52
Spotswood, Robert, 52

INDEX

Spring Garden, 66-71, 75-76, 82, 87, 89, 92, 94, 115, 137, 141, 143-144, 150, 163, 165, 176, 194, 239-242, 248
Springer, Sarah "Sally" (Crawford) Harrison, 5, 49, 69, 240
Springer, Uriah, 240
Squaw Campaign, 141, 146-148, 152, 225
St. Clair, John, General, 38
St. Joseph, Mission of, 192
Stanwix, John, General, 54-55
Stephen, Adam, 18-24, 27-28, 35, 37, 42-43, 47-48, 50, 97-98, 127, 129
Stephenson, Honora (Grimes) Crawford, 1-2, 4
Stephenson, Hugh, 66-68, 117
death of, 117
Stephenson, John, 2, 76, 87, 113
Stephenson, Richard, 1-2, 4, 8, 64
Stewart, Robert, Captain, 52
Stewart's Crossing, 66
Stirling, Lord William Alexander, Major General, 127, 129
Stone, Jabez, 237
Sullivan, John, General, 125, 127, 129, 132-134, 136
Surphlitt, Robert, 149
Tahgahute "John Logan", Chief, 93-94, 105-106
Tanaghrisson "Half King", Chief, 14-16, 19-23, 25, 31
Teague, Elijah, 5
Teanaostaiae (Indian village), 192
Third Virginia Brigade, 135
Thirteenth Virginia Regiment, 116-118, 124, 127, 129, 135-136, 153-154, 156(i), 161, 181
Tionontati Tribe, 193
Treaty of Camp Charlotte, 106
Treaty of Easton (1758), 65
Treaty of Fort Finney, 238
Treaty of Fort Harmer, 238
Treaty of Fort McIntosh, 238
Treaty of Fort Stanwix, 72, 92
Treaty of Greenville, 235
Treaty of Hard Labor (1768), 72
Treaty of London (1604), 30
Treaty of Paris (1763), 64, 103
Treaty of Paris (1783), 165, 234-235
Trenton, battle of, 119
Turner, Elizabeth, 221, 229, 231, 238
Turner, John, 100-101
Turner, Mary (Girty), 100-101
Turney, John, Lieutenant, 217-218
Tuscarawas River, 157, 159, 161, 167-168, 184, 186, 228
Tygart Valley, 84
Tymochtee Creek, 193, 229, 239, 242
Valley Forge, 137, 152, 178
Vance, Elizabeth, 5
Vance, John, 4-5, 9, 69
HMS *Vigilant*, 122
Virginia
  Alexandria, 17-18, 26, 64
  Augusta County, 16-17, 52, 155
  Berkley County, 155
  Culpeper County, 8
  Fairfax County, 74
  Frederick County, 2, 5, 16-17, 27, 50, 64
  Fredericksburg, 75
  Hampton, 11
  Hampton Roads, 32
  Richmond, 115
  Rockingham County, 155
  Shenandoah Valley, 2-4, 7-8, 18, 28, 48, 52, 64, 68, 96
  Springfield, 6
  Westmoreland County, 1, 75
  Williamsburg, 11, 13-17, 62-63, 74-75, 89, 113-116, 235
  Winchester, 8, 18-19, 22, 24, 26-28, 48, 50-52, 55, 59, 84, 85
  Yorktown, 163
Virginia Company, 11, 90
Virginia Executive Council, 154
Virginia Gazette, 116
Virginia General Assembly, 8, 115
Virginia House of Burgesses, 18, 71
Virginia House of Delegates, 235
Virginia Regiment, 17-18, 26, 28, 48, 50, 55, 73, 76, 84
Walters, John, 209
Walters, Michael, 220
War of 1812, 204
Washington, Augustine, 7
Washington, Charles, 84
Washington, George, 6-9(i), 14-16,

295

17(i)-28, 34, 42-46, 48, 50-56, 59-65, 69-76, 79-82, 84-85, 89, 91-92, 98, 101, 105, 108-109, 112-113, 116-123, 126-127, 130-133(i), 135-136, 139, 145, 152-153, 161-163, 165, 178, 233, 235, 240-241, 248
   death of, 235
   elected first POTUS, 235
Washington, Lawrence, 7-10
Washington, Martha (Custis), 63
Washington, Mary (Ball), 7-8
Washington's Bottom, 76, 109
Watkins, Evan, 50
Wayne, Anthony, General, 124, 235
Weedon, George, General, 124, 129
Wells, Sam, 222
Wendake "the island", 191-193
Wendat Tribe, 191
West Augusta Committee of Safety, 141
West Virginia
   Hampshire County, 155
   Harpers Ferry, 2
   Paden City, 81
   Point Pleasant, 82, 98
   Raven Rock, 81
   Wheeling, 93, 96
Western Department, 139(i), 145, 152(i)-153, 163, 165-166(i), 175, 233
Wheeling Creek, 96
Whitehall, seat of British Government, 28, 31-33, 48, 109, 165
Whitemarsh Church, 136, 137
Widow Myer's Tavern, 76
William and Mary College, 74-75
Williamson, David, Colonel, 169-175, 177, 180, 187, 193, 197, 199, 208, 210-211, 214-216, 218, 221-222, 225, 227-228, 233, 236, 247-250
   death of, 236
Wingenund, Chief, 194-195, 220, 223-229, 238-239
Wyandot Tribe, 150-151, 167-169, 174, 189-195, 197, 200-201, 204, 207-208, 217, 221, 235, 238, 242
Yorktown, battle of, 165, 236

Youghiogheny River, 66, 69-70, 75-76, 87, 116, 177
Zane, Jonathan, 184, 187-189, 193-194, 197, 199

ABOUT THE AUTHOR

ROBERT N. THOMPSON is a historian living in the St. Louis, Missouri area. A former career military officer, he has a bachelor's degree in history from Texas Tech University, and was a Distinguished Graduate of American Military University, from which he holds a graduate degree in military studies. His first book, *A Woman of Courage on the West Virginia Frontier: Phebe Tucker Cunningham*, was published in 2013. His other works include "William Averell's Cavalry Raid on the Virginia & Tennessee Railroad," published in the November 2000 issue of *America's Civil War* and "Battle of Cold Harbor: The Folly and Horror," which appeared in the November 2006 issue of *Military History*. He has also written seven book reviews for Michigan State University's Civil War H-Net Web site.

www.ingramcontent.com/pod-product-compliance
Lightning Source LLC
Chambersburg PA
CBHW070607170426
43200CB00012B/2613